Reimagining the Civic

Yale School of Architecture
The Louis I. Kahn Visiting Assistant Professorship

Yale School of Architecture
180 York Street
New Haven, CT 06520
www.architecture.yale.edu

Distributed by Actar
355 Lexington Avenue, 8th fl.
New York, NY 10017
www.actar.com

Reimagining the Civic was made possible
through an endowment from the Louis I. Kahn
Visiting Assistant Professorship at the Yale
School of Architecture. It is the tenth in a
series of publications of the Louis I. Kahn
Assistant Professorship published through
the dean's office.

Editors: Nina Rappaport and Stav Dror
Design: Manuel Miranda Practice
Copy Editor: Cathryn Drake

Library of Congress Control Number:
2022936513
ISBN:
978-1-638400-17-2

Reimagining the Civic

Fernanda Canales

Yale School of Architecture

The Louis I. Kahn Visiting Assistant Professorship

Stella Betts

Luis Callejas

and

Charlotte Hansson

Table of Contents

Preface

The Louis I. Kahn Visiting Assistant Professorship is Yale's second endowed chair to honor Kahn. Established in 2004, the professorship brings to the school younger architects who practice and teach, offering them the opportunity to lead advanced design studios and seminars. The Kahn Visiting Assistant Professorship carries with it the expectation that the work of the visiting professors and their students will be published so that others may benefit from the ideas developed and exchanged in the studios and seminars.

Louis I. Kahn (1901–1974), perhaps the greatest American architect of the post-World War II era, was closely associated with Yale as a teacher and practicing architect. Yale is home to his first important building, the extension to the Art Gallery (1951–1953), and his last, the Center for British Art (1969–1977). Kahn was fresh to teaching when he came to Yale, in 1947, to begin what would be ten years as chief critic in the architecture school. As a teacher, he worked closely with students and encouraged them to go beyond their initial ideas about architecture, as he himself was trying to go beyond his own ideas. Kahn inspired a generation of architects, leading them to new insights that became the basis of their independent work.

Over thirty studios have been offered by Louis I. Kahn Visiting Assistant Professors, whose works have been published in the book series listed here by year of publication.

Layered Urbanisms 2007

Gregg Pasquarelli (SHoP Architects)
Galia Solomonoff (Solomonoff Architecture Studio)
Mario Gooden (Huff + Gooden Architects)

Negotiated Terrains 2009

Jeanne Gang (Studio Gang)
Sunil Bald (Studio SUMO)
Mark Tsurumaki (LTL Architects)

Turbulence 2011

Christopher Sharples (SHoP Architects)
William Sharples (SHoP Architects)
Ali Rahim (Contemporary Architecture Practice)

Architecture Inserted 2012

Eric Bunge (nARCHITECTS)
Mimi Hoang (nARCHITECTS)
Chris Perry (Pneuma Studio)
Liza Fior (MUF Architecture and Art)
Katherine Clarke (MUF Architecture and Art)

Renewing Architectural Typologies 2013

Makram El Kadi (L.E.FT)
Ziad Jamaleddine (L.E.FT)
Tom Coward (AOC)
Daisy Froud (AOC)
Vincent Lacovara (AOC)
Geoff Shearcroft (AOC)
Hernan Diaz Alonso (Xefirotarch)

Cultural Cues 2015

Joe Day (Deegan Day Design)
Tom Wiscombe (Tom Wiscombe Architecture)
Adib Cure (Cure & Penabad)
Carie Penabad (Cure & Penabad)

Against the Grain 2016

Marcelo Spina (Patterns)
Georgina Huljich (Patterns)
Dan Wood (WorkAC)
Lisa Gray (Gray Organschi Architects)
Alan Organschi (Gray Organschi Architects)

Future Real 2018

Kersten Geers (OFFICE Kersten Geers
David Van Severn)
Michael Young (Young & Ayata)
David Erdman (davidclovers)

Mexican Social Housing: Promises Revisited 2019

Tatiana Bilbao (Tatiana Bilbao Estudio)

Within or Without 2020

Scott Ruff (RuffWorks Studio)
Florencia Pita (Pita Bloom)
Jackilin Hah Bloom (Pita Bloom)
Omar Gandhi (Omar Gandhi Architect)

This volume, *Reimagining the Civic,* shows projects ranging from editing landscapes to reinventing familiar types and designing a house, while converging on the civic as a multiprogrammatic space that allows a polyphony of activities, asking — what is the architect's agency in the civic discourse of space?

This book was made possible through an endowment from the Louis I. Kahn Visiting Assistant Professorship at the Yale School of Architecture. It is the tenth in a series of publications of the Louis I. Kahn Assistant Professorship published through the Dean's office.

Introduction

Reimagining the Civic investigates and describes the design challenges of three studios led by the three Kahn Visiting Assistant Professors: architect Fernanda Canales, of Mexico City, with David Turturo, critic in architecture; Luis Callejas and Charlotte Hansson, directors of LCLA office, based in Oslo and Medellín, with Marta Caldeira, lecturer; and Stella Betts, of LEVENBETTS, in New York. Each studio focused on different environments and social contexts while scrutinizing age-old questions pertinent to the architectural discipline's understanding of civic space.

Fernanda Canales's studio, "Postprivacy," took a critical look at the housing dichotomy in Mexico, where empty homes coincide with a shortage in dwellings. Stella Betts's studio, "Free Library," focused on the politics of freedom and information, considering the library as a catalyst for the organization of social programs. Luis Callejas and Charlotte Hansson's studio, "The Forest," studied the woods of Norway as both a mythical space and site of the civic parliament.

While diverging in methodology and technique, the studios intersected in functional approach and the possibilities that emerged by multiplying the program. All of the programs were condensed through the design of a single building, dissolving a monolithic type whether it be a house, a library, or a parliament building. Through the cross-examination of all three studios, the multiprogram's pluralism of activities emerges as a tool for defining the civic. Whether through manipulating trees in a forest, expanding the definition of the house in Mexico City, or shifting the discourse in reimagining the library, the students regarded existing cultural and spatial contexts as transformative conceptual and physical materials, defining the act of editing as a mode of civic responsibility and invention.

The editors would like to thank all of the professors and students for helping to make this book possible: Fernanda Canales, with David Turturo, and Michelle Badr, Emily Cass, Camille Chabrol, Clara Domange, Shuchen Dong, Miriam Dreiblatt,

Layla Ni, Alex Pineda, Limy Rocha, Armaan Shah, and Xiaohui Wen; Stella Betts and James Bradley, Daniella Calma, Shuang Chen, Elaine Cui, Gordon Jiang, Max Ouellette-Howitz, Jenna Ritz, Limy Rocha, Jen Shin, and Brenna Thompson; Luis Callejas and Charlotte Hansson, with Marta Caldeira, and Elise Limon, Natalie Broton, Stav Dror, Kate Fritz, Jiaming Gu, Lillian Hou, April Liu, Naomi Ng, and Daoru Wang.

Special recognition goes to Cathryn Drake for her guidance and precise editorial work and to Manuel Miranda Practice we express our utmost appreciation. We hope this volume signals a new way of thinking about what a civic space can be in various contexts today.

Postprivacy: Designing New Centralities at the Border

Fernanda Canales

Conversation with Fernanda Canales

Elena Garro Cultural Center, 2012, Mexico City. Photo: Sandra Pereznieto

NINA RAPPAPORT I am very curious as to why you took on such a large-scale research project on the entire history of twentieth-century Mexican architecture in your book *Mexican Architecture 1900–2010: The Construction of Modernity.* How did that project evolve from your PhD?

FERNANDO CANALES The book started just as a single map during my PhD at the Escuela Técnica Superior de Arquitectura de Madrid. I was mapping so many different layers that it became impossible to put them all together. It was important for me to understand architecture in a broader sense, beyond buildings and architects, so I pursued the research to look at different things that related architecture to science, art, and urban planning. I started unfolding that multilayered map into different diagrams, and it resulted in twenty-five timelines showing the interrelationships between history, ideas, buildings, and art, such as the Muralist movement. It was a process that unfolded in an attempt to understand the broader reality and culture.

NR How does this intensive research inform your own architecture? Does it inspire you, or is it a burden to have so much knowledge?

FC I am using this research method for current projects. It wasn't clear how to read such a complex country and the histories behind the streets I cross every day. It was difficult to work in a place that I didn't understand, but to try to make sense of the growth of the city and its public policies clarified the relationship between different movements and eras. This has become a way of working, not just with the city but also with the mind-set of the context that I'm working in.

NR What are your major concerns right now in Mexico in terms of housing and social issues?

FC I think the issues really changed after the earthquake in 2017. The growth of our cities has been so big that we are usually focused on urban development. After the earthquake the architects of my generation realized that the contrasts between buildings and territories, along with the rural exodus of past decades, have been devastating, not only in terms of the infrastructure but also in the way architects have forgotten to deal with different geographies, climates, and cultures. After the earthquake it became evident that we are failing to understand local building methods. As a result, I am working more directly with the communities and trying to adapt to different approaches.

Bruma House, 2017, Estado de México. Photo: Rafael Gamo

NR I see that in your practice you collaborate with architects and engineers as consultants. Does that give you more time for your research and writing?

FC Yes, that's actually what has made me shift. When I began my career I thought I should have a big office, but I think this smaller scale is better for me in order to adapt to the informal conditions of Mexico. I've been spending more time on-site and working on small projects as a way to understand local conditions. I focus on research and writing because the velocity of client-based projects has nothing to do with the rhythm of exploration. I can only combine those worlds if I can shut myself off and work in a more personal manner.

NR I'm really interested in your analysis of ideas about public and private space and, in general, your attitude about what is public and what is private space. If you live in an apartment building in a dense city, when you look out the window, like I am now, you can see into your neighbor's apartment. Even the neighbor's sounds and scents are public, so how do you provide the necessary private space while also making space for the public and the community? And how do you incorporate your theoretical ideas into a project?

FC That's a wonderful way to put it. It is difficult to combine theories on dwelling and the relations between private and public with the need to respond to clients and construction processes. When projects are not interesting in terms of typology or experimental design, I ask myself if I should even participate, and I always try to include a utopian framework and question the ways cities are built. The main challenge is to try to put all of that together: the site, the commercial considerations, the economic restrictions, and the desire to make

Terreno House, 2018, Estado de México. Photo: Rafael Gamo

profound changes. The biggest challenge for me is how to make sense of what I am trying to construct in theory through design.

NR How would you describe the difference in the way you approach public or private space in the multiunit buildings in Mexico City versus the Casa Bruma, in the rural setting of Reserva el Peñón? And how do these different projects build on each other?

FC The differences help to emphasize certain priorities despite varying spatial allocations and densities. I think this contrast is recurrent in my work, which ranges from very small-scale projects to urban developments, and helps me to incorporate the generosity of a large weekend retreat into small housing projects for local communities with minimum budgets. It may sound crazy to shift between such different situations, but it is the reality of a country characterized by contrasts—in terms of social, geographical, and economic conditions. I'm often working on a house that can fit into the closet of another house I have designed.

NR How did you foresee the idea of making the community library into a new type of public space?

FC The library project started as a commission to remodel an abandoned apartment in order to house one thousand books donated by the Ministry of Culture in a plan to improve large housing estates characterized by violence and segregation. But I was afraid to transform the apartment into a public space because no one would be able to see what was happening inside and take care of the space. So I asked if it would be possible to make it a public space that would be really accessible to everybody. The response was, as usual: "We don't have any space, and we don't have any money." After I visited different housing units, they all shared a similar condition: public space that had been illegally occupied and turned into private parking spaces and storage areas. I thought we could reclaim one abandoned parking space that could become a public space and then apply that prototype as a self-built project adapted to different needs.

NR How do you think the project has transformed the sense of community?

FC At first these small structures provided the only shade and safe public space in the area. During the evenings, they became sort of lamps, where everyone could always see what was happening inside. They're built from typical concrete blocks that are placed tilted in order to form a latticework so the inside is always visible; there's no division between the public and the private realm. They are flexible spaces that have become not just reading rooms but also the place for baptisms and weddings, where people from different generations meet.

Productive House, 2018, Hidalgo.
Photo: Rafael Gamo

NR In addition to urban work you also have a strong relationship to rural landscapes and forests that enclose and embrace the house as a private space or open it up to the environment, but how is this achieved?

FC One topology that fascinates me is the patio and the possibilities it has offered throughout history of relating the private and the public realms. Especially in Mexico—rural settings have bigger problems with a lack of safety, so patios become an opportunity to provide an exterior space that is in some way controlled or linked to interior space. They help provide transitions that broaden the thresholds between inside and outside. Rather than fighting violence with more violence, I attempt to make smoother transitions by using patios, halfway between a public space and the private sphere. It is a way of molding the different gradients of people coming into a house.

Reading Rooms, 2015, Nayarit.
Photo: Jaime Navarro

NR How does this issue of public versus private play out in a public commission?

FC In the Elena Garro Cultural Center, in Coyoacán, the idea was to tear down the existing wall of the abandoned house and transform the site into a public building. I designed a bookshop and library for people who have never read a book or felt invited into the city's public buildings. The idea was to make the sidewalk enter directly into the building and take the books outside the building. The vegetation played an important role because there are no boundaries between trees that are outside and trees that become part of the new interior space. Also, designing a series of patios helped to make those transitions more inviting without losing the sense of an enclosed, silent space. It's a way of opening buildings to the city without feeling a loss of privacy.

NR In terms of the Bruma House and Casa Terreno, you discuss the building disappearing into the landscape. Are you opening urban buildings up to the city but closing in the rural houses?

FC It's a dual condition. The fun part of designing those two houses was that it became like turning a sock inside out. The inside of the house is actually an outside space—a patio. There is a contradiction in that the inside space is the most exterior part of the project and the outside disappears, so the house does not obstruct the landscape. The idea is that you see only vegetation, not buildings. When you are inside the house you have an inside that is an outside. That play between interior and exterior, private and public, is what fascinates me.

NR How are you exploring this in the Monte Albán housing project?

FC The structure with twenty-four housing units and mixed-use spaces that I am building in Mexico City has been a challenge because it is very dense. The L shape connects two streets through the inside of the building, linking two parts of the city instead of using closed-off spaces and private corridors. All of the hallways are open to the exterior. Patios, terraces, and balconies are inserted into a very narrow, highly dense project in the city, resembling in different ways some of the spatial qualities of the large houses I have designed in rural landscapes.

Postprivacy: Designing New Centralities at the Border

Fernanda Canales planned the studio "Postprivacy" at a time when the U.S. government announced the most aggressive policies against migration in decades, along with the construction of a wall along the Mexican border, to be paid for and built by Mexicans—precisely those who were in favor of border crossings. It was also a time when the Mexican government finally acknowledged the failure of public-housing policies that had led to five million abandoned homes, most of them new, financed with public funds, and characterized by lack of services, infrastructure, links to public transport, public space, schools, and jobs. The paradox of having one out of every seven homes abandoned in a country experiencing a lack of housing evidenced the inadequacy of urban policies and housing projects.

Mexico was the first laboratory for gauging the urban and social repercussions of the demographic explosion, pollution, and traffic on a vast megalopolis in the twentieth century. It is characterized as an active space for experimentation with dramatic economic and territorial contrasts offering an immense opportunity to work with an array of situations that challenge the ways we usually understand architectural practice.

Aerial context, Paseos del Vergel, Tijuana, Baja California, Mexico

With the Yale students we posed a critique of single-family

Paseos del Vergel, Tijuana, Baja California, Mexico

housing developments based on the American dream. Poor planning and a lack of services and infrastructure triggered dystopian developments indifferent to people's needs on the peripheries of cities worldwide. As a result, many Mexican residents spend more than three hours per day and 30 percent of their income on transportation. Against the predominant housing models and urban schemes, "Postprivacy" advocated the reconstruction of abandoned territories and fragmented communities by maximizing space, production, supply, trade, education, and recreation. Students transformed abandoned structures to promote a sense of community. Significantly these projects incorporated self-built techniques and local dynamics rather than imported models.

Ángeles de Puebla. Mexicali, Baja California, Mexico

The central goal was to provide housing schemes that could adapt to the specific needs of families and incorporate spaces for work, commerce, and culture. The studio assignments aimed to redensify horizontal

Backyard, Paseos del Vergel, Tijuana, Baja California, Mexico

Border line, Tijuana, Baja California, Mexico

developments and narrow the gap between informal settlements (accounting for more than 70 percent of what is built) and monofunctional, single-family housing. In the early 2000s the Mexican government launched an ambitious effort to provide affordable dwellings to millions (sponsored by INFONAVIT, the Mexican Federal Institute for Worker's Housing), spending more than $100 billion on thousands of sprawling developments that are now landmarks of violence and abandonment. The intention was to restructure these ghettos by working within the existing fabric and narrowing the brutal mismatch between how the city is built and the way people use it. The hope was to promote an incremental approach that would adapt to continuous changes through responsive and flexible architecture.

By reusing existing structures, optimizing densities, and linking housing to different activities and services, the studio aimed to foster pluralism, flexibility, participation, income generation, equity, public space, and connectivity.

Massive housing developments in Escobedo, Mexico, and abandoned houses. Image by Jorge Taboada

Aerial context, Paseos del Vergel, Tijuana, Baja California, Mexico

Our cities are criticized continually yet projects fail to diverge from the monotony built around the world. The same architectural solutions are replicated in different geographical conditions, climates, cultures, and economies, extending uniform shapes that accentuate the contrast between peoples, territories, buildings, and activities. For the past 200 years the disparities between these four realms have grown, amplifying oppositions between owners and users, rural and urban, private and public, and living and working. This disparity has led to increasingly segregated environments. As a result, there is little relation between individual desire and collective consequences, and nobody is in charge of the space that lies between a bed, a sidewalk and a water system. These gaps are visible in the oppositions that exist between resources and waste, centers and peripheries, formal and informal, and dispossessed people and vacant houses.

El Laurel, Tijuana, Baja California, Mexico

Through a sequence of exercises the students aimed to transform typical forms of housing for more flexible and

El Laurel, Tijuana, Baja California, Mexico

Border line, Tijuana, Baja California, Mexico

abstract ways of living. They engaged, for example, in the design of a minimum living cell, starting from one bedroom and extending to correlating spaces—bathroom, dining, work, social, and so on. The projects comprised as many living units as desired and followed concepts chosen by each author (water systems, maquiladoras, and marketplaces, among others). The emphasis was placed on utopian proposals that explored what lies between a partition and a habitable space, the place that exists between sleeping and living and between what-belongs-to-one and what-belongs-to-all.

Inhabiting a Wall The students looked at the wall as an architectural tectonic that exceeds its definition as a limit (border, line, surface). As such, the wall provides infinite relationships between seclusion and enclosure, positive and negative space. The aim was to critically rethink forms of subtraction and addition (acts of building, unbuilding, and reuse); to open new connections and bring different realities of the same territory together; and to build cities and societies no longer divided by walls. Students were asked to imagine the minimum elements of a house (just a wall), challenge the common definitions and meanings of home, expand the possibilities of liminality and in-between spaces, and reconsider what are they willing to share. The studio analyzed different degrees of privacy and the relation between spaces, objects, landscapes, and activities.

***Vecindad* Project** Each student designed a *vecindad* (a multiunit urban housing complex), comprising as many units as desired, linked to a program chosen by a team. As with the previous assignment, projects could be designed for a specific site or as a prototype for an abstract setting. Students were asked to rethink the studio research and propose new possibilities for collective dwelling focused on homes and cities. Visiting and researching historic *vecindades* fostered a deeper exploration of shared space and the private realm. The projects presented an opportunity to discuss issues regarding collective services, density, privacy, and public space. Concepts such as kitchenless cities, courtyards, living/working, owning/sharing, and interior/exterior became subjects of constant debate.

Collective Housing The next prompt was to reimagine *vecindades* for the scale of mass housing developments. The process began with the design of a minimum dwelling unit, leading to large-scale projects that enriched relationships between the public and private spheres. This involved research of extreme situations pertaining to violence, immigration, and mobility. Each of the eleven schemes addressed issues such as: How can we foster continuity and connectivity within fragmented territories? How can we convert peripheral developments into new centers? How can we transform abandoned buildings into safe communities? With strategies ranging from discrete improvements and minor interventions to mass replacement, students attempted to subvert oppositions between temporality and permanence, isolation and cooperation, habitation and work, construction and landscape, and identity and repetition. In some cases the house was understood more like a piece of furniture; in others it was akin to a tent or camping structure. At times homes were spaces to intensify the relations between working, socializing, and sleeping; at others they were simple structures used to store rainwater or bridges employed to reunite divided topographies. *House* in any case remains a word to be defined.

Massive housing developments in Garcia, Mexico. Image by Jorge Taboada.

Studio Brief

Fall 2019, with David Turturo

Aerial context, Ángeles de Puebla. Mexicali, Baja California, Mexico

Introduction

While the housing shortage in the world increases, the number of empty homes is also growing: millions of people are without houses while millions of homes are abandoned. Countries both rich and poor suffer housing shortages and build ghost towns. From Detroit to Keelung and Ciudad Juarez, our built environment reflects the incongruities of a system in which architects become gradually less useful. Mexico exemplifies this dramatic scenario: despite being a country with a vast scarcity of homes, it has one of the highest rates of abandonment—more than five million homes, most of them new. One out of every seven houses is empty due to massive developments of single-family homes at urban peripheries, in areas lacking public space, collective services, and links to transport systems. Urban expansion no longer follows population growth; instead development mimics market-driven decisions that benefit only a few: produce more to sell more. In the past 30 years the population of Mexico increased 210 percent while urban sprawl grew 700 percent.[1] This worldwide phenomenon, based on the American dream of the suburban single-family house, has become the nightmare of the periphery.

Still today in the United States most residential land is destined exclusively for detached single-family houses. These are required by law on 75 percent of residential land in many cities (Los Angeles, Seattle, and Chicago), so that residential developments are built hours away from places of

1 Sergio Trejo, "En 70 años creció 700 veces la mancha urbana," in *La Razón*, July 6, 2013; available at www.razón.com.mx, accessed September 2, 2015.

Abandoned houses, Ángeles de Puebla. Mexicali, Baja California, Mexico

Ángeles de Puebla. Mexicali, Baja California, Mexico

work and schools. The only apparent alternative to this perpetual model is the apartment building. Housing advocates ask: Are there options for dwelling other than suburban homes or apartments in the twenty-first century? Can we depart from these two predominant typologies, the first derived from the misunderstood Garden City movement, proposed by Ebenezer Howard in the late nineteenth century, the second based on the influence of Le Corbusier's Ville Contemporaine, developed almost 100 years ago and also misconstrued? Can we imagine projects that revoke the oppositions between living and working, urban and rural, and individual and collective?

Program

This advanced design studio focused on new housing alternatives for abandoned neighborhoods in Mexico. It presented the opportunity to work near the Mexico-U.S. border to address issues dealing with migration, identity, temporality, privacy, housing, and production. What can be done with five million abandoned homes in Mexico? How can a place be made for immigrants who want to cross into the United States but visit Mexico intermittently? How does one build a sense of identity and prosperity in places lacking local appreciation and hope? The students considered urban, political, social, and cultural issues in an attempt to reshape communities and territories.

The studio looked back at the *vecindades*—mixed-use multifamily tenements arranged around central courtyards with shared services—a primary typology in Mexico for the past three centuries that was essentially forgotten after the 1950s. The *vecindades* started as improvised subdivisions of grand colonial houses during the eighteenth century. They accommodated many tenants, along with commerce for a range of social classes. During the last decades of the nineteenth century *vecindades* were built as urban alternatives for transitory dwellers and rural immigrants. They are a historical example of flexible design promoting a shared sense of belonging oriented toward the space between public and private spheres.

We also studied the concept of the wall and various definitions of boundary. The goal was to dismantle binary categories such as exterior/interior and seclusion/sharing. The studio engaged new ways of understanding collective dwelling as the main instrument for making cities.

Border line, Tijuana, Baja California, Mexi co

Border general context

Site

The students in the "Postprivacy" studio traveled to Mexico to investigate *vecindades* in the historic neighborhoods of Mexico City and then traveled to Tijuana and Mexicali to visit abandoned housing complexes in the outskirts and near the border. The aim was to repurpose the vast underused territories of suburban dwellings, producing alternative ways of living where neighbors are not seen as a threat and architecture does not accentuate boundaries. The studio collaborated with SEDATU, the Mexican government agency in charge of urban development, agrarian land, and living space, and INFONAVIT, the National Institute for Social Housing.

The Mexico-U.S. border, the target of our work, is the most frequently traversed border in the world, with more than 350 million documented crossings per year and an estimated 2,500 illegal crossings every day. The border extends from the Pacific Ocean to the Gulf of Mexico through urban areas and deserts displaying diverse economic, cultural, and geographical realities. Despite policies against immigrants, unauthorized crossings have nearly doubled in recent years. Additionally, more people are migrating from South and Central America and Africa but are staying near the border indefinitely. Migration into Mexico is occurring on an unprecedented scale. This issue is being treated as a temporary emergency, but its consequences are imprinted on the culture, economy, and territory.

The idea of the studio was to seek out new architectural strategies and designs for real issues and employ radical experiments to transform abandoned housing into sustainable communities and centers of production. The projects explored new types of collective living without the boundaries that characterize contemporary life and imagined cities without walls.

Border wall, Mexico-USA

Border line, Tijuana, Baja California, Mexico

Objective

The challenge presented to the students was to question the way we consume territory, buildings, and resources. The ambition was to produce alternative housing capable of building new centralities at the border, new spaces that pose different understandings of conservation and destruction, growth and use, identity, and coexistence.

Organization

The aim was to imagine projects that revoke the oppositions between rich and poor, living and working, formal and informal, and individual and collective. The studio was divided into two parts: the first consisted of research and the design of two speculative projects, "Inhabiting a Wall" and "Vecindades." The students worked in teams to develop historical research on collective housing projects and *vecindades* while designing housing projects that address the idea of border or limit. The fundamental task was to create housing between the scale of the unit and of mixed-use complexes.

The second part of the studio was centered on the analysis of seven specific sites of mass housing developments. Through these examples—in Tijuana, Mexicali, Nuevo Laredo, Reynosa, and Ciudad Juárez—the students investigated architectural conditions that contribute to high rates of abandonment, design solutions that had lasting positive effects, and ingenious adaptations designed by residents. Each student designed a project that would transform typical forms of housing into more flexible structures that foster collaborative infrastructures and acknowledge air, water, and culture as shared resources.

Case Studies and Projects

Students addressed the issue of abandonment as a corollary of dwelling multiplication, with a focus on dissolving walls, scales of sharing, typological variation, and expanding limits between public and private space. Each student chose a main theme to anchor the project and make it sustainable in social, economic, and ecological terms. The projects focused less on imagining homes and more on understanding how to live together with shared infrastructure, resources, resources, and production.

Vecindades. Edificio Jardin, Francisco Serrano, 1931

Massive housing developments
in Cadereyta, México.
Image by Jorge Taboada

Student Projects

The Neighborhood as House

Michelle Badr
Clara Domange
Shuchen Dong
Layla Ni

The House as a Collective Infrastructure

Armaan Shah
Alex Pineda
Limy Rocha

Plug and Play Houses

Emily Cass
Xiaohui Wen
Camille Chabrol
Miriam Dreiblatt

Shared Work

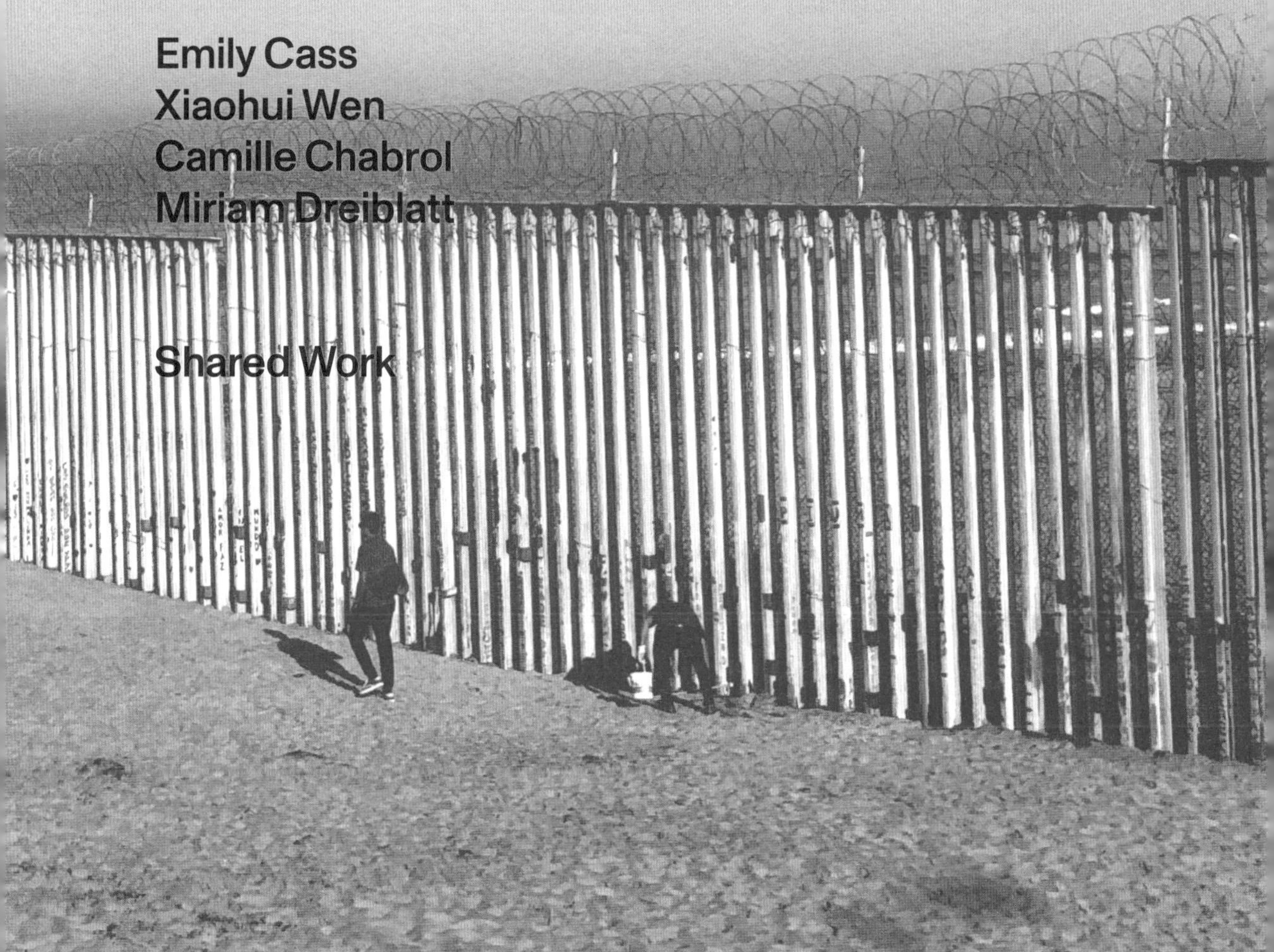

The Neighborhood as House

These projects focus on the relationship between house and community, fostering different ways of relating to the need for privacy and the benefits of sharing. The main strategies consist of improving connectivity within fragmented topographies and rethinking the *vecindades* as places where the private and the public realms don't accentuate divisions. By reclaiming residual spaces for collective amenities, educational facilities, commerce, and public gathering, the existing housing complexes characterized by abandonment are transformed into protected and lively spaces.

Michelle Badr: A Privada within a Privada

Paseos del Vergel comprises a series of fragmented residential enclaves, or *privadas*, sprinkled across an extremely steep slope. Each *privada* includes a strip of 80 homes marked by a gate at either end of the street defining it as an enclave. While the front sides of the *privadas* are visibly valued, the backs of many homes appear underutilized and poorly maintained. This project proposes to reclaim these residual spaces as communal amenities for the public domain. The new landscape permeates the rigid monotony of the *privadas* through the act of carving, creating an entirely new ground condition that reorients the focus from a formal street to an interwoven landscape of shared amenities and inverting the existing front-back relationship. By relinquishing unused remainders of private space to the public domain, residents gain access to amenities such as communal bathhouses, kitchens, and dining areas that facilitate a sense of community. As the residents come to share the horizontal, an opportunity to densify the vertical arises—homes are renovated, subdivided, and enlarged to accommodate several new residential typologies.

Paseos del Vergel

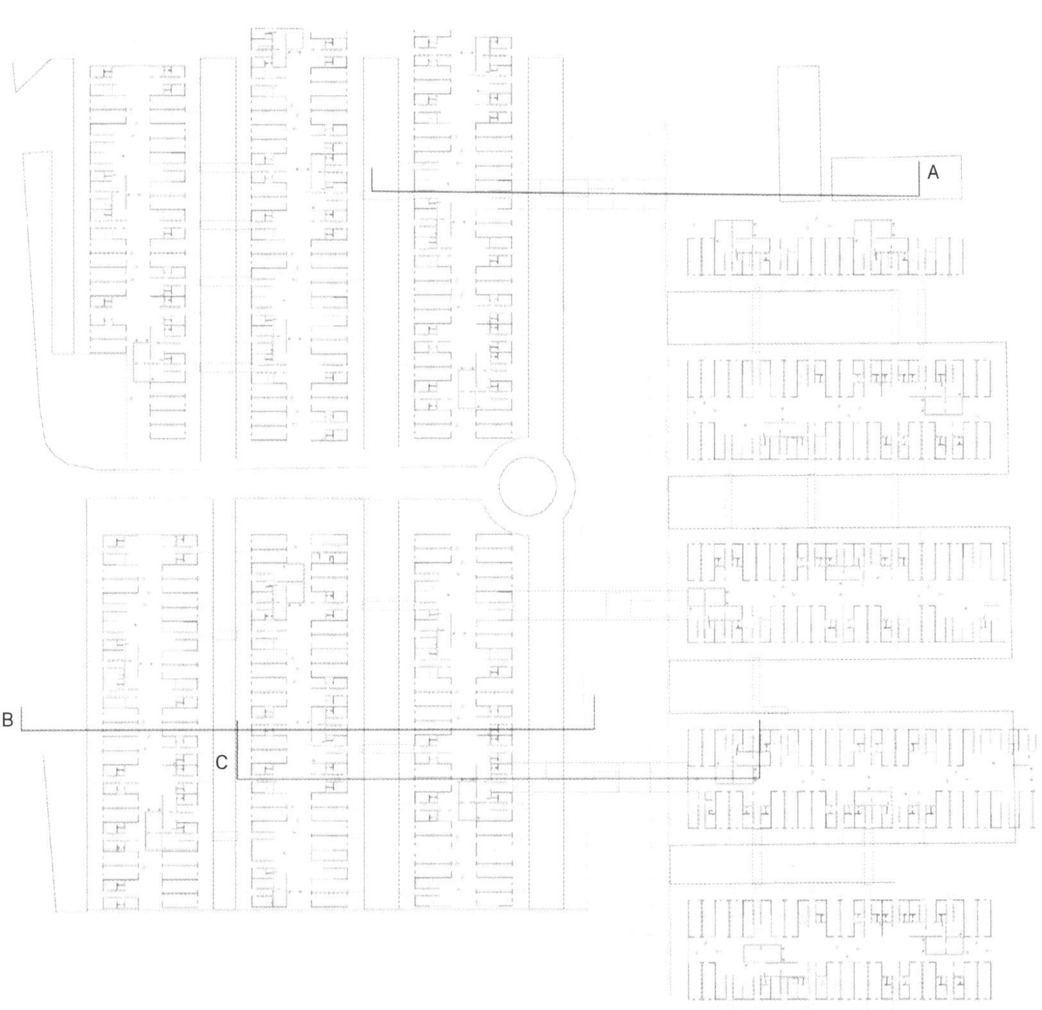

Michelle Badr

Carving and restitching forgotten private areas for public amenities

Inserting new program to connect isolated *privadas*

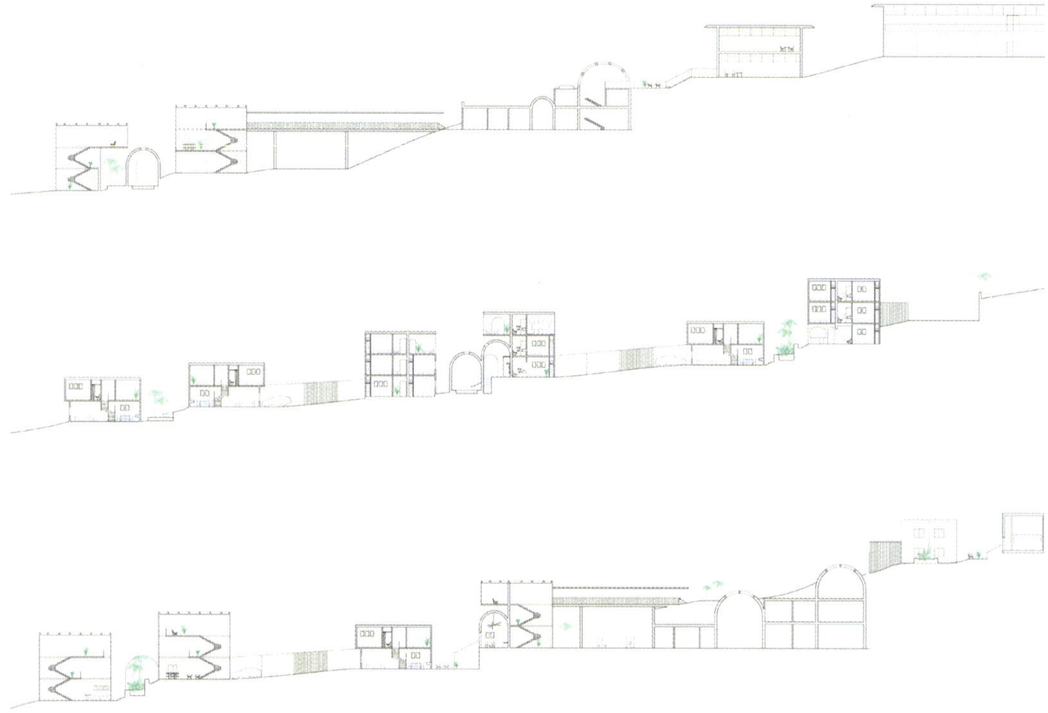

A Privada within a Privada

Reorienting the site through shared amenities

Unit pairs transformed into six new housing typologies with gradients of privacy

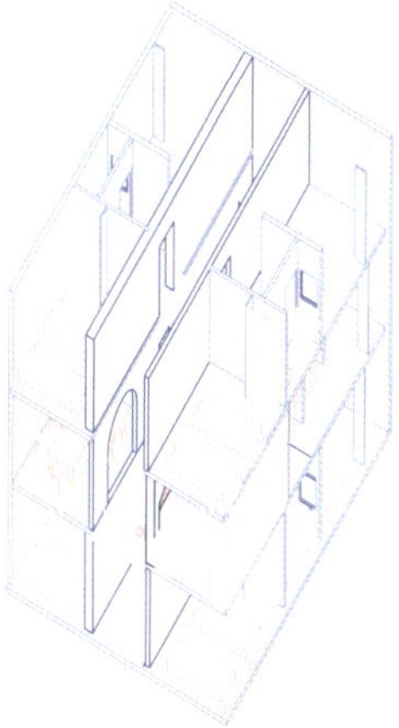

Type 1

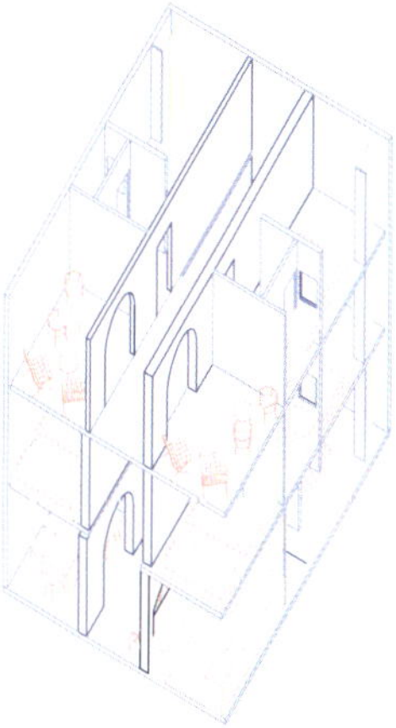

Type 3

Type 2

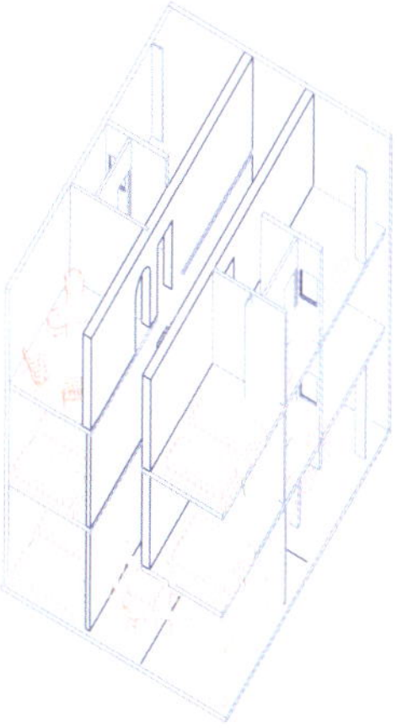

Type 4

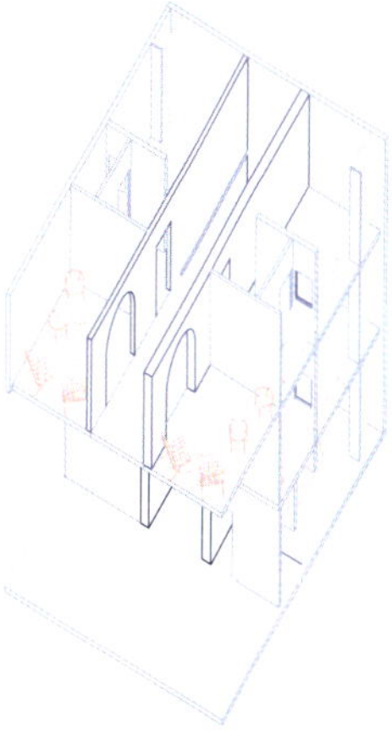

Clara Domange

This project sits atop a hill in the Tijuana neighborhood of El Laurel, located in the center of a homogeneous residential landscape. It proposes to break up and rearticulate a rigid formal grid to optimize private and public living while prioritizing community, flexibility, and business opportunities for inhabitants.

Housing units are grouped into clusters with different parts of the home fragmented into one-to-three-story volumes of single domestic programs: bathrooms, bedrooms, and living spaces. In response to the local predisposition to living outside, there are communal outdoor spaces between the volumes. The articulation of volumes provides complete privacy within the homes while maintaining an open relationship with the outdoors. Similarly the various unit typologies range from one to three bedrooms and remain private by virtue of fragmentary spaces interconnected via porous passageways. As one navigates upward the plan dissolves from floor to floor.

The project replaces the existing 185 housing units with 500 units organized through a system of 20 identical clusters of 25 homes. Each individual cluster can be seen as an independent community within a larger ecosystem. Every community includes three additional programs at ground level. The first is a large laundry room open to the exterior to reflect the social nature of traditional laundries seen in Mexican housing developments, which promote interaction among neighbors. The second is a multipurpose community space for events and gatherings. The third is a commercial space designed for inhabitants to grow their own businesses, in turn activating the surrounding area. These hubs respond to the multitude of makeshift businesses that inhabitants of El Laurel have created inside their own homes, on the sidewalks, and in temporary stands.

The interstitial spaces between clusters are open to the public, comprising larger, more open spaces and smaller, more intimate zones. The housing clusters are interwoven with a marketplace, a sports complex, a large open park, and a community hub with a day-care center, employment services, community spaces, and a shared open work space. The site is surrounded by an array of existing institutions including supermarkets, schools, and churches that are easily accessible and can be seen as part of a larger network. Through the regrouping of programs and clustering of homes, this project aims to activate circulation and interaction with the site, engaging the community to create new ways of living together while maintaining the privacy of each residence.

Clusters of Living, Sharing, and Working

Cluster axonometric view into one-, two-, and three-bedroom apartment typologies

1 Community space

2 Laundry room

Clara Domange

Contextual site plan

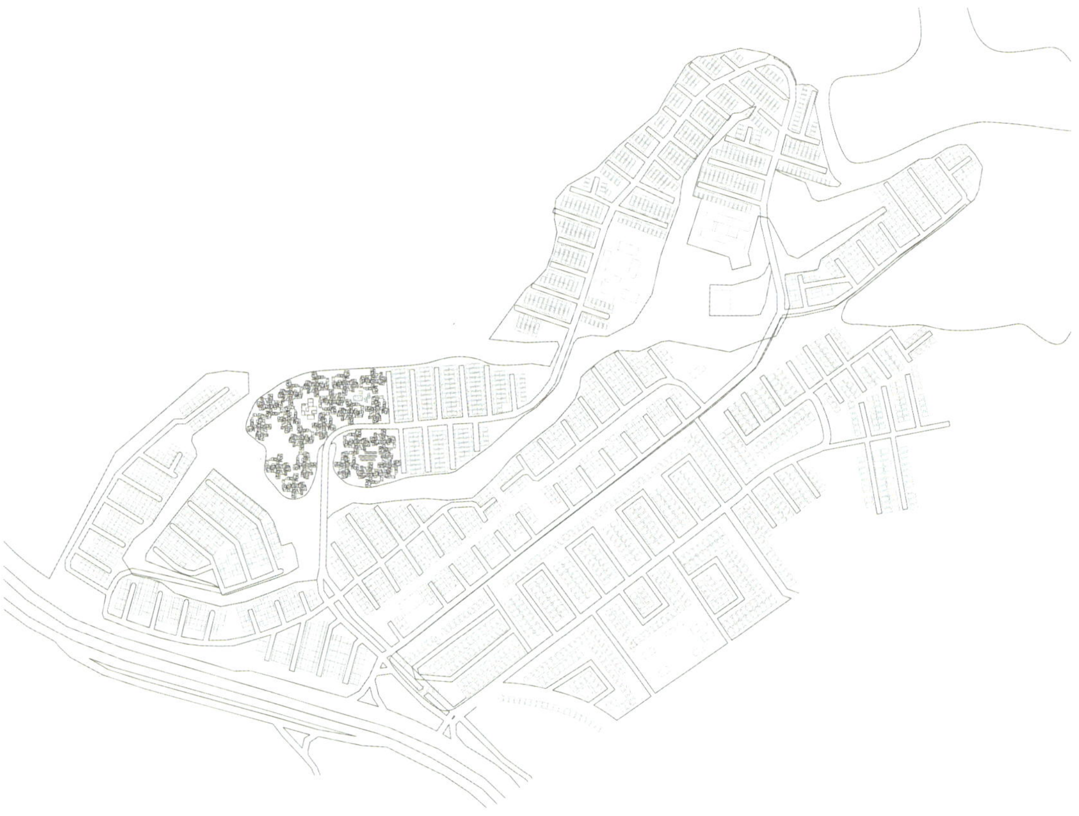

Section of adjacent clusters showing stacked, interconnected domestic programs

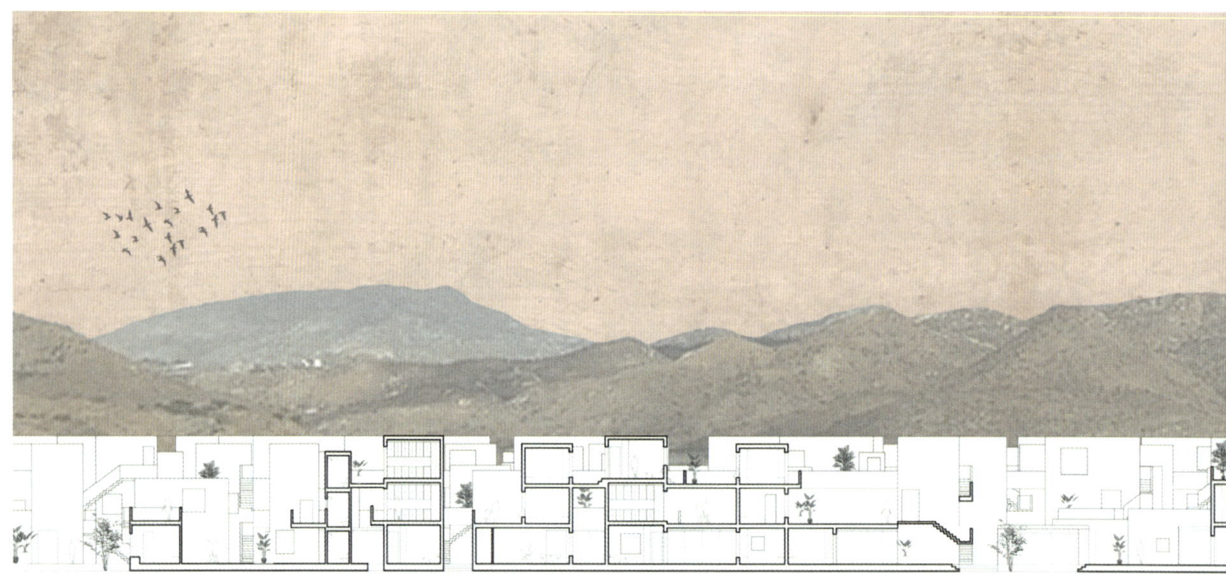

Clusters of Living, Sharing, and Working

Site plan

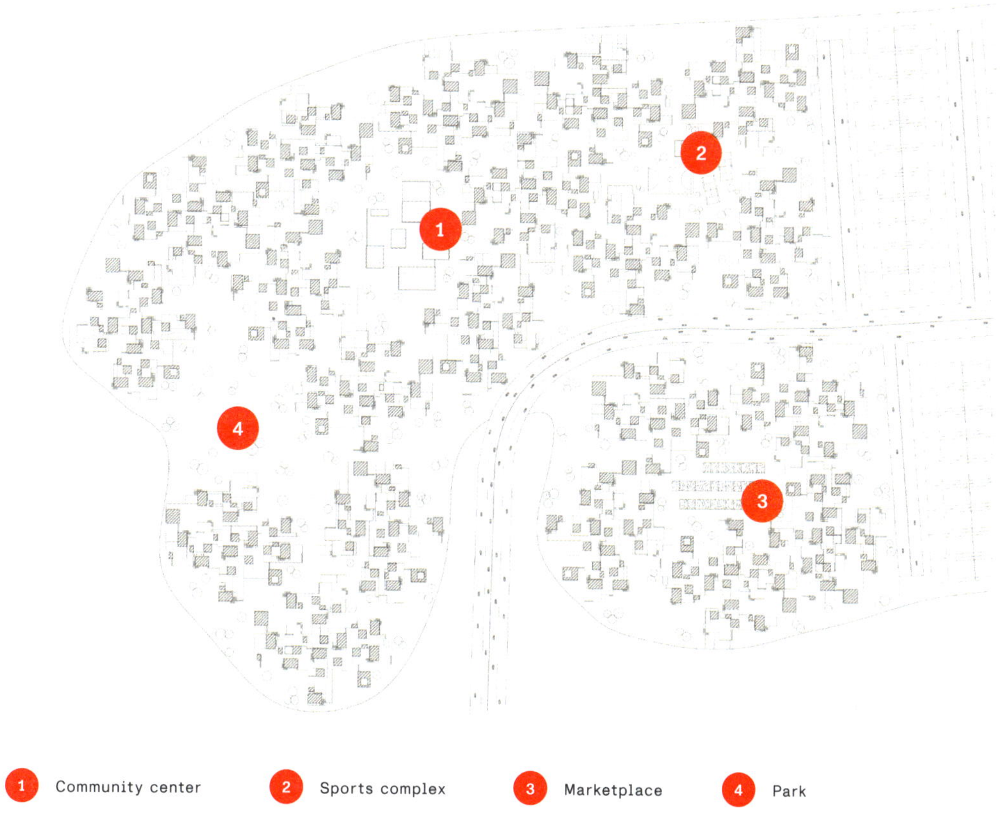

Section glimpses of housing clusters

Clara Domange

Ground-floor plan of housing cluster and enlarged unit plan

1 Community space

2 Laundry room

3 Commercial space

Clusters of Living, Sharing, and Working

Large open spaces and smaller intimate zones

Shuchen Dong

Tijuana is one of the fastest-growing cities in Mexico and is experiencing serious housing shortages. The population growth stimulates a need for housing, causing the city to expand east and south, where squatter homes appear on the periphery. As businesses strive to fulfill basic needs in those peripheral areas, they become more habitable and attract new migration. This trend fuels a vicious cycle of endless growth that the project aims to break by employing the slopes as a buffer while densifying residential areas. The strategy is designed to control rapid urban expansion at this site and in other communities with similar conditions.

This project is located in a suburban community named El Laurel, on the edge of Tijuana. The community is divided into two sections by a long slope traversed by improvised stairs and narrow paths that are dangerous for those who have to climb the hill every day. There are other problems, such as unsafe outdoor spaces, undeveloped collective and commercial areas, and a lack of green public spaces, despite the hot, dry summer months. The project aims to reform the spatial structure of the community by developing the concept of a boundary-house that works both as connector and protector. On the one hand it creates paths connecting the upper and lower levels of the slope, for example, the schools to the community. These connectors also provide informal collective business areas and thus comprise a new community center. On the other hand, the boundary-house proffers a feeling of security for adjacent dwellers, along with protected outdoor spaces and gardens with various levels of privacy and shade.

To accommodate various site conditions, the boundary-house is constructed with a modulated structural system featuring repetitive units of four types. These units provide sub- and superstructure, contain vegetation, offer shade, and support balconies. The buildings can be developed with flexibility while upholding communal amenities.

Sectional perspective showing shared light between levels and uses

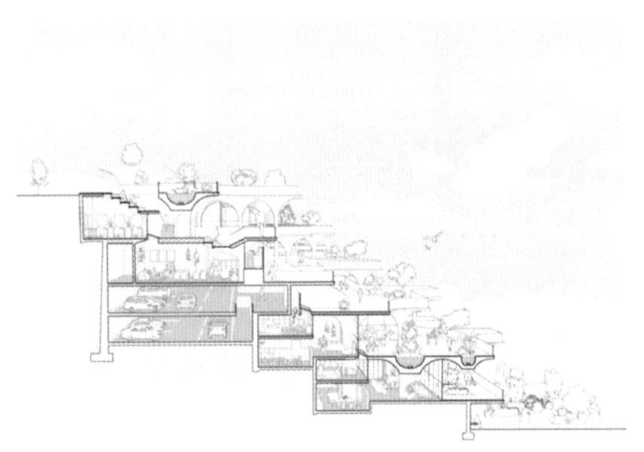

Layered community diagram

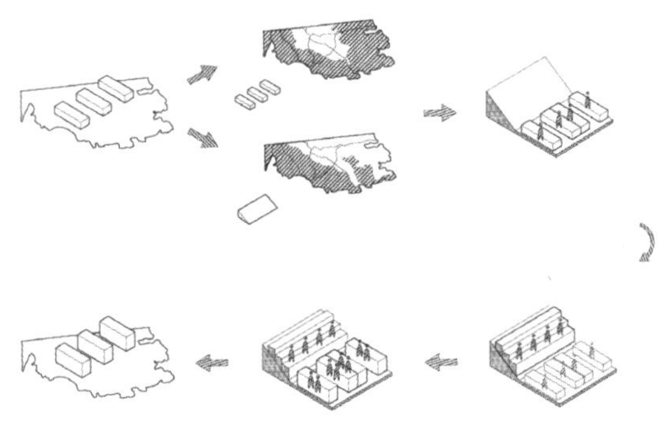

Residence as a Polysemous Boundary

Residence on the unused slope and modified path network

Connection, protection, and different levels of privacy

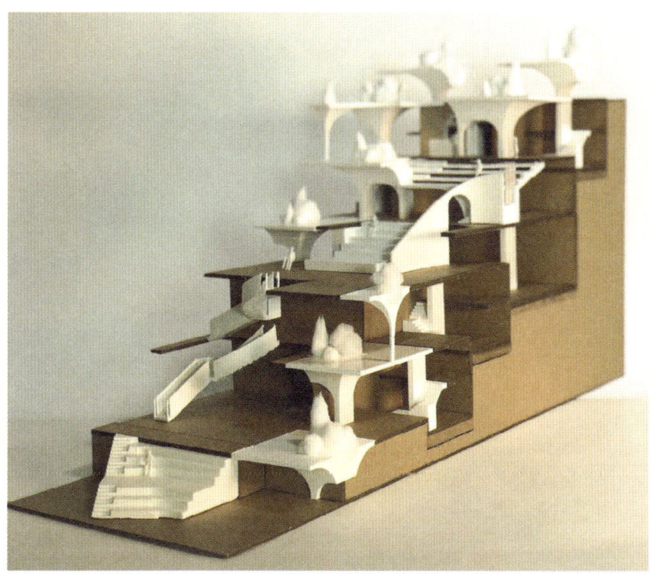

Site strategy to connect dead-end streets

Before

After

Route to School

Shuchen Dong

Axonometric view of various levels and circulation

Residence as a Polysemous Boundary

Shuchen Dong

Strategy to control urban expansion through densifying communities

Residence as a Polysemous Boundary

Layla Ni

To integrate closely with the steep site, this project explores ideas of cohabitation at different scales, from individual units to small arrays of houses and larger communities. At the largest scale the project proposes cohabitation that celebrates semi-enclosed shared spaces such as playgrounds and libraries between layers of houses. Taking advantage of differences in topography, public spaces are carved into the earth. These programmed spaces double as circulation points between the dense layers of topography and housing. At the medium scale the end of each housing cluster forms a *vecindad*, where increased levels of community interaction can be anticipated. These community centers are amplified by rooftop bridges connecting different rooftops to the next street up the hill. At the smallest scale living spaces are carved within flexible, transformable walls. These walls contain furniture and extend coliving possibilities that negotiate the boundary between public and private space.

Conceptual model or public-private interweaving

House-Scape

Interior section of a unit

Section showing different levels

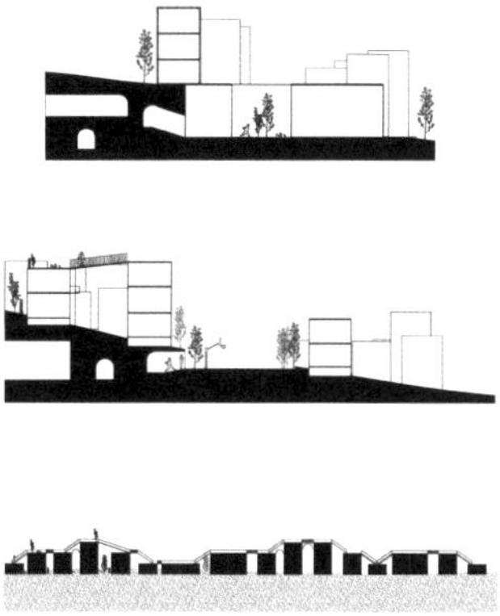

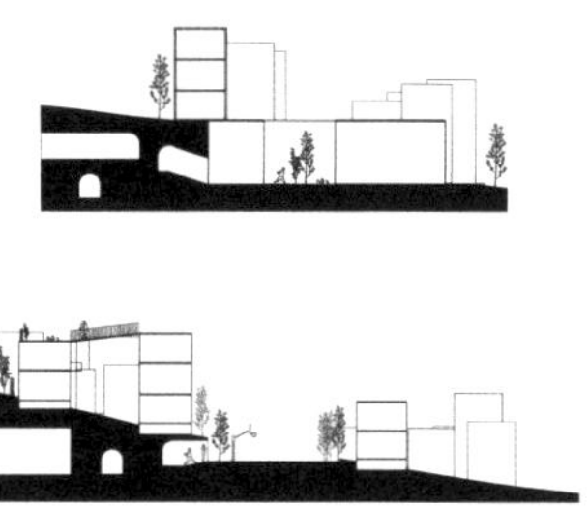

Inhabitable wall possibilities

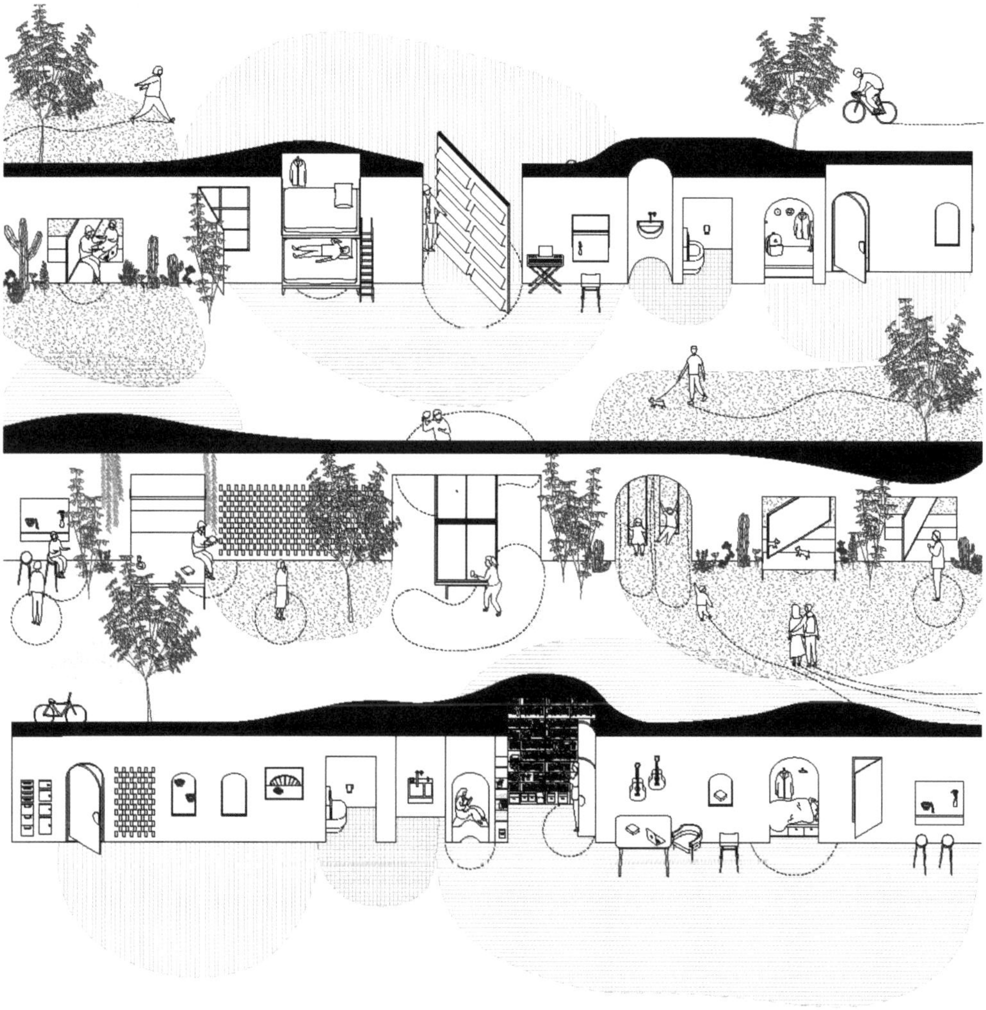

The House as a Collective Infrastructure

The work in this section emphasizes the relationship between infrastructure and domesticity. Considering water and electricity as communal services and potential place makers, these projects are based in the possibilities of linking living spaces to resources by coupling infrastructural hubs with social and collaborative programming. The idea is to promote self-sustainable developments, give visibility to services, and empower the community.

Armaan Shah: Community by Infrastructure

In response to the predatory cellular tract developments in Tijuana, this strategy of densification prioritizes collective infrastructure. Paseos del Vergel residents often grapple with unreliable access to basic utilities such as water and electricity. In response, "Community by Infrastructure" provides scales of access to water and electricity by coupling infrastructural hubs with social and collaborative programming within new multifamily residences. The intervention breaks the rigid block structures of low-cost developments by inserting various community services through micro power stations that double as commercial nodes and micro water tanks that serve as domestic servicing hubs.

Building utilities coupled with everyday domestic and commercial needs

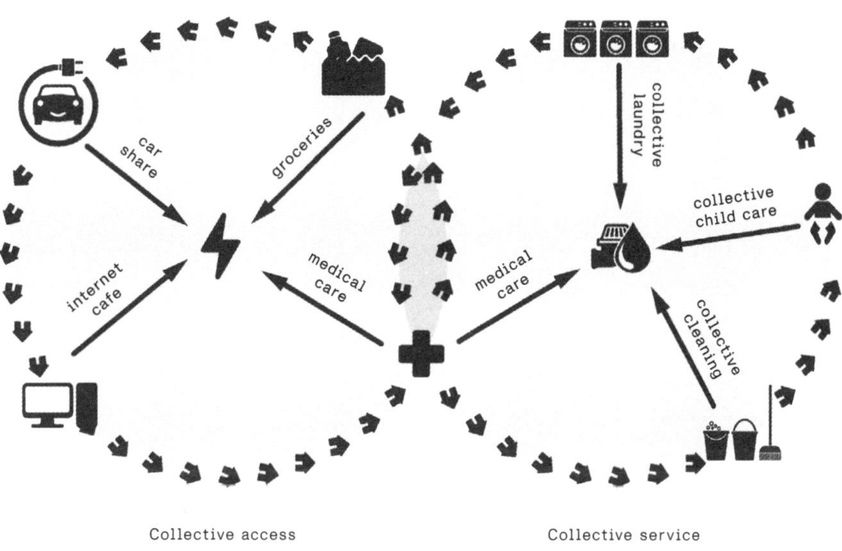

Diagram: framing microgrid and infrastructure-driven densification

Armaan Shah

Master plan: breaking up cellular blocks with defined neighborhood regions and infrastructural nodes.

Community By Infrastructure

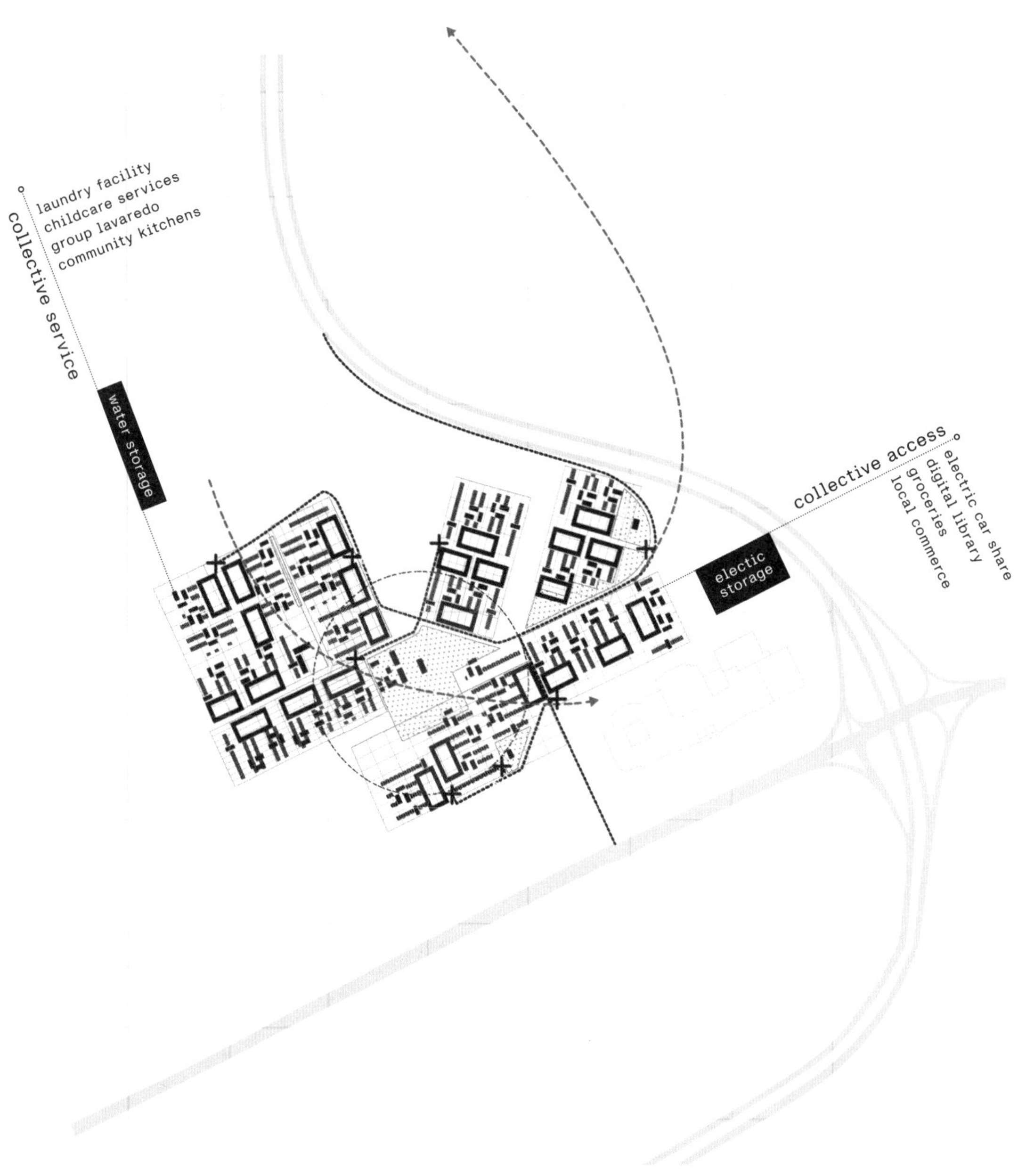

Breaking the Homogeneity
1:4000

Community by Infrastructure

Typical plan: densified 500-unit neighborhood subdivided around large community access nodes and small service hubs.

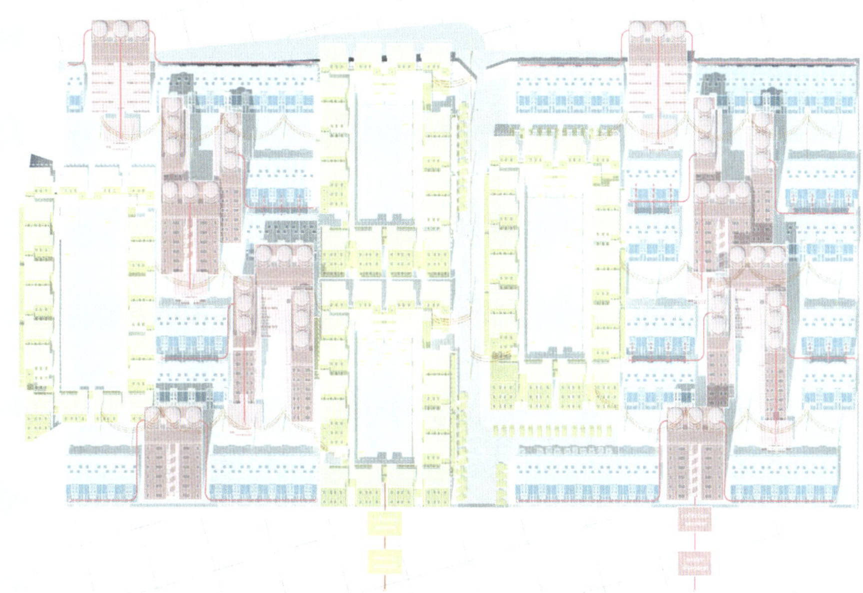

Two new multifamily building types break down the relationship between shared and public spaces through a covered marketplace courtyard and sheltered laundry and play areas across the *vecindad*.

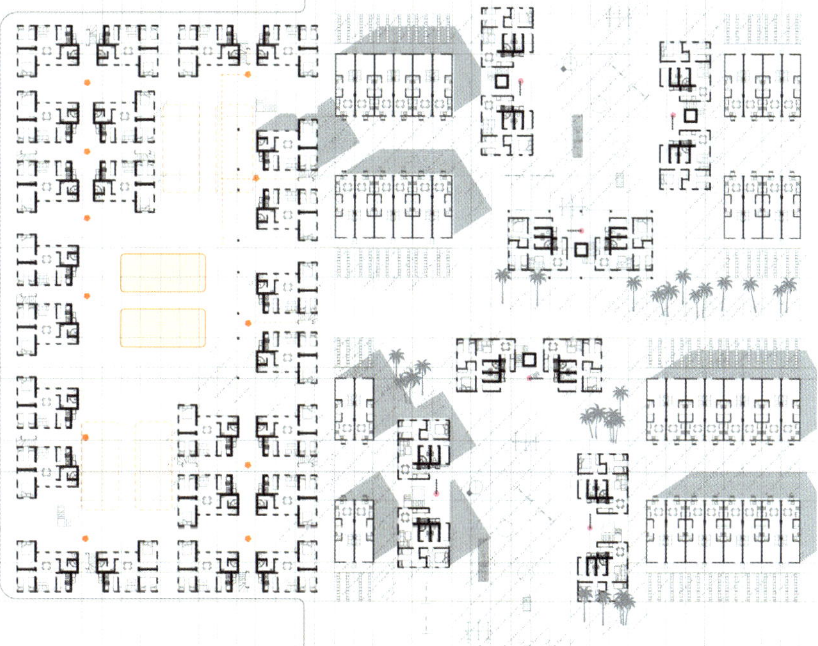

Armaan Shah

Community access hub: provides backup battery power. Paired program activities include a marketplace, electric car-sharing, and community Internet access.

Unit cluster: aggregated in groups of three, allowing multigenerational living. Lower levels are accessible and share *lavaredos* with neighboring clusters.

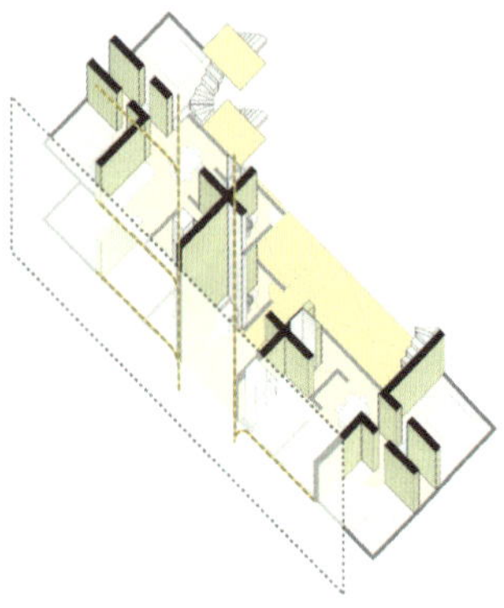

Commercial courtyard: shared space providing local vendors a central neighborhood location to earn wages as well as resident access to goods and services such as supermarkets and hair salons.

Community by Infrastructure

Community service hub: provides neighborhood water tank when pipes run dry. Paired program activities include shared laundry, a semicovered playground, and a higher density of *lavaredos* across units.

Service playground: shared amenities deep within the *vecindad* that serves as both sheltered playground and laundry facility, encouraging shared community responsibility for child safety in a safe social hub.

Alex Pineda

“Domestic Waterways” is a project for 1,000 “units” of housing within Angeles de Puebla, a development on the outskirts of Mexicali. The project responds to high levels of abandonment by infilling and densifying emptied areas, particularly the central 70-unit blocks and the development’s edge. Units with direct access to a “water room” are built up over time around infrastructural supply walls, creating a variety of exterior spaces organized around overlapping configurations that challenge norms of ownership and collectivity. The internal condition of the block is inverted around the newly collectivized core. Ultimately the cores are leveraged systematically, pairing the collectivized water resource with domestic social life.

Dispersion of units across a collaged site

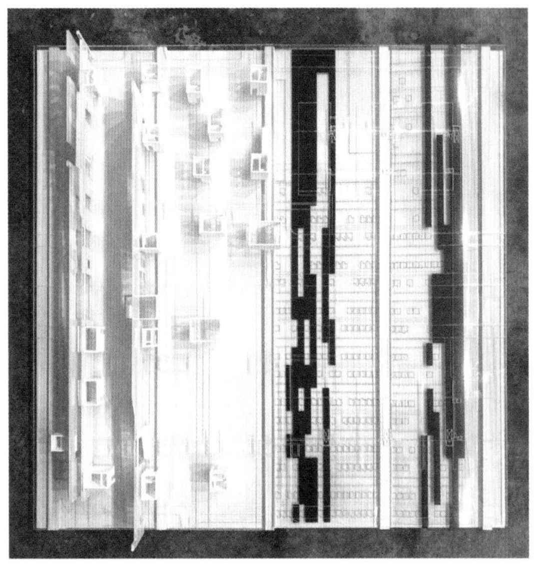

Interconnectivity of units

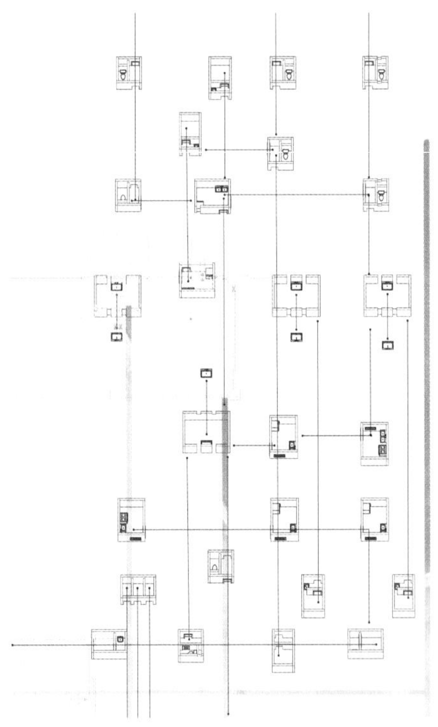

Domestic Waterways

Infilled abandoned lots and resulting waterways along the edge

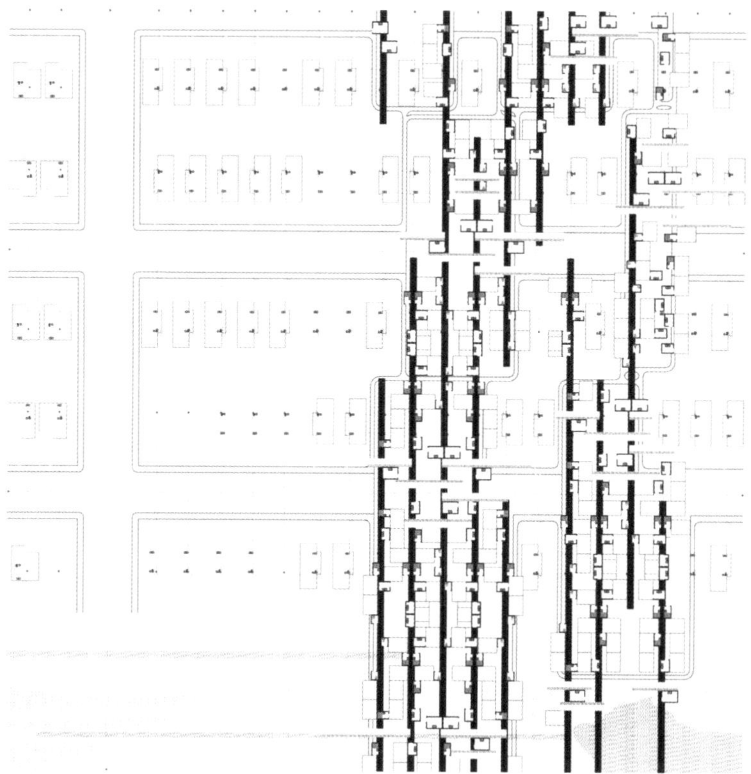

Infilled abandoned lots and resulting waterways

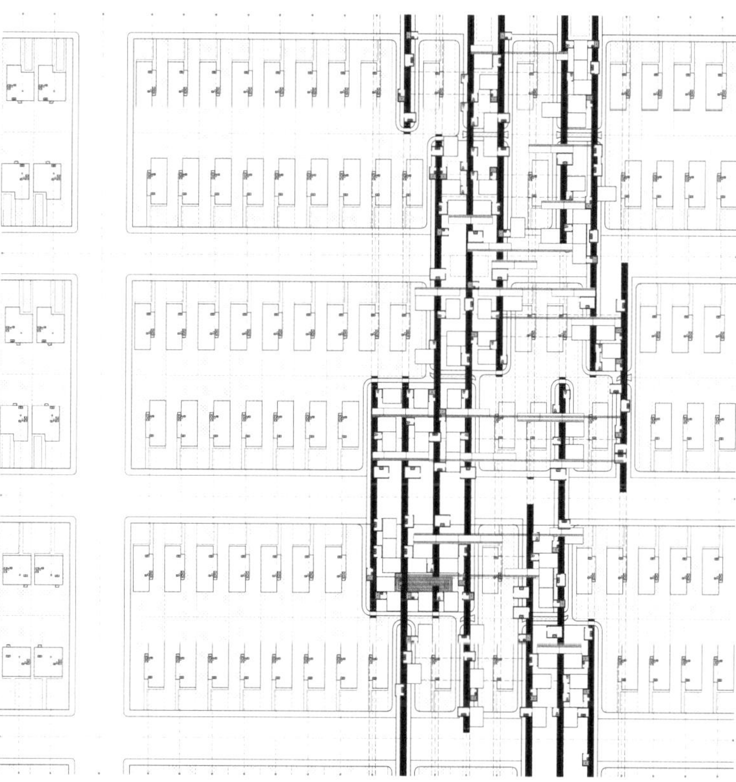

Alex Pineda

Everted *Vecindad*

Documented individuated frontage

Regional water systems

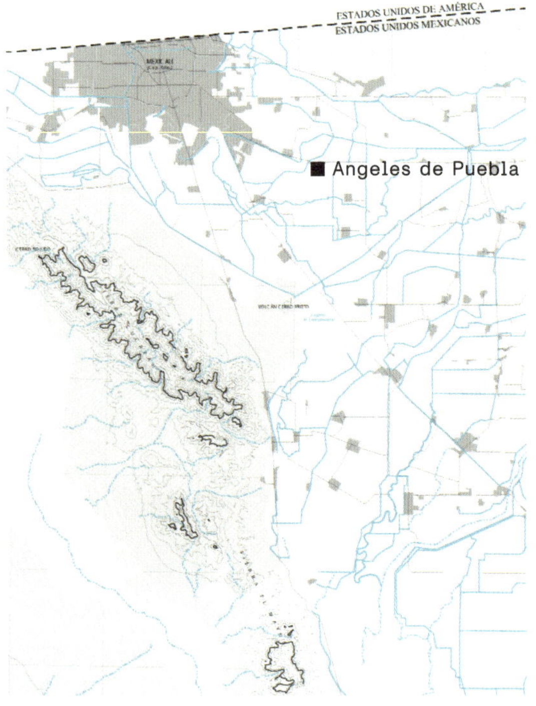

Domestic Waterways

Infrastructural, public,and domestic sections

Conceptual section: domestic landscapes

NS section: public path scale

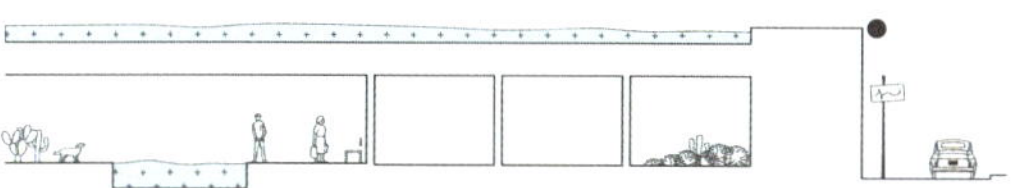

NS section: infrastructural scale

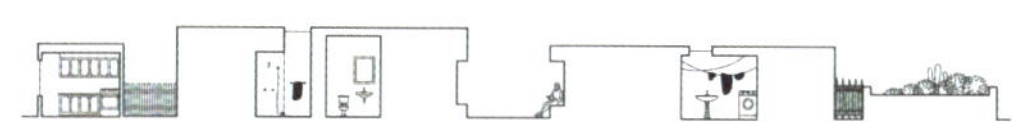

NS section: domestic scale

Stitching across developed edges

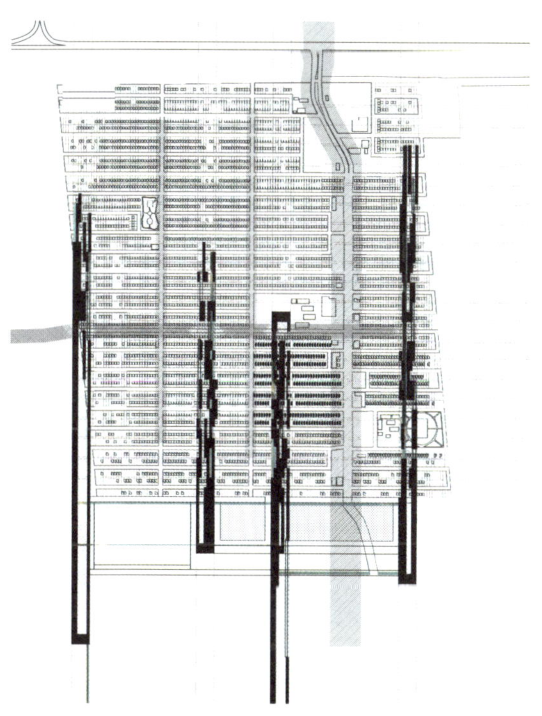

Water-room modules

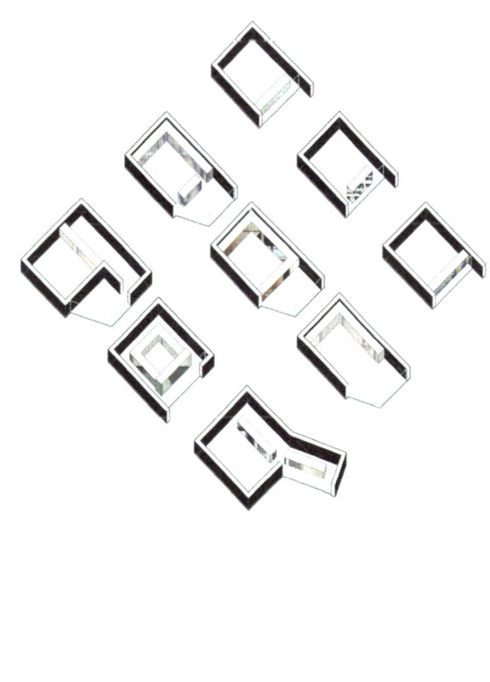

Limy Rocha

Angeles de Puebla is a housing development on the periphery of Mexicali, about 17 km from the city center. It is comprised of roughly 4,500 standardized one- and two-bedroom units, more than half of which are abandoned. High and rising rates of abandonment due to violence and lack of services have created fragmented street fronts, blocks, and neighborhoods with large swaths of empty houses that are often concentrated within the middle of blocks, which are made up of 70+ houses each. The block fragmentation is most evident in personalized front yards, creating a street frontage that portrays a highly individualized form of living, lack of infrastructural support, and absence of communal well-being for Mexicali's working class.

"Fixture Constructs" challenges the idea of standardization as a unit that is whole and independent, fostering different scales of grouping to form collectives by means of sharing resources such as water. This project challenges the idea of home/land ownership, proposing rather a transparent understanding of resources; and adding value to water availability. It challenges the idea of identity based upon private boundaries, preferring an understanding of interstitial space as communal grounds following the *vecindad* model. By utilizing existing water access points (i.e. toilet, shower, sink, and *lavaderos*), a domestic frame can be derived from the water grade—thus the spectrum from gray to potable water becomes vital to the organization of the block, street, and ultimately collective living within the *ejido*. Each water access point is given a room dimension that corresponds to its domestic program, which is then connected to the others through a plumbing supply wall. From this logic, the "unit" emerges: a single interior space (dry) with direct access to a water room (wet) and to the exterior.

The supply of potable water manifests itself as infrastructural lines located above the plumbing walls, allowing rainwater collection. At the other end of the system, the urban equipment of the wet-wall transports gray water into bio-swale interventions that then revitalize the once-active irrigation streams. Through the extremity of potable and gray-water access points, and their corresponding dry rooms, *vecindad*-like spaces emerge as shared exterior space for multiple uses by the community. This suggests groupings that, rather than proliferating, organize public spaces around systemic resource conditions perpetuated in domestic space, like water management, thus erasing the individualized "lot line."

Fixture Constructs: A Water Syntax

Memory collage of ownership, identity, and dwelling urgency

Limy Rocha

The proposed site plan highlights above-ground incisions via north-south infrastructural domestic lines that supply potable water, while east-west ground-carvings create bio-swales to recycle gray water that washes into a revitalized irrigation stream to the west of the *ejido*.

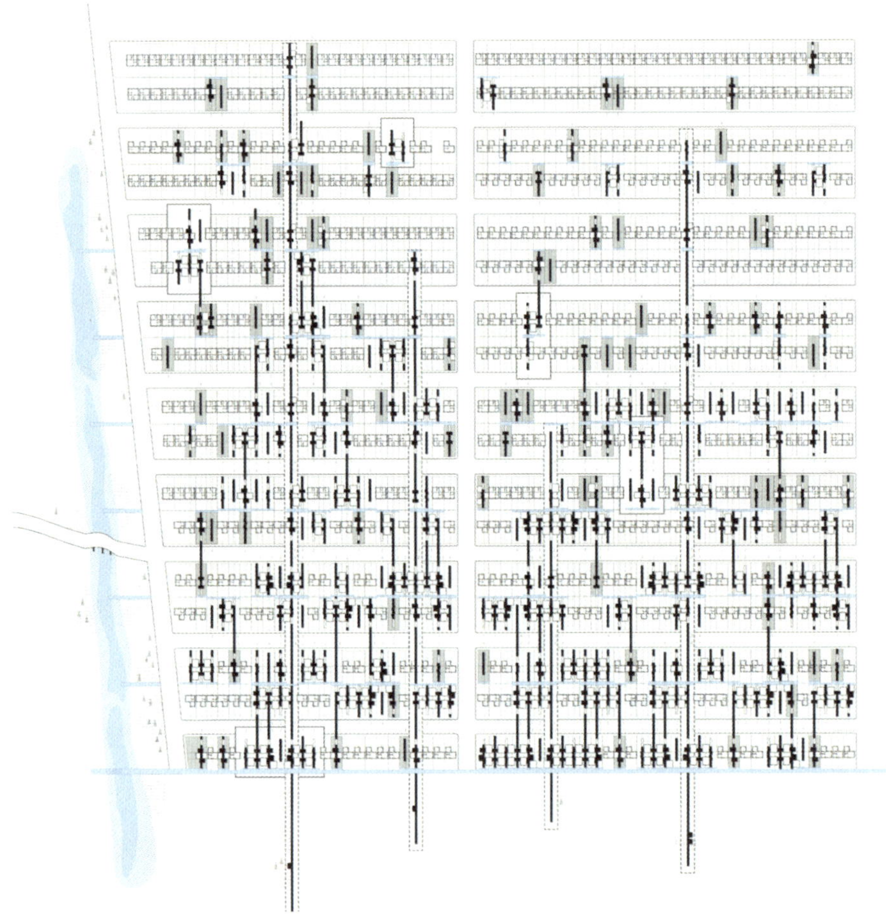

Satellite images of razing *ejidos*—communal farmland in a Mexican village—bound by irrigation streams of various sizes

Site photos demonstrating the deteriorating abandoned conditions of mirrored backyard spaces, also referenced as a shared mid-block space.

Fixture Constructs: A Water Syntax

Plan progression (left to right) from a typical unit to a housing commons that is comprised of dry rooms surrounding water-access points that manifest as domestic fixtures: sink, toilet, shower, *lavadero*.

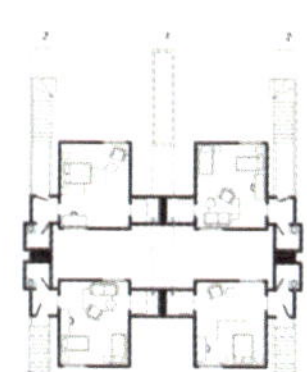

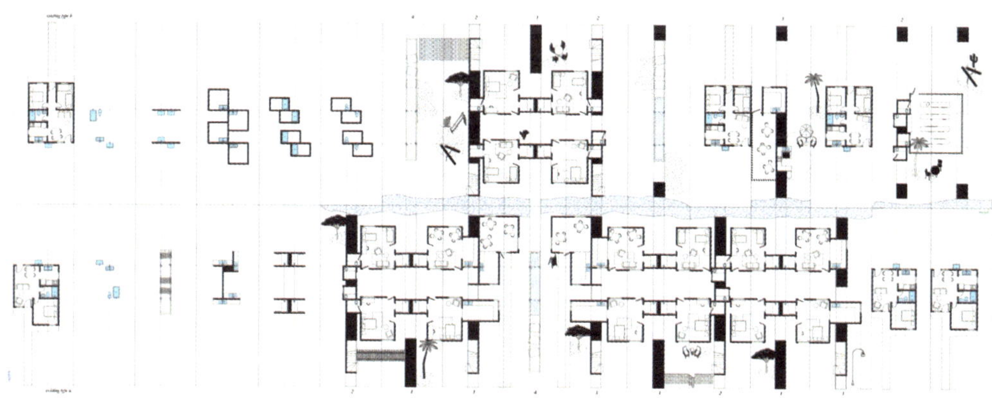

Growing abandonment rate in Angeles de Puebla is visible in three conditions of intervention throughout the housing complex: abandoned single lots, lots within the block, and lots across the street.

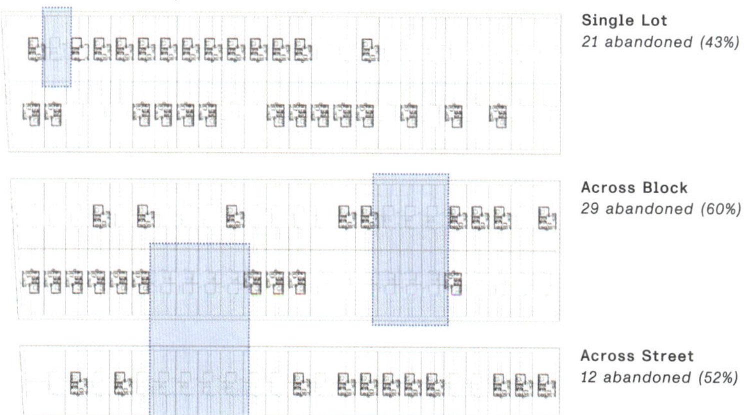

Plug-and-Play Houses

The personalization of the home through carving, moving, adding, and completing constitute the basis of these projects. The interest lies in the flexibility of living spaces and fostering mixed-used strategies that correspond to economic and social realities. While some of the projects attempt to bridge the contrasts between the formal and the informal, inspired by the ways residents have adapted their homes employing local construction methods and incremental growth, others offer adaptability within a singular system that allows for various interpretations of interior space.

Emily Cass: Building Blocks: An Incremental Housing Strategy

"Building Blocks" proposes an intervention into the flawed megahousing complexes built on the perimeters of borders and cities in Mexico. These housing complexes suffer from extreme bouts of abandonment because of lack of resources, faulty water supplies, and the residents' inability to pay monthly mortgage payments. Developers build the housing complexes and residents are encouraged to purchase individual units through housing tax credits from employers. The system creates perverse incentives that contribute to the appalling deficiencies that in turn imperil the resulting communities. The proposal stems from collective research on *vecindades* completed in the first half of the semester. This examination informed a conceptual study that sought to utilize formal moves as drivers of alternate ways of living while challenging traditional domestic roles in terms of more nuanced relationships between infrastructure and domesticity.

The focus was Paseos del Vergel, a housing complex in Tijuana, Mexico, with nearly 5,000 residents, primarily single mothers. It was constructed with 3,000 identical homes scattered across a steep and disconnected topography that impedes communal continuity and circulation between home and school, housing project and city. Moreover, the faultily constructed homes have been delaminating and collapsing. Despite these issues, residents continue to personalize their homes and bring life to the otherwise sterile development. Inspired by the ways residents have adapted the site, this project seeks to create formal and informal interventions that support community making.

The project is an incremental mixed-use housing strategy that invests in the entire site through a series of discrete improvements that homeowners can make to their dwellings. Through carving into and adding to the existing grid, this project seeks to be neither top-down or bottom-up but rather a critical intervention and catalog of possibilities that allow plug-and-play elements based on residents' needs and desires.

Existing blocks are carved into and break the relentless grid, adding green space, passageways, and spaces for communal living.

Emily Cass

Changing landscape of an existing block at Paseos del Vergel. A phased approach of carving, adapting, and adding to the existing landscape allows communities to develop at multiple scales.

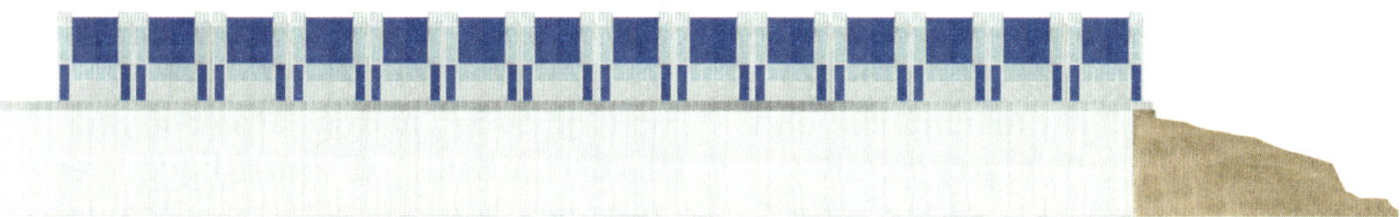

Existing

Carve

Add

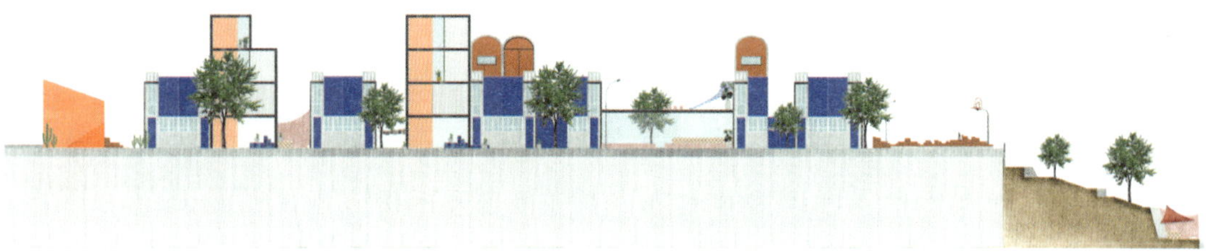

Adapt

Building Blocks: An Incremental Housing Strategy

A catalog of possibilities allows residents to plug-and-play based on personal needs and desires.

Carve

Breaking grid
with green space

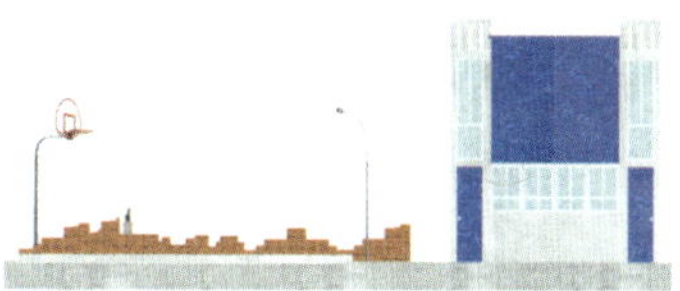

Carve

Creating dedicated
space for play

Carve

Creating paths
to shorten commutes

Add

Local factory that will facilitate
construction

Add

Structural reinforcing
for at risk units

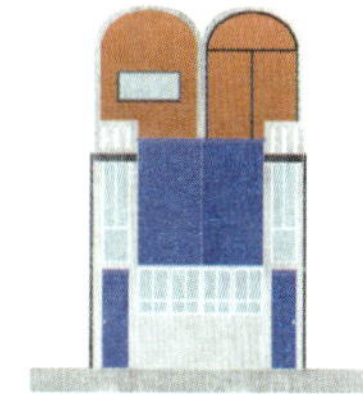

Add

Expanding existing properties

Add

Program to insterstitial
dead zone

Add

Educational spaces

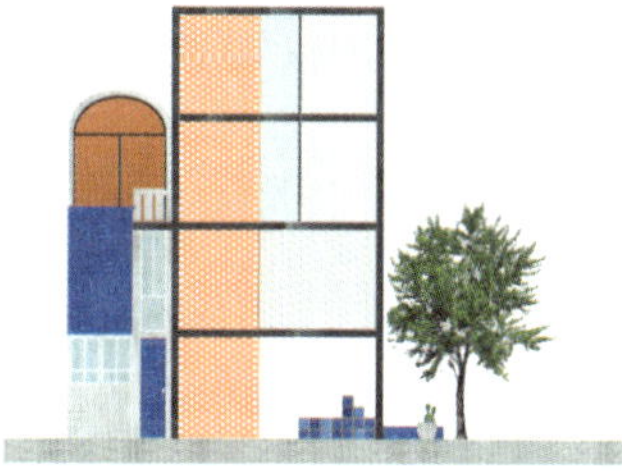

Add

New communal dwellings with
increased density

Emily Cass

Incremental mixed-use housing strategy that invests across the entire site through a series of discrete improvements that homeowners can make to their dwellings

Building Blocks: An Incremental Housing Strategy

Emily Cass

A *vecindad* is formed through carving into the landscape, adding additions to existing units, and constructing entirely new structures that serve as hubs for essentials such as water and Wi-Fi.

Paseos del Vergel: Vecindad

Addition of new higher-density communal dwellings that provide resources such as Wi-Fi and potable water

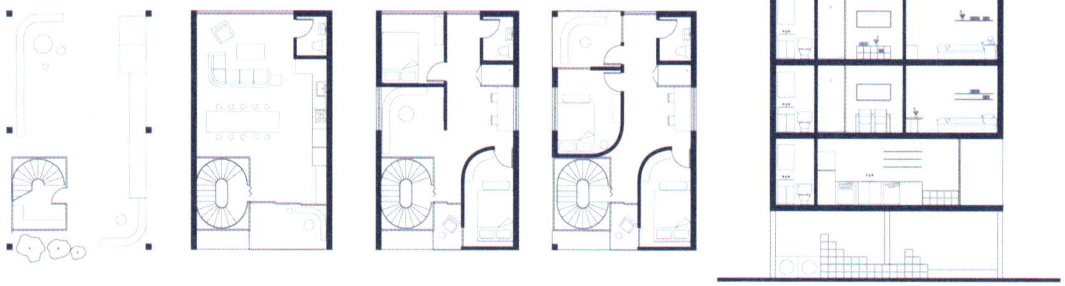

Aerial view of Paseos del Vergel

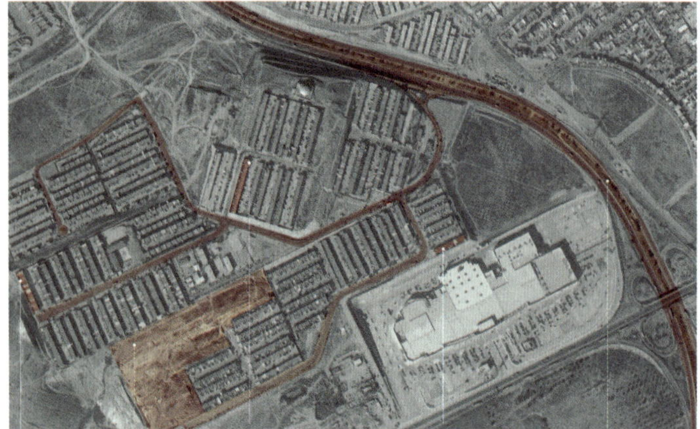

Building Blocks: An Incremental Housing Strategy

Paseos del Vergel was constructed with around 3,000 identical homes scattered across a steep and disconnected topography. Breaking the relentless grid through various architectural and programmatic moves makes the community function more at the scale of an individual.

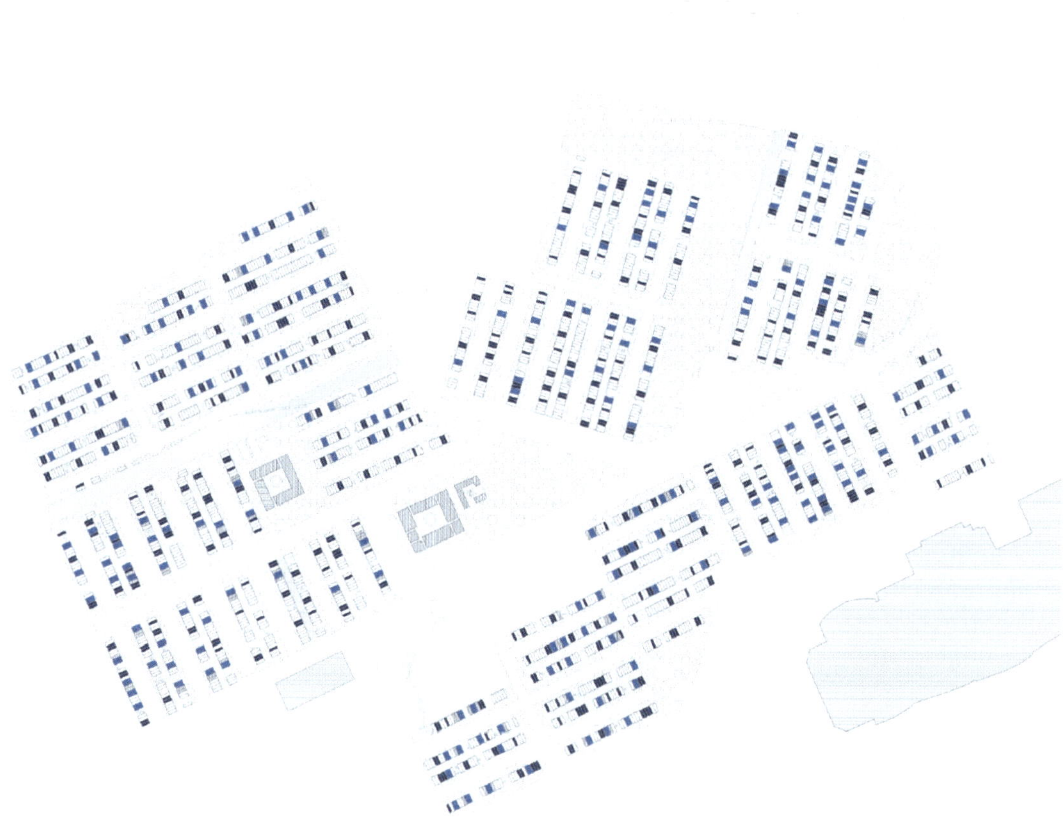

Model illustrating the myriad interventions along a single block

Model depicting the roof as a space for communal living

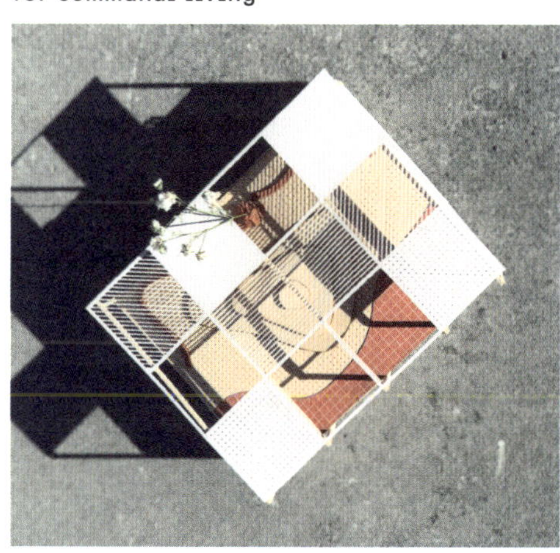

Xiaohui Wen

To explore the potential of the *vecindad* typology, this project examined shared housing in square form, creating a courtyard that is essential to coliving and social interactions that energize the architectural form. Residents do not fix purposes on specific spaces but rather share the free public areas and occupy private pocket rooms as needed. This sharing and occupying allows a reconsideration of the privacy required for each life activity, manifested in the curved walls that work as capsules and host activities, only some of which require enclosure. The sense of neighborhood is fluid and changing, and the architecture is meant to free the inhabitants from formal constraints and territorial boundaries.

The concept leads to vertical stipulation whereby a shifted alignment creates opportunities for an activated facade that calls for domestic and social adventures. The curves in the wall correspond to bumps and cutouts in the interior spaces, where furniture and furnishings echo and accommodate lovely moments.

Conceptual model revealing practical use of curves as a continuation of the square concept

View of units from top

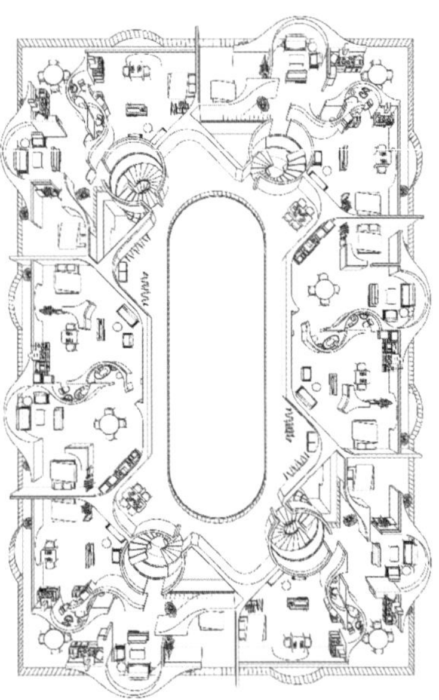

Squared

Conceptual prototype of a square *vecindad*

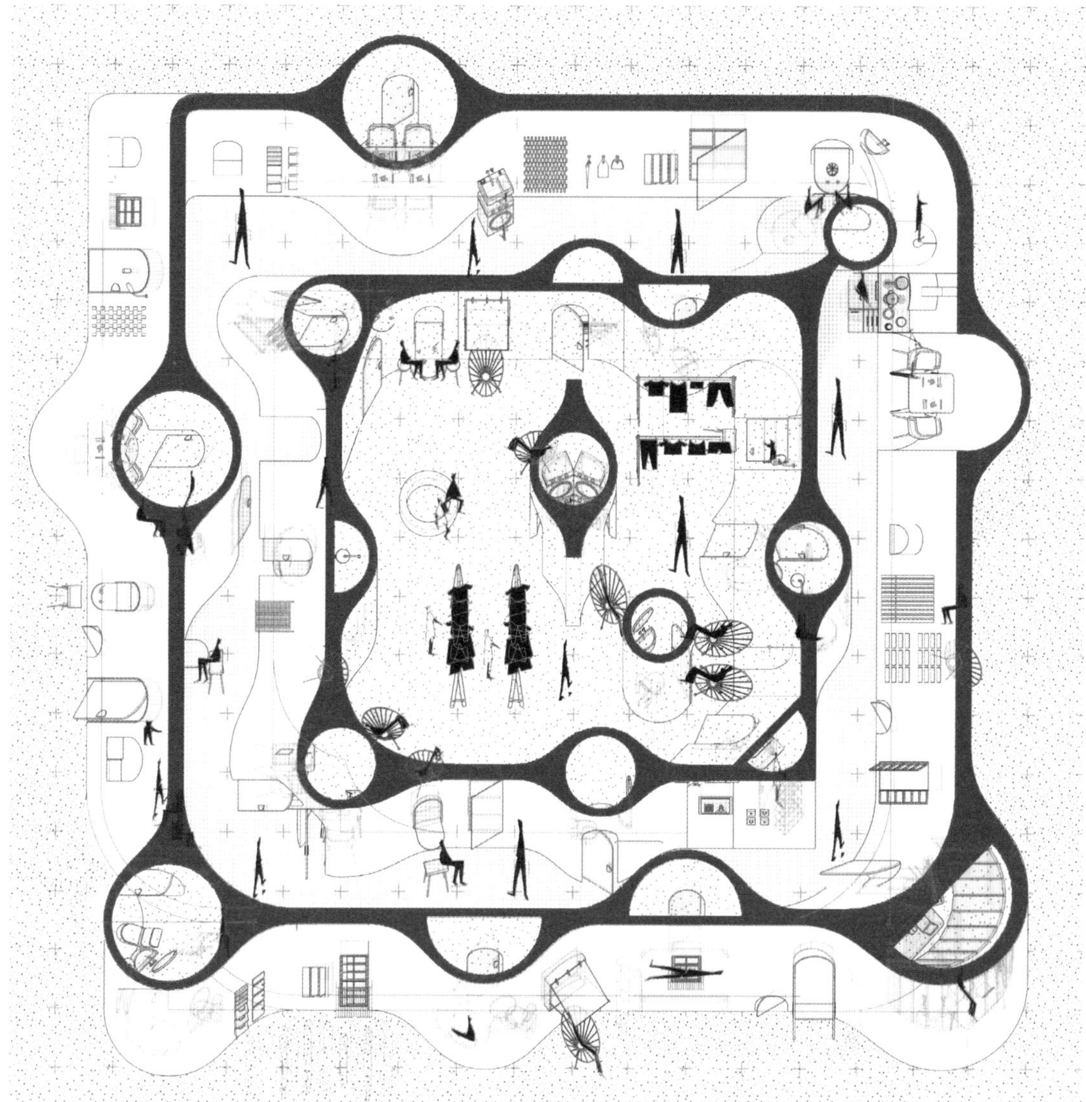

Xiaohui Wen

Vertical exploration of aggregated *vecindades*

Squared

Interior life

Camille Chabrol

Angeles de Puebla is an INFONAVIT affordable-housing development on the western periphery of Mexicali, Baja California, Mexico. The desertion of single-family homes began only six years after its construction, in 2009. The units were abandoned for a variety of reasons: poor infrastructure, lack of amenities, distance to city center, overcrowding in the tiny 40-square-meter houses, dearth of safe public spaces, and lack of connection between neighbors.

Today Angeles de Puebla, a development of 4,400 units, counts about 20 percent of its housing as abandoned, a rate that continues to increase since abandonment begets abandonment. This project develops a strategy for revitalizing the abandoned lots while fostering a new public life. New forms of communal ownership can be created through repurposing abandoned lots and rethinking property lines, thereby bringing services to people already living in the development.

The urban strategy behind "City of Pathways" is to subdivide the existing street grid with a meandering path that increases connectivity throughout the community. This path links together new plots of land and consolidates several smaller existing plots. A portion of these plots are communally owned and occupied by bedrooms clustered around collective kitchens. Another portion of land is reserved for public parks and buildings such as libraries and health centers. Small commercial spaces line the new pathways throughout the collectively owned plots. Residents can rent them to start businesses and then move to larger spaces on different plots as they grow. The variously sized plots of land and kitchens and different quantities of bedrooms enable diverse communal living patterns and allow "social groups" to buy into shared properties also enabling new groups to form.

Incremental repurposing of abandoned lots

Consolidating small privately owned lots to host public amenities such as day care, libraries, communal housing, and spaces for small business

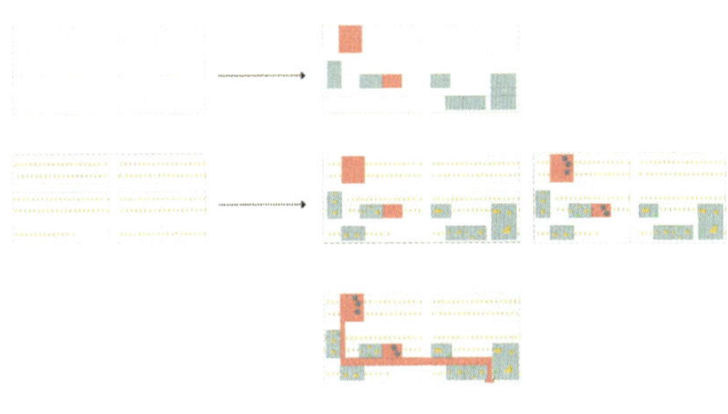

City of Pathways

Axonometric of pathways linking consolidated plots

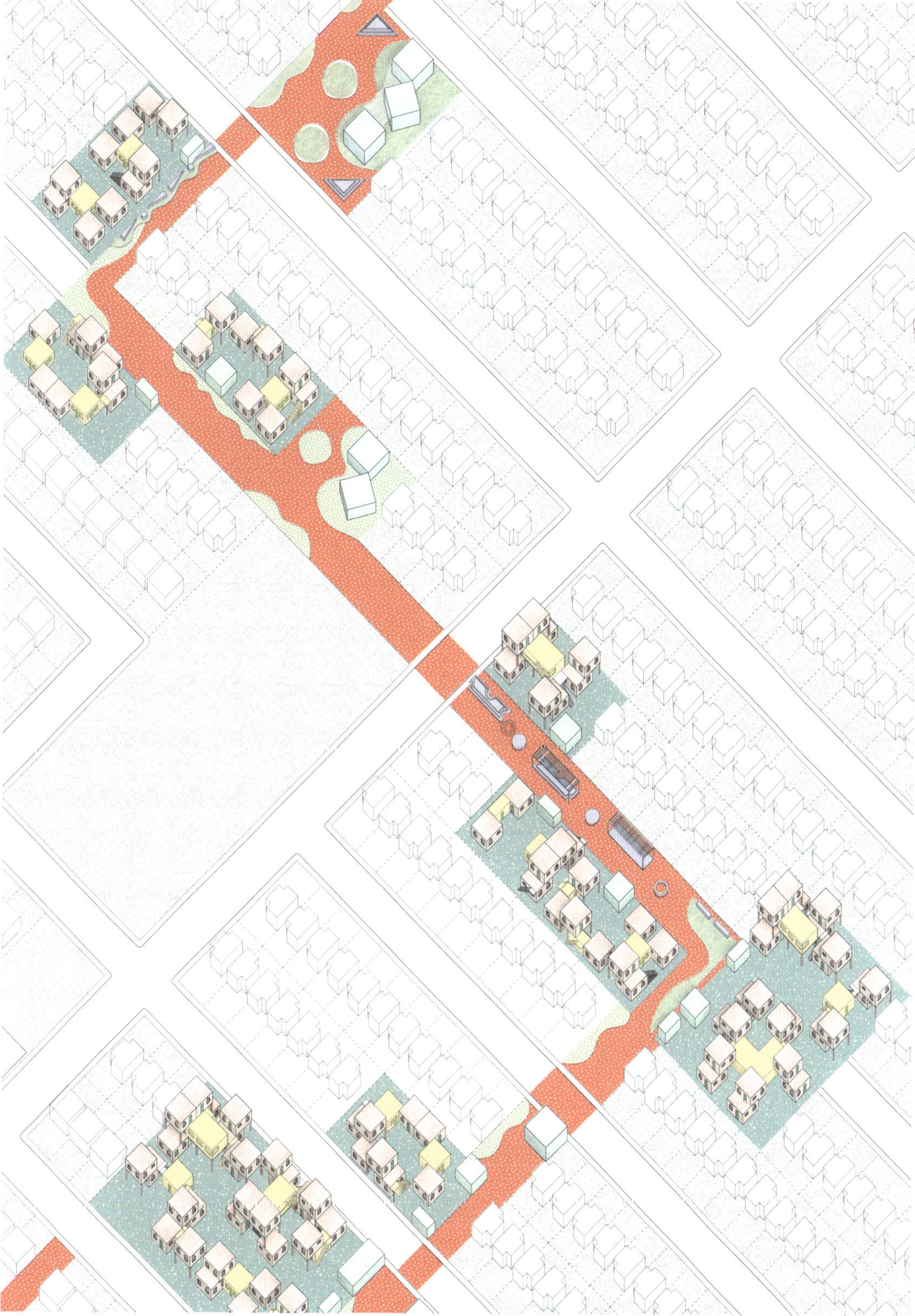

Camille Chabrol

Model showing how public pathways and lots (in red) form a linear park, connect communally owned lots (in light blue), and bring amenities to existing residences.

New *vecindades* combine flexible "bedroom units" with kitchen units of various sizes

Two-kitchen, eight-bed configuration with large central courtyard and small commercial space with restaurant

City of Pathways

Configurations feature large courtyards and stacking to create balconies and patios. Maximum circulation allows maximum flexibility.

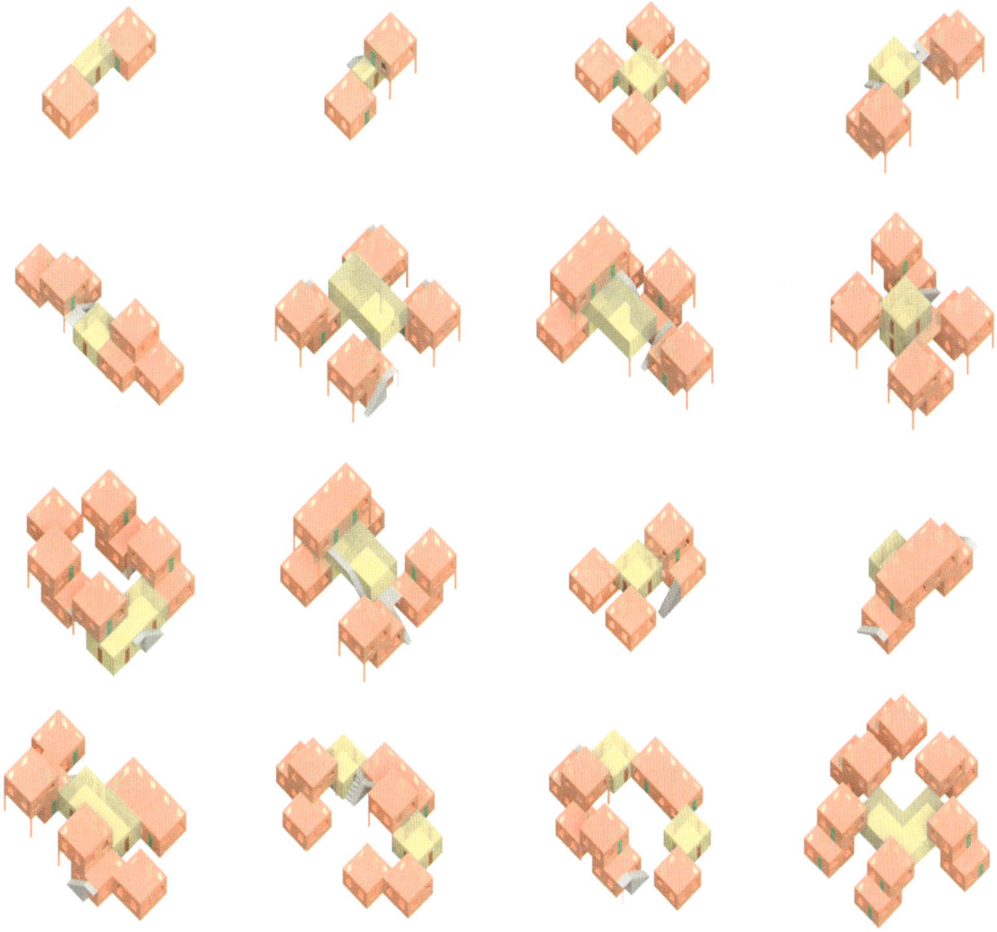

Model photo of a *vecindad* on communal land

Public buildings on consolidated lots: library, day care, and small businesses open onto communal spaces, diversifying the existing residential-only condition.

Miriam Dreiblatt

This project disrupts the domination of privatized land in Ángeles de Puebla, Mexicali, through the establishment of Community Land Trusts (CLTs). With more than 16 percent abandonment concentrated along the periphery of the development, the site is emblematic of the failure of single-use zoning to foster community life. This proposal recaptures abandoned lots through the INFONAVIT protocol, decoupling land from private homes to empower the community via collective landownership and densify the typical block with varied housing typologies and collective services. CLTs are formed around a group of formerly abandoned homes and occupied residences, reflecting the tripartite organizational structure that links existing and new residents with INFONAVIT members. The CLTs are located adjacent to existing public infrastructure such as parks and public schools as well as new areas for compressed earth-block production. The new housing is constructed with this material and hinges upon the vestigial wet walls of the former abandoned homes. This partial-preservation strategy reduces the expense and difficulty of new construction and retains a physical memory of the existing built fabric.

Live-work cluster

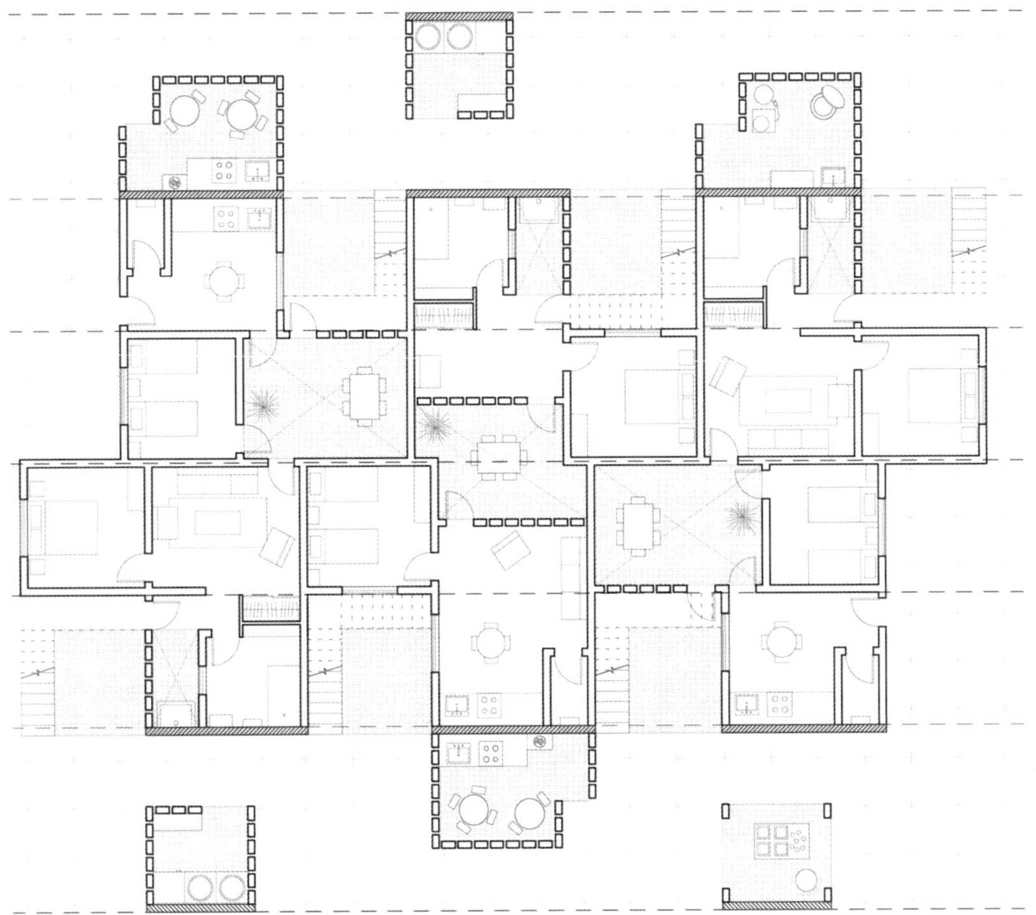

Breaking the Pattern of Privatized Land

Regenerating abandoned lots

Creation of Private Parcels

Contruction of Single-Family,
Private Homes

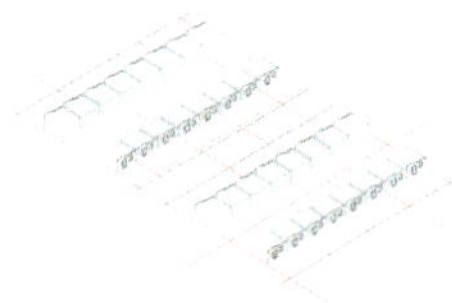

Expansion of Abandonment

Amalgamation of Formerly
Abandoned Land

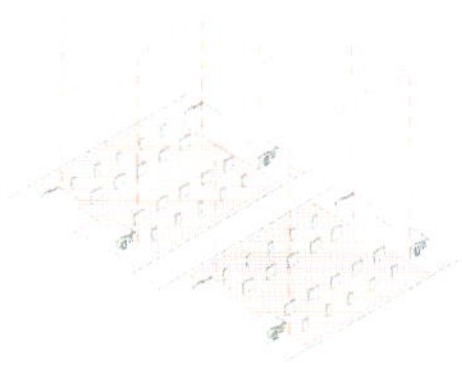

Separation of Abandoned
Homes and Land

Preservation of Abandoned
Homes' Wet Walls

Multiscalar units

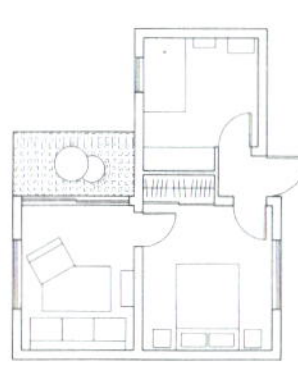

Studio—Square
2/building complex

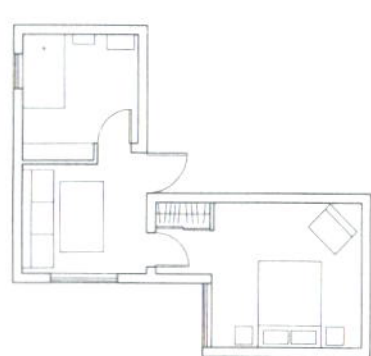

Studio—Square
2/building complex

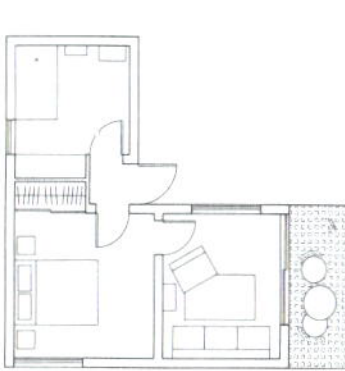

Studio—"L" Shape
2/building complex

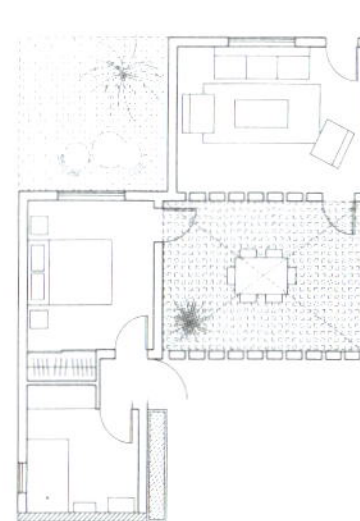

One Bedroom
6/building complex

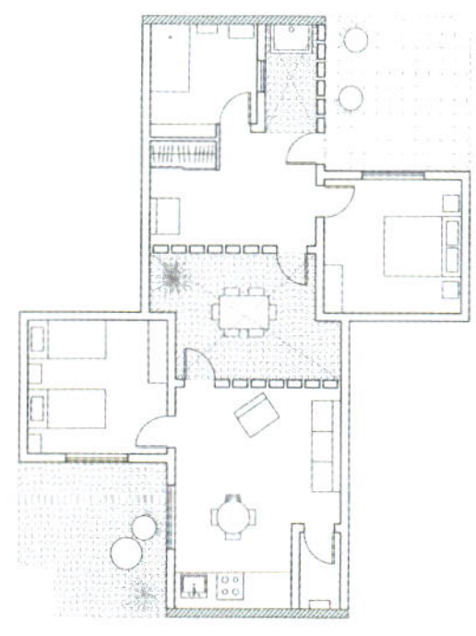

Two Bedroom—Central
1/building complex

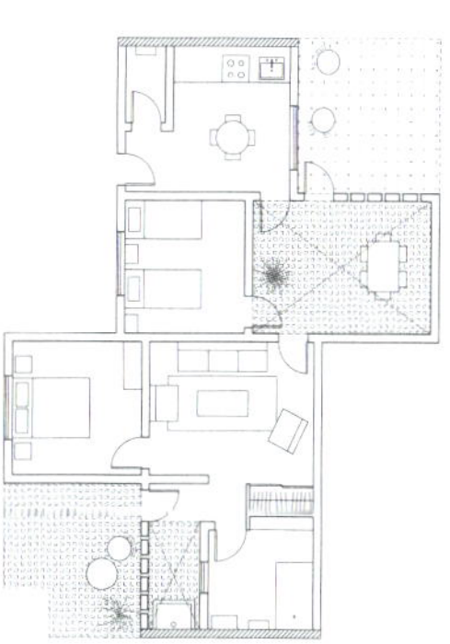

Two Bedroom—Edge
2/building complex

Miriam Dreiblatt

Public trusts in a privatized landscape

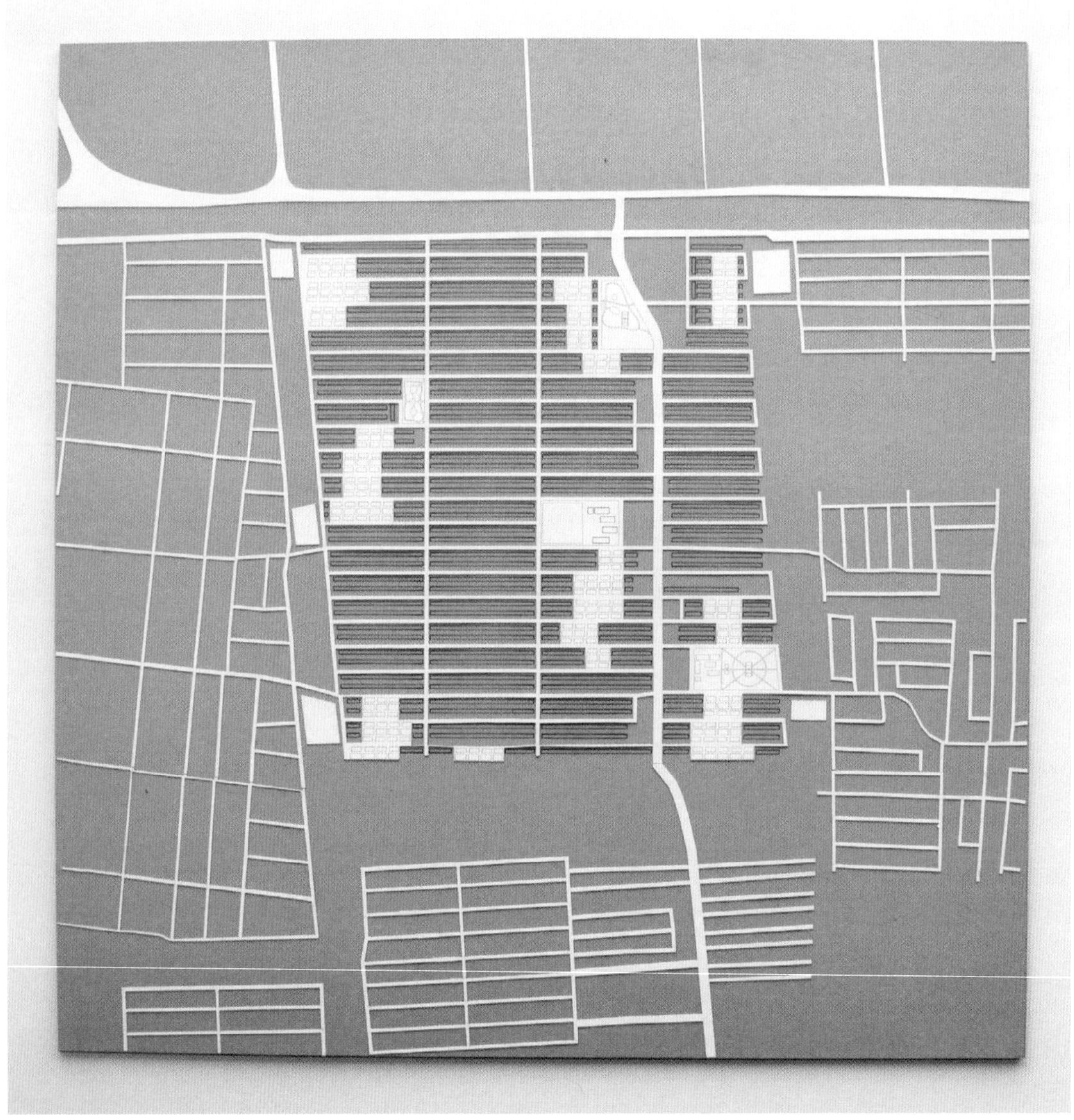

Breaking the Pattern of Privatized Land

Inverting the block

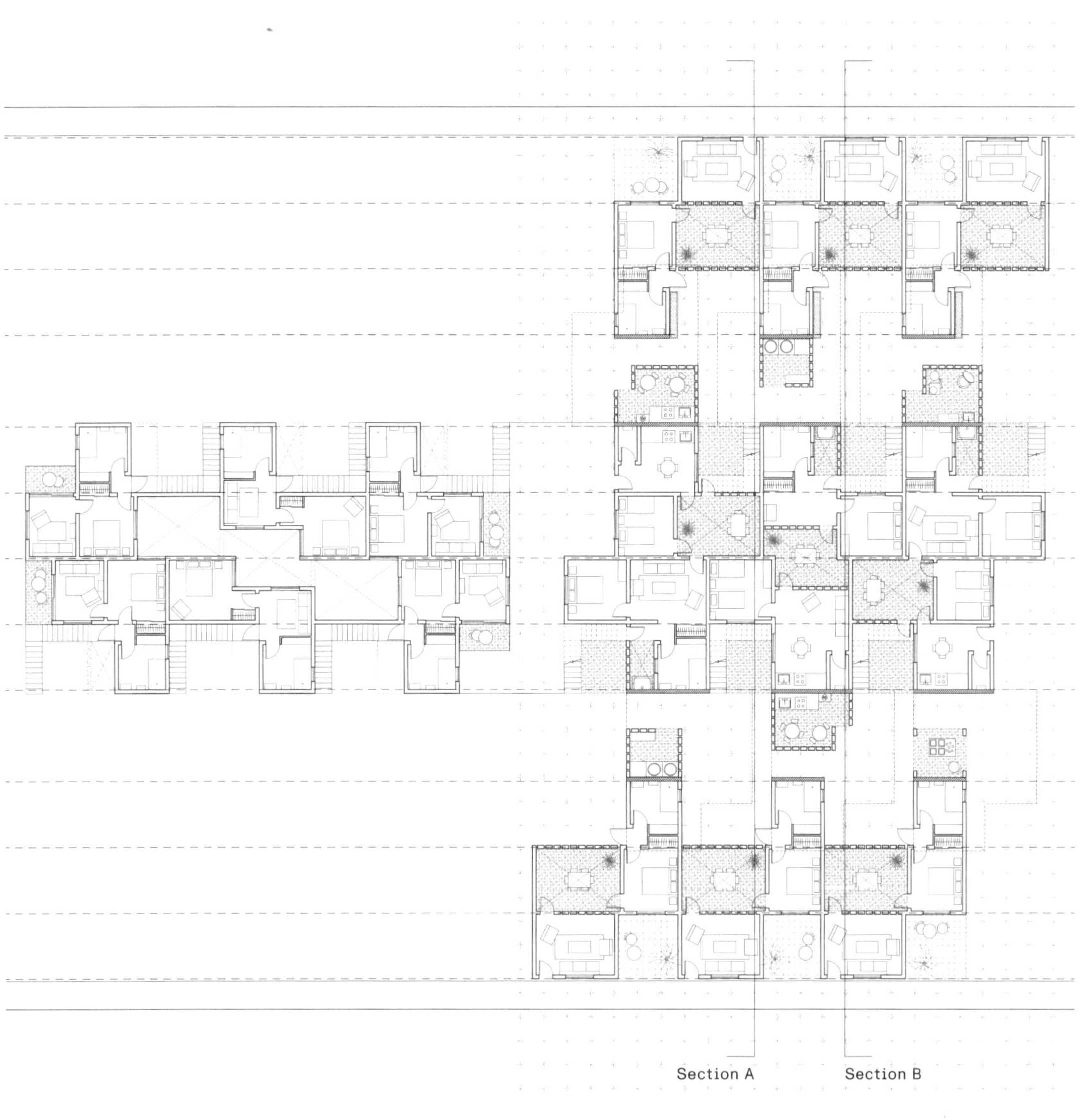

Shared Work

Michelle Badr and Camille Chabrol

Cohousing axonometric

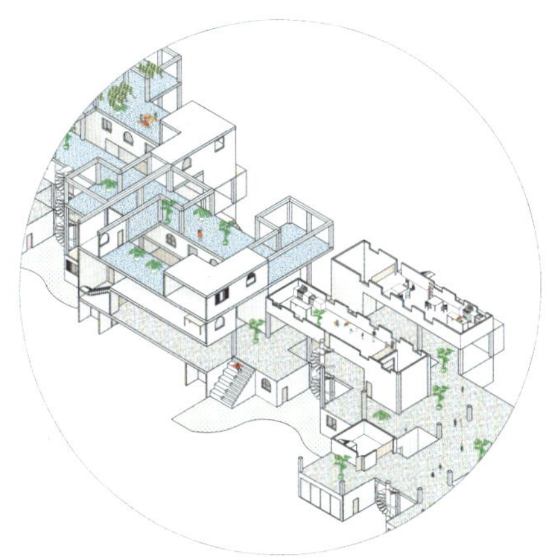

Cohousing module

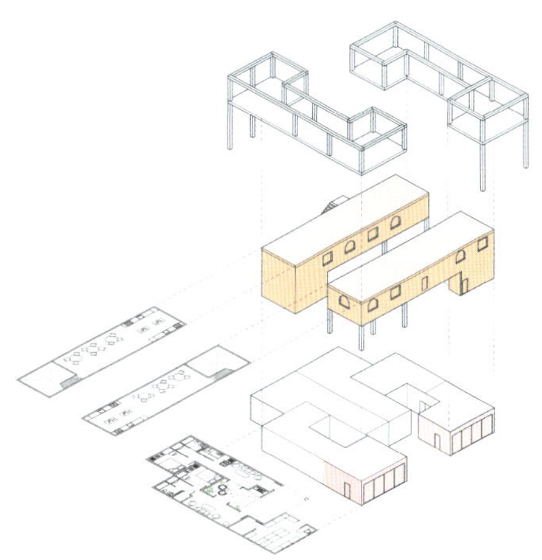

Cohousing axonometric

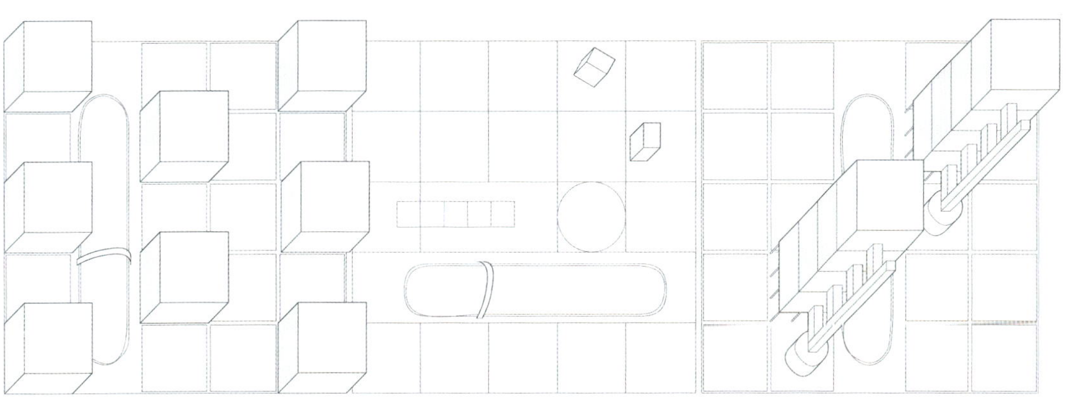

Magnitogosk plan

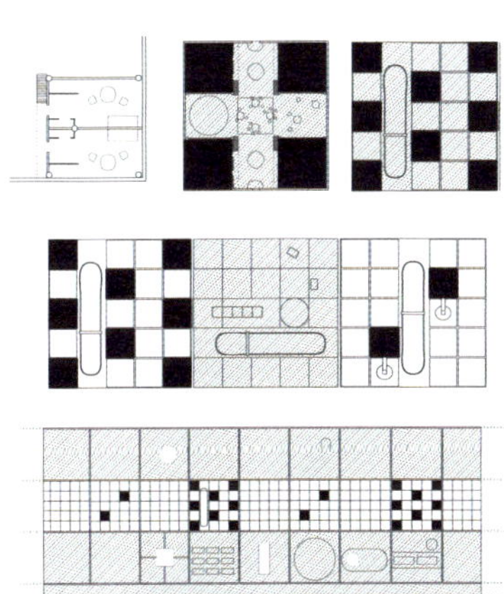

What is a wall?

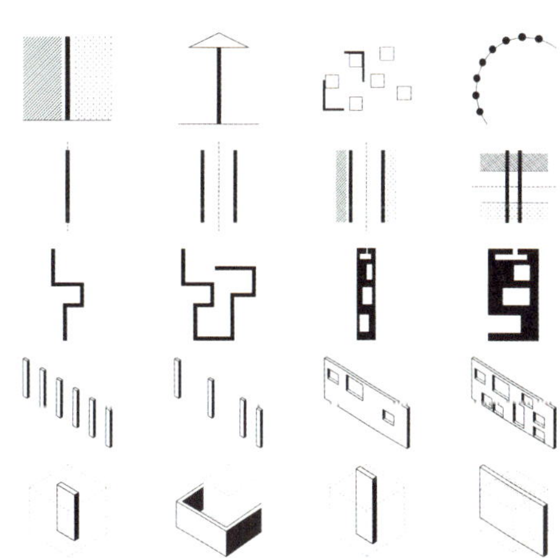

Michelle Badr and Camille Chabrol

Courtyard

Inner street

Garden view

Emily Cass, Shuchen Dong, and Armaan Shah: Liminal Expressions

Permeable thresholds, nesting of private and public spaces

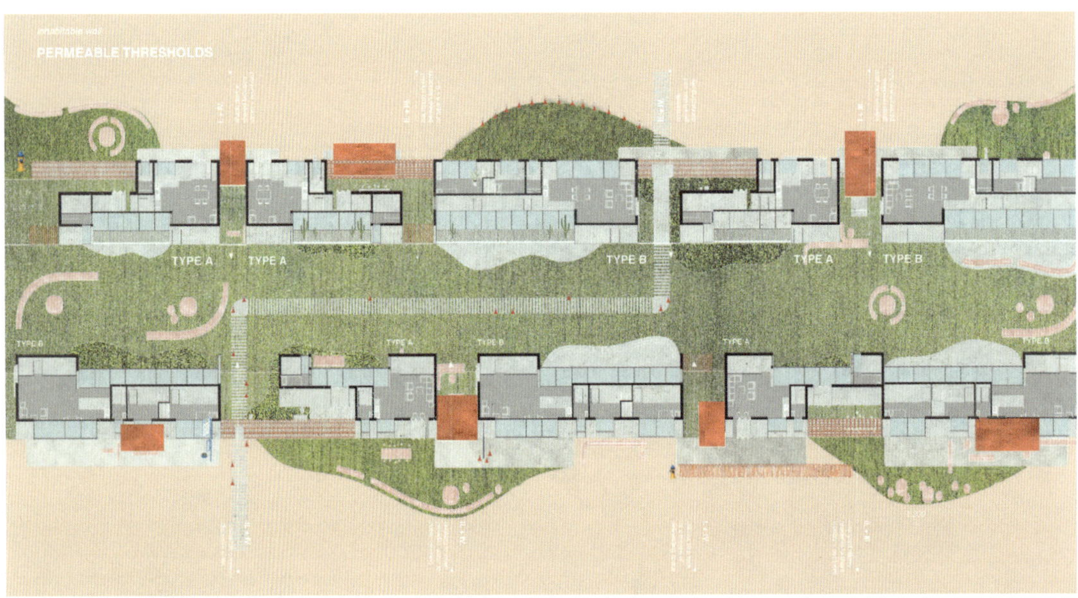

Softening the public periphery

Shared continuous yard and street

Blending home with community play

Clara Domange and Miriam Dreiblatt

Inhabitable wall

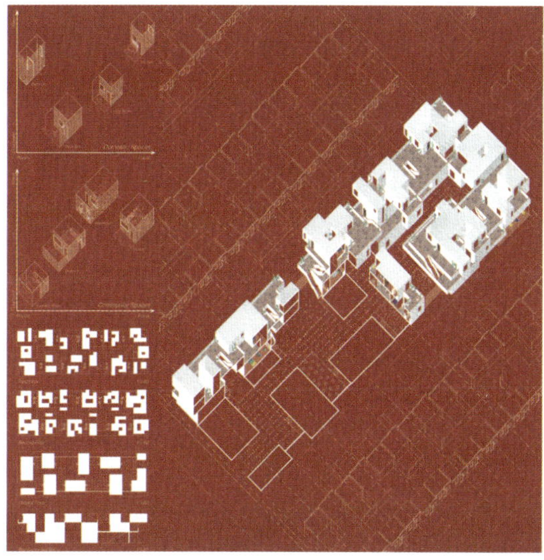

Vecindad

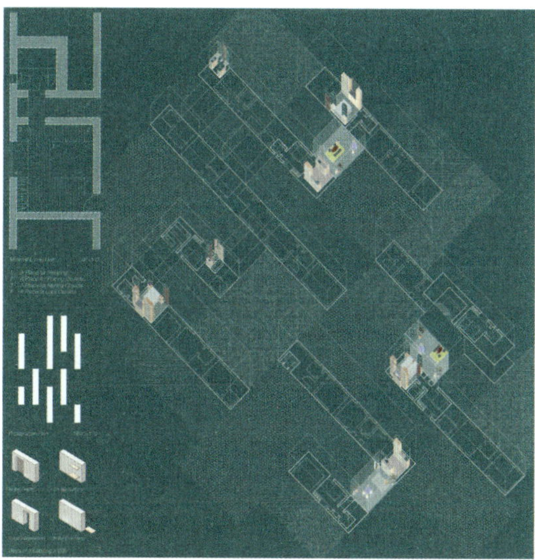

Alex Pineda and Limy Rocha: Individuality

Documenting a fragmented block in Mexicali

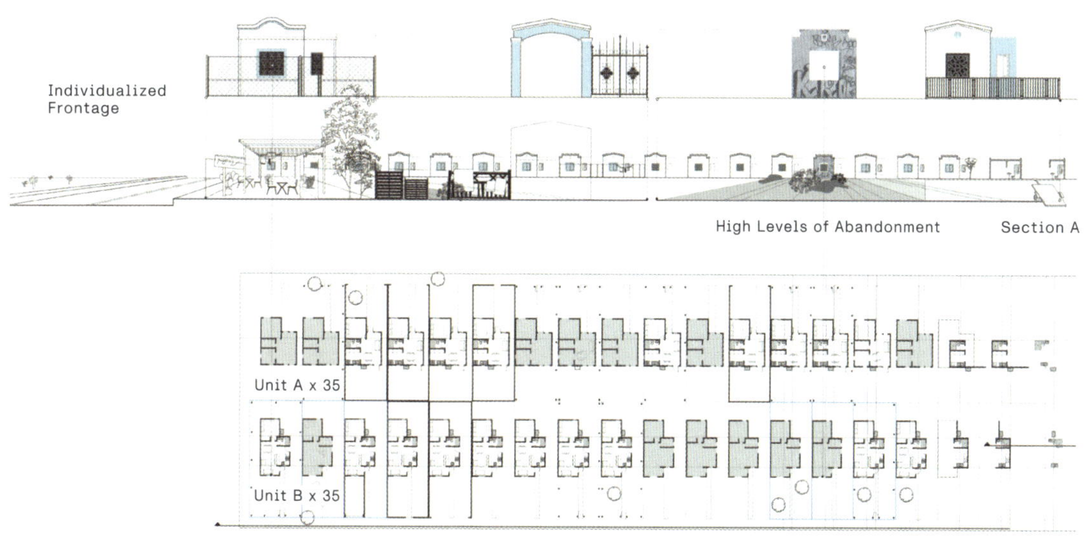

Free Library

Stella Betts

Conversation with Stella Betts

Cornell University East Sibley Hall, Cornell University Campus, Ithaca, NY. Photo: Naho Kubota

NINA RAPPAPORT Let's talk first about the organization of your firm and how you and David, your partner in every way, started out.

STELLA BETTS We were a little bit different than some of our colleagues. We didn't start off teaching. We decided to get married, start a practice, and move into a Chinatown loft that we renovated, all in one month. We basically used our loft as a building laboratory. We both came from fine-arts backgrounds and wanted to be artists. We started our practice together slowly by making custom furniture. Since we were always reconstructing our residence and moving things around, as if we were camping,it made us think about domestic space. We designed a few small projects, and then we were commissioned to do a project for a 13,000-square-foot two-story printing plant.

NR David had construction experience as a Yale graduate student working on the Building Project.

SB Yes, and after he moved to New York he worked for Vito Acconci and then in a wood shop, in a metal fabrication shop, and in construction. I first worked for what was one of the few women-owned construction companies. I learned a lot, including the tough aspects of running a business doing construction projects in Bedford-Stuyvesant.

NR How do your hands-on experiences play out in your house designs in terms of construction and detail development as well as model making? Has it become a more iterative process?

SB I think it's really integrated for us so that the details are at the forefront. We approach many of our projects with the idea of an "open house" and the informality of a campsite. Many of our houses—most of them are around 2,000 square feet—have no formal front door. Sometimes they have all doors and no windows, allowing you to drift in and out effortlessly. We make tons of models and work through the details in the process, using 1:1 mock-ups produced in our own shop. Designs evolve through making and a trust in the process. We set up open-ended parameters and see how it evolves.

For instance, we were layering chipboard for the Square House and realized it should be board-formed concrete, a texture that we like that relates to the context, which is about heaviness and steps into the ground with a recessed central living space. The Catskills House, constructed of a wood and stick frame, is elevated above the ground like a tree house, so it is about lightness.

East Flatbush Branch Library, Brooklyn, New York

NR You discuss the informality of programs and spaces, in contrast to a formal geometry and hierarchy of spaces. Yet from your house models in the office it is evident that you have made a collection of forms. How do you unify these different approaches?

SB We construe life in a house as informal—for example, the front door is not celebrated, even in the large three-pronged house in Amagansett, Long Island. You kind of slip into the house from the side, negating the formal front yard-back yard arrangement. The informal comes into the organization and relationship to the site.

NR How have you been attracted to the primary form of the trapezoid, seen a few years ago in your piece for the exhibition *Unpacking the Cube*, at the Chamber Gallery, in New York? I remember discussing with you how it could be a building.

SB We have been kind of obsessed with it since we responded to curator Andrew Zuckerman's prompt to do whatever we wanted relating to cubes. We made the project "Not to Scale," with a trapezoid shape that nests. It was also about the idea that as architects we are always working with models. So the piece became a toy, and then furniture, and then it grew into a pavilion at Art Omi and a house in the Hudson Valley, as well as benches in the Miami Design District. We have been fascinated with the process of scaling it up and down.

NR Why is that form so interesting to you?

SB I don't know really! I think it is the way it opens on one side and pinches on the other. The Hudson Valley house opens to the east, the west, and the north, so with each room you get a different perspective and focus.

NR It also can be assembled in different ways, like a hexagon.

SB Exactly. You can kind of turn it into a snaky wall or a linear shape. With the piece at Art Omi we let the roof vary so it opened in both plan and section but was still the same shape in plan. We have designed houses in a variety of shapes, including ovals and triangles, but began with a series of linear bar houses.

SQUARE House, Stone Ridge, New York. Photo: Naho Kubota

NR You have also been working on adaptations of existing buildings, including historic landmarks. How do you design new insertions, and do you feel you are liberating the existing buildings in a way?

SB We often say it's harder to do projects in existing buildings because of the constraints and resistance presented by the existing structure. On the other hand, there is an opportunity in the challenge of working with the building's DNA.

NR How did these challenges create a trigger for something totally new in Cornell University's East Sibley Hall, where you had the pressure of an architecture school as a client and OMA's Millstein Hall design to compete with?

SB Actually it was funny, because when we were invited to submit for the RFP, the person from Cornell asked, "Do you want to do a project where your client is a group of architects, and you have to deal with a building that has structural and mechanical problems?" But they were wonderful to work with. Since it's landmarked, it was like putting a ship in a bottle, and fitting in the HVAC system in what is now hidden in the attic space was a huge challenge. We wanted to open up the third floor into a more collaborative space, creating transparency between the dome and East Sibley Hall, and then make a connection through the egress stair that connects down to the OMA project. We used fire-rated glass to produce transparency, adding new windows and forming a dynamic relationship between the historic envelope and the new insertions.

SQUARE House, Stone Ridg, New York. Photo: Naho Kubota

NR How did you use the structure to set up the idea of closed and open frames, and how did that play out in terms of new ways to program the spaces?

SB We thought of it in terms of urban interiors and campuses as well as how we could pick up where OMA left off, so it became an urban campus with transparency. We removed three masonry walls and inserted three open frames: a large moment frame from end to end; a smaller, intermediate frame between the faculty office area along a wide corridor-like gallery space; and a smaller frame connecting to the Dome. Silman, the structural engineers, said that the first thing needed was to structurally stabilize the building, and we responded that we wanted to knock out all the walls.

NR For your next project at Cornell, at Rhodes Hall, were you able to continue the idea of openness?

SB The hall had two floors connecting the department of computer sciences that they wanted to expand with more flexible space for a cross-disciplinary computer hardware lab and digital computation. The existing offices were on the perimeter, leaving the corridors in darkness, so instead we continued the idea of the interior urban campus. We moved the private spaces away from the window-wall to bring natural light into the shared spaces and floor plate of the building.

NR Themes of light, both natural and artificial, have been apparent in your work, particularly in your adaptive-reuse projects. How have you carved into and out of spaces to increase light in recent projects such as the Brooklyn libraries?

SB We often joke that early in our practice we worked only on projects in basements. In the printing plant the employees were on the street level, but with the arrival of a new printing press they had to move to the basement, so we cut into the floor plate to create a lightwell. Our second project was a furniture showroom, half of which was in the basement, so we approached it like Gordon Matta-Clark, cutting out surfaces to bring light down. For the East Flatbush Library we are inspired by Henri Labrouste's naturally lit reading rooms. We carved three large north-facing skylight monitors in the main reading space.

NR Besides natural light, what are your spatial and organizational concerns in the branch libraries?

Taystee Building, 450 West 126 Street, New York

SB One thing that was really important to us was not to create a "back of house" separating the staff from visitors. In East Flatbush we got rid of corridors and created a light-filled central reading room, which everyone crosses through so that there is more interaction. In the Red Hook project we are removing almost everything except for the concrete slab, the columns, and the roof, which is made out of concrete T-beam panels. We are celebrating its structure, which is like a parking garage, by leaving it exposed in an informal way. We are removing the horrible glass-block and brick facade and using a light gray salt-and-pepper perforated brick pattern to connect to the community context. So it's about understanding the materiality of the context and the project's DNA.

NR How have you extended that to community participation and the local review process?

Zoid, Art Omi, Ghent, New York. Photo: Richard Barnes

SB With each of the libraries, which are usually under the city's Department of Design and Construction (DDC) or Economic Development Corporation (EDC), we have a review process with the librarians, the community, the Brooklyn Public Library, the Public Design Commission, and the DDC. The more you do public projects the more you realize how much there is to appreciate in an amazing project because you know how many people have had to buy into it financially, emotionally, and creatively.

NR You also have your largest new building almost finished in Harlem, on the site of the former Taystee Bakery factory. How did that come about?

SB The developers are unusual in the sense that they didn't parachute into Harlem and drop in a building but have been developing and renovating a group of structures, including the Mink Building, all on the same block. They came to us ten years ago, and one of the owners, Scott Metzner, asked us to unify the ceiling in two buildings. We thought of it as a ceiling art installation, and then later we renovated their offices. Then they asked us to work on the RFP for a site on 126th Street. The most important part of the project is not the building but a midblock urban garden passage that reorients the structure and connects 125th and 126th Streets. It is very much about making sure that it isn't just a new building but also a community connector.

Free Library

There are many definitions for and uses of the word *free.*

free country
free to do as you please
free to go
problem free
carefree
duty free
free fall
free speech
fancy free
free-form
free of charge

The list goes on...

Politics of Space

What in the physical environment is free? The answer is: not much, especially these days. In the United States we have a right to free air and, for the most part, free water. In theory, we are guaranteed by the Clean Air Act (1963) and the Clean Water Act (1972) that the air and water are safe to breathe and drink, although sadly we have seen that in

Bibliothèque Sainte-Geneviève, Henri Labrouste, 1850

different parts of the country air and water are neither free nor safe to consume.

Natural light is free and a codified right. In New York City, for example, the residential building code mandates legal levels of light and air. In other words, you have a right to light.

Education is free. All citizens can send their children to public school from kindergarten to grade twelve. Although education is free, it is important to note that it is not always equal. The quality of education differs depending on where you live, and many school districts suffer deficits in educational support spaces such as libraries.

Public space is free. A large majority of public space is outdoors in parks, recreational facilities, and civic and urban spaces. Civic buildings such as the post office, the courthouse, and the city hall are free for public use. Of course there is also the free public library. Somehow, even in our commercialized contemporary culture, the library remains a free space to sit, read, check out a book, and access free Wi-Fi and information. A place to learn, the public library functions as a supplemental education space for schools and universities.

The studio, focusing on the politics of space, began with an examination of free civic space. Our study aimed to go beyond the simple distinction between public versus private to include a deeper awareness of embedded

Bibliothèque Sainte-Geneviève, Henri Labrouste, 1850

NY Public Library, Bobb, Cook & Willard, 1905

hierarchies as well as formal and informal definitions of space. Where are these public spaces located? Who are they serving? How are these spaces designed to promote inclusion, equity, diversity, and accessibility?

Centre Pompidou Library, Piano & Rogers, 1971

The goal of this studio was not to become experts (necessarily) on the history and politics of civic space, but rather to recognize that as architects we are responsible for the politics inherent in the places that we create. How a building is organized, positioned, and designed reflects the power of architecture to transform social culture, challenge norms and conventions, and allow a more open democratic civic society.

This studio focused specifically on the architecture of the free library as an urban public building that houses a collection of free books and varied public programs and, as part of a larger campaign for public education, provides access to information.

History and Transformation of the Public Library

The students studied the history of the library with particular focus on the emergence of the public library institution. In the nineteenth century, the popularization of book publishing in many parts of the world transformed libraries. Books were no longer produced in limited quantities for an elite readership. The ability to print large numbers of books changed not only the scale of the library but also its spatial organization, allowing direct access to its collection and strengthening its role as a public amenity. In addition, the public face of the library changed along with the urban spaces around it.

Seattle Public Library, OMA, 2004

One of the very first public libraries was Henri Labrouste's Bibliothèque Sainte-Geneviève in Paris, built in 1850. The library made a wide range of publications available to a population that previously did not have access to private book collections. The advent of gas lamps allowed the library to stay open into the evening hours, providing university students and the working-class public access to the books and a quiet reading space.

Only three decades later, beginning in the 1880s, the Scottish-American philanthropist Andrew Carnegie began his campaign for free libraries throughout the United States and in the United Kingdom, Ireland, Canada, and many other parts of the world. He located libraries in small urban centers and underserved neighborhoods as well as in large cities. During the period of segregation in the

Centre Pompidou Library Public Plaza, Piano & Rogers, 1971

Sendai Mediatheque Library, Toyo Ito, 2001

United States, when African Americans were denied entrance to public libraries, Carnegie circumvented the law by financing separate libraries for these citizens. Carnegie also made the stacks open and accessible to library visitors for the first time: previously visitors would have to consult the catalog and then make a request to the librarian to take a book from the collection. Like his contemporary F. W. Woolworth, who radically changed the shopping experience by making merchandise accessible for customers to browse on the store floor, Carnegie allowed library visitors to browse open book stacks . With more than 2,500 libraries built in nearly 50 years, Carnegie created a "chain-store" version of the public branch library located in outer neighborhoods at a time when these institutions were located predominantly in the center of major cities.

In the twentieth century public libraries became containers for continually expanding book collections with large reading rooms and public spaces. A significant exception to this was Renzo Piano and Richard Rogers's

Centre Pompidou, in Paris, built in 1977. The building and program represented a radical departure from traditional library design. Conceived as a multi-programmed building that included a new free library, a center for contemporary art, and a music research center. Moreover, the "inside-out" design created a new image for civic buildings, with a large public plaza in front.

Another new library model emerged at the very beginning of the twenty-first century, one of the most notable examples of which is Toyo Ito's Sendai Mediatheque, in Japan (2001). In 1989 the city of Sendai initiated a study to organize an open competition for a new library concept dedicated to culture with a library, cinema, café, and art gallery. The library as an institution was no longer to provide only books but also information and gathering spaces for the community. Ito's design concept was a "fluid, barrier-free" environment both in function and structure. Like the Centre Pompidou, the project combined the library with a civic art gallery and an audiovisual media center for people with visual and hearing disabilities. The radical idea was to create a nonhierarchical open civic space that blurred the boundaries between city and building by marrying traditional library programs with community services. It was a catalytic project that reflected the ambitions of the twenty-first-century library to offer diverse programs and flexibility for future changes. Only a few years later, in 2004, OMA completed the Seattle Public Library. The architecture of the library has not been the same since.

Today the mission and scope of the public library extends well beyond traditional reading rooms and book stacks. Libraries are constantly incorporating more social programs, maker spaces, vocational education, literacy classes, arts and crafts, and children's after-school programs. These additional functions are changing the architecture of the library and its role as a civic space in the city.

The studio invited students to consider the architecture of the future public library: What are the opportunities to rethink the free library? How does it operate as an urban building? How does it foster civic space? What are its organizing principles? How is it structured? How does it perform environmentally? What is its public face?

Reflecting on the Semester

Almost immediately following our midsemester review, the COVID-19 pandemic closed down nearly every aspect of life as we knew it. After a restructuring over spring break, the second half of the semester began and ended with remote teaching: in-person studios were not permitted, and there would be no more group pinups and no physical models. This was devastating in many ways and on many levels. The world had turned upside down.

While COVID-19 was spreading, there was a movement taking place in spring 2020—a revolution that highlighted racial, social, economic, and cultural injustices. From the onset the studio was focussed on public space and equity through the lens of the public library. Now these issues were taking center stage globally in ways that we did not anticipate. Yet these issues are not new, they just have a brighter light shining on them demanding us to take action. Free libraries are more important than ever as examples of equitable, accessible, welcoming free spaces where everyone can attain new knowledge and be part of a community.

Studio Brief

Spring 2020

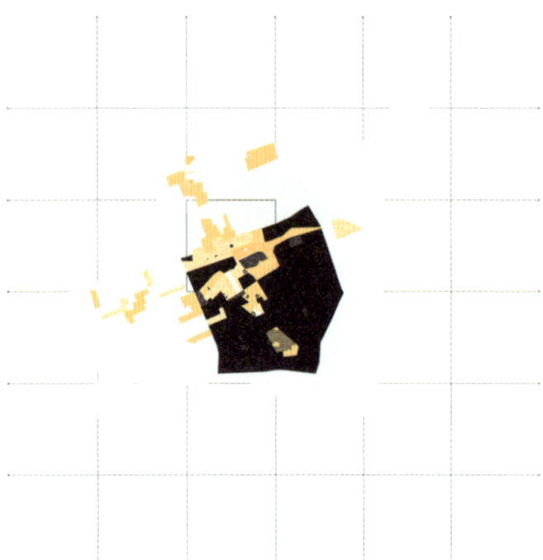

Limy Rocha "Vulnerable Populations"

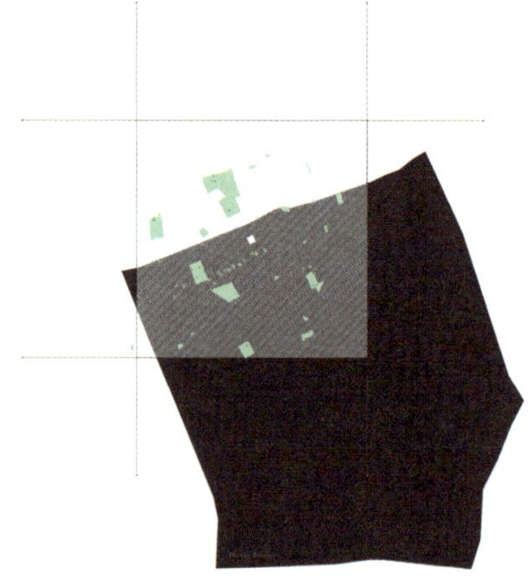

Limy Rocha "Free City Resources"

Studio Project and Site

The studio analyzed the New York City Public Library system, including New York Public Library (NYPL), Brooklyn Public Library (BPL), and Queens Public Library (QPL). The proposed project was a redesign of the Queens Central Library, in Jamaica, Queens.

Jamaica is a vibrant middle-class neighborhood with a highly diverse demographic represented predominantly by Black, Caribbean, and Central American communities. The neighborhood serves as a civic anchor for the area, hosting a number of local government functions as well as several regional transit hubs. The site consists of two plots straddling Merrick Boulevard between 89th and 90th Avenues. One- and two-story commercial and residential districts surround the east, south, and western sides of the site, while a NYCHA high-rise housing block bounds the edge immediately to the north. A low-rise pedestrian shopping corridor flanks the west edge, and a vital regional bus depot occupies the service area just behind it.

Travel Week

The studio traveled to New York and Paris for inspiration and case study analysis. In New York students visited several recently built libraries including Steven Holl's Hunter's Point Branch Library, TEN Arquitectos 53rd Street Branch Library, and Work AC's Kew Gardens Hills Branch Library, as well as the Central Book Ops, the book-sorting facility for NYPL and BLP, in Long Island City, Queens. Finally, the students met with the librarians at QPL's Central Library. In Paris they visited Labrouste's Bibliothèque Sainte-Geneviève, the central reading room in the Bibliothèque Nationale, Perrault's Bibliothèque Nationale de France, and the Centre Pompidou, by Piano and Rogers, as examples of both historic and forward-thinking contemporary libraries.

Research and Analysis

Work commenced with a series of quick iterative exercises that began with a focus on the book as an object, followed by more in-depth site analysis and aggregation studies as well as a series

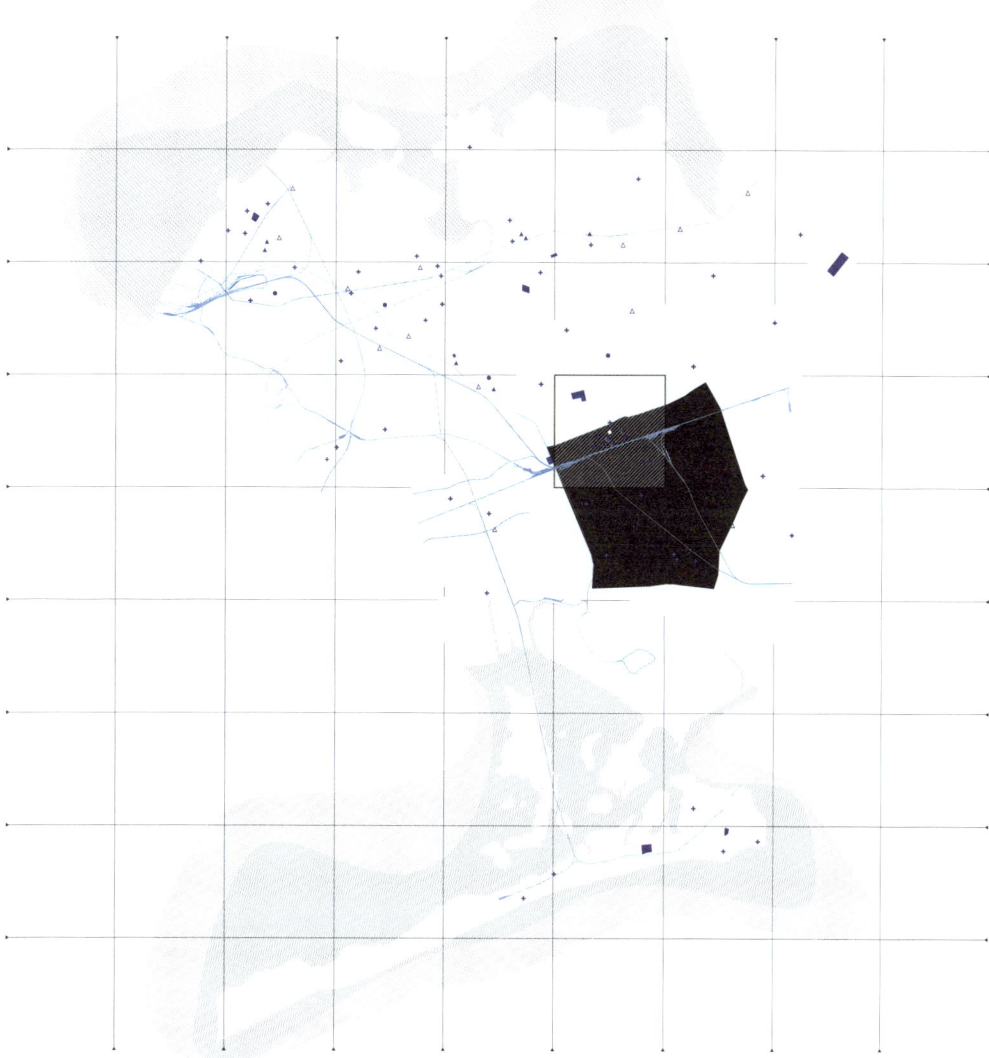

Limy Rocha "Health Facilities"

of massing strategies. Each exercise introduced constraints that informed and transformed the original study and functioned as a series of operations and strategies for students to develop their own library proposals.

Book Transformation

For the first exercise, each student was asked to purchase a used book and transform it to create a new artifact. The goal was twofold: as a warm-up for remaking and rethinking a found object (a site for intervention) and as a way to begin to think critically about the structure, narrative, and accessibility of the book, and in turn the library.

Site Analysis and Obsession

Working both individually and as a group, the students studied the site in Jamaica, Queens, and curated a collection of obsessions or interests related to the neighborhood and the city. During this phase they studied the area and noted the existence or absence of nearby green spaces and parks, public services, public schools, health facilities, transit, and sound and movement to determine ways in which their

Brenna Thompson, “Schools”

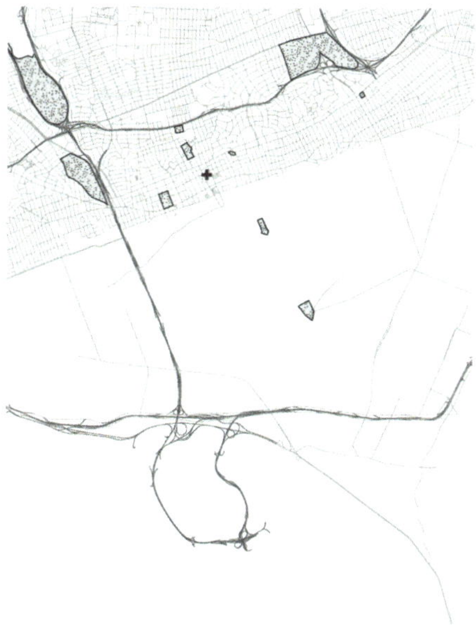

Brenna Thompson, "Parks"

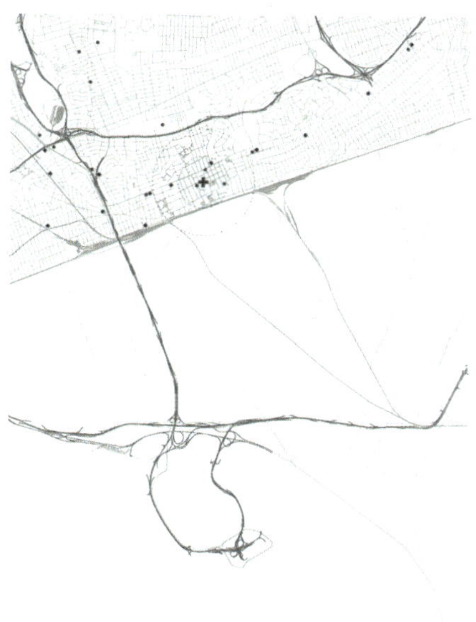

Brenna Thompson, "Transit"

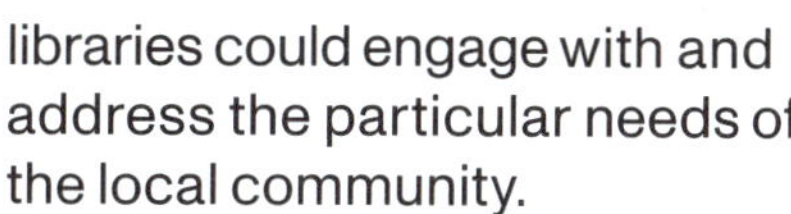

libraries could engage with and address the particular needs of the local community.

Library Precedent Study and Transformation

Precedent Study Part I: Analysis

The students were given a list of suggested library precedents to choose from and also had the option to select any other library to study. They were asked not to reproduce the library in plan and section but to diagram, model, draw, and distill the core ideas. As part of the study the students were required to consider the site, orientation, and environmental strategies employed in their library precedents.

Precedent Study Part II: Transformation

Following the precedent analysis, students were asked to place the case study buildings on the Queens site. Because the orientations and urban contexts of the precedent libraries were different, students were required to make transformations and manipulate them to "fit" in the Queens site while maintaining some of the core concepts of the original buildings.

System Aggregation and Massing Strategies

The students were prompted to create, modify, and iterate several aggregation studies that addressed space, structure, and surface through a series of operations loosely based on the program for the new central library. These studies developed the massing strategies for their library proposals.

Bibliotheque Nationale, Paris, February 2020

Centre Pompidou, Paris, February 2020

Queens Public Library, Hunters Point Library, Queens, NY, February 2020

Student Projects

Library as Social Infrastructure

Limy Rocha
Jen Shin

Library as Site Intervention

Daniella Calma
Gordon Jiang
Jenna Ritz

Library as Third Space

James Bradley
Elaine Cui
Max Ouellette-Howitz
Shuang Chen
Brenna Thompson

Library as Social Infrastructure

These projects focused on the library as social infrastructure with the capacity to address deficiencies in existing social-services programs in the neighborhood and city, thereby strengthening and fostering a more supportive and equitable community.

Limy Rocha: Library Commons

Queens is home to a large foreign-born population, one of the highest percentages among the boroughs, particularly undocumented immigrants. The educational attainment of this population, along with other minorities nationally, is primarily a high school diploma. There are few health services available to them and little to no access to health insurance. New York City's Sanctuary Movement addresses these complexities at the scale of the city, working to provide refuge and civic services to residents regardless of legal status, gender, race, and more.

A "Sanctuary City" subverts space and provides refuge in the public realm. It is made possible by and for impacted communities, positioned within a gradient of publicness and refuge; it is the reclaiming of land and its growth; it is a place that nurtures, educates, and protects its community. It is commoning at the scale of the city. From temporary living spaces and community food gardens to health and educational resources, sanctuary spaces highlight the public realm as a place that honors everyone's humanity. At the scale of the district, the Queens Public Library has the potential to provide social infrastructure to surrounding vulnerable communities. Within the immediate context, the library can carve out itself to open up free outdoor space that is not privately owned or commissioned.

These series of fabrics, networks, and spaces coalesce on a range of dimensions from both interior and exterior, providing a grid that weaves together the commonalities and familiarity of the Jamaica district. The tartan grid produced from a precise context analysis creates a rule set of weaving programs, adjacencies, and leftover urban rooms found amid Jamaica's density. The mapping of these spaces and their relationships to the site promote the tartan grid as a familiar-unfamiliar relationship, as seen in process collages of the Oita Prefectural Library in Queens.

The Central Library manifests as a series of nested spaces with dematerialized boundaries onto the surrounding context. The plan consists of city services—from legal support, English classes, and CityMD services to a bus terminal. The opposite lot provides places more in tune to the needs of the stereotypical library: a reading bar spans above bookshelves that act as structural support and shift to provide various reading and study areas.

Connecting to the Jamaica Colosseum Mall to the east, a pedestrian throughway allows autonomy for storefronts along the northern part of the site and more discreet spaces toward the middle. The exterior shell is composed of brick—solid, porous, or paired with glazing—following an interior wooden shell. The nesting of materials and spaces provides a sense of anonymity and refuge within the public sphere. These autonomous and semiautonomous spaces are flexible to the program necessitated by the community, even in times of emergency.

"Library Commons" is a place that nurtures, educates, and protects the community at the scale of the city. The proposed free library is a space of freedom and refuge within the sanctuary city—characterizing the next wave of urban spaces that provide for the most vulnerable populations, engage the surrounding city, and challenge the stigma of public services.

Limy Rocha

View of Library Commons hovering above

Ground-floor plan of Library Commons

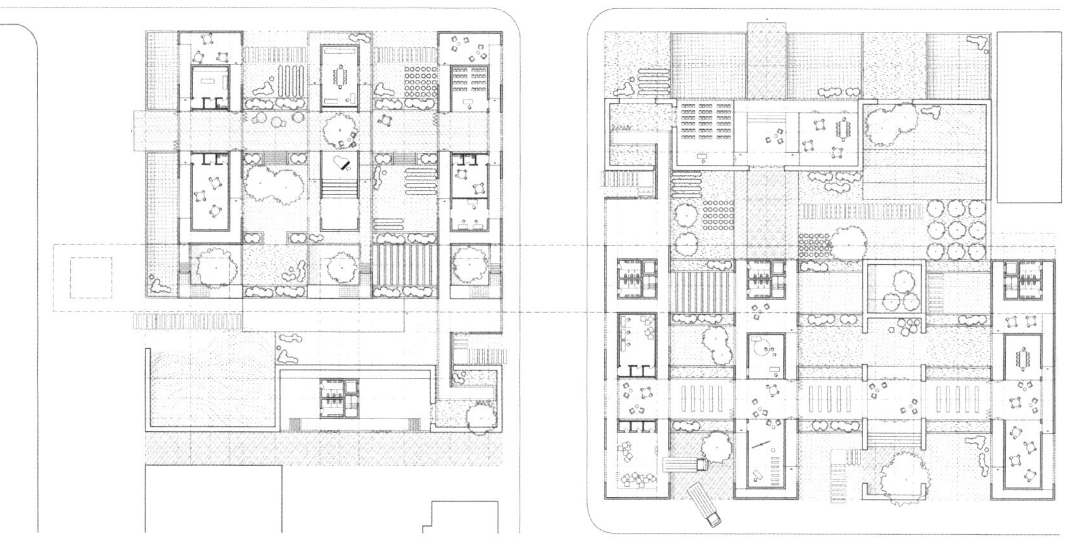

Second-floor plan of Library Commons

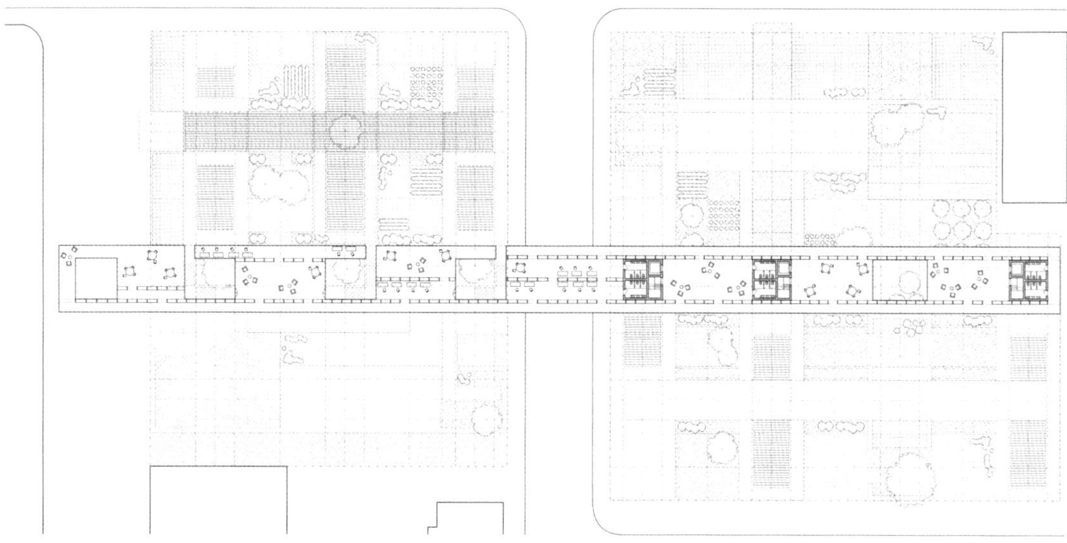

Limy Rocha

Rooms along a gradient of private-public spaces and interior-exterior conditions

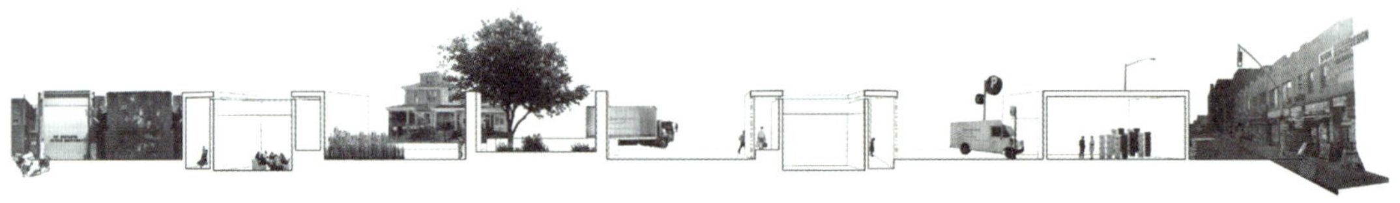

Reading bar bridging city and institutional sites above Merrick Boulevard

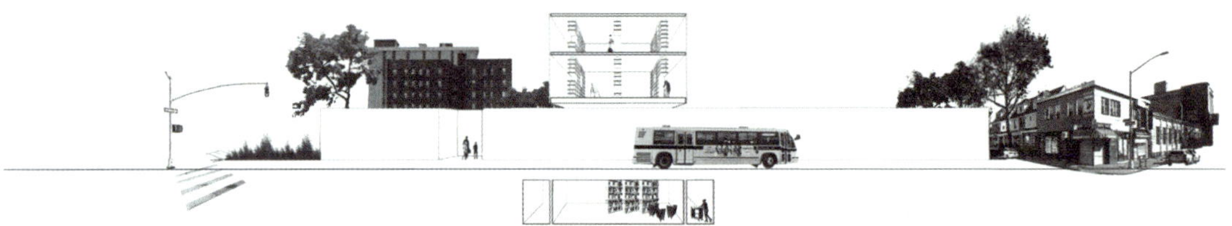

Process model of Library Commons

Library Commons

View of brick screen and walls along an interior-exterior topography

Familiar-unfamiliar collage of void space in Jamaica, Queens

Jen Shin

"Queens Table" gives form to the work of the Queens Public Library (QPL) as a way to strengthen the great democratic experiment and nurture a robust social infrastructure. By assuming the best in each individual and supporting each patron unconditionally, QPL destigmatizes free social services and dignifies the work of building social cohesion, beginning with the individual and extending to the neighborhood, borough, and city. To reflect and enhance these simple life-affirming principles, this proposal houses the myriad pursuits of self-improvement under one roof, a free zone through which people, ideas, and aspirations can arrive, dwell, and pass. These pursuits might include reading the news, obtaining immigration services, or simply being out and about.

Organized around two urban courtyards, a combination of covered areas, porous operable glass membranes, and articulated organelles form both ambiguous and specific spatial zones for selective programs. The low roof promotes the democratization of public space and sensitivity to a low-rise context. The horizontal line remains consistent as spaces shift in section beneath the roof, providing for dynamic activities and multiple centers to emerge within the complex.

By allowing for all components of civic life to happen below one free space, "Queens Table" provides the setting for deep participation in public life. It is monumental and ordinary all at once. The library's approachability lends nobility to patrons as they pursue growth and personal development while augmenting the unfolding democratic project that is the Queens Public Library.

Ground-level plan

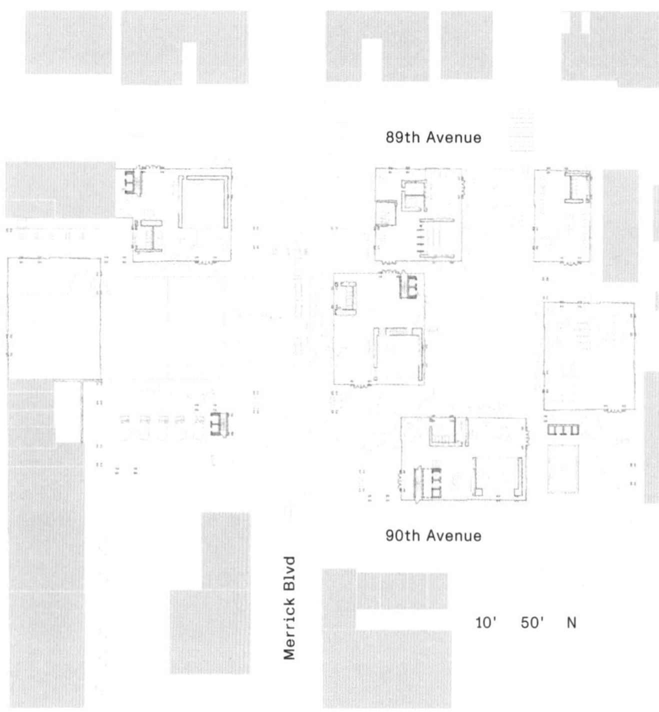

Queens Table

Main entry

Courtyard elevation

Jen Shin

Site section

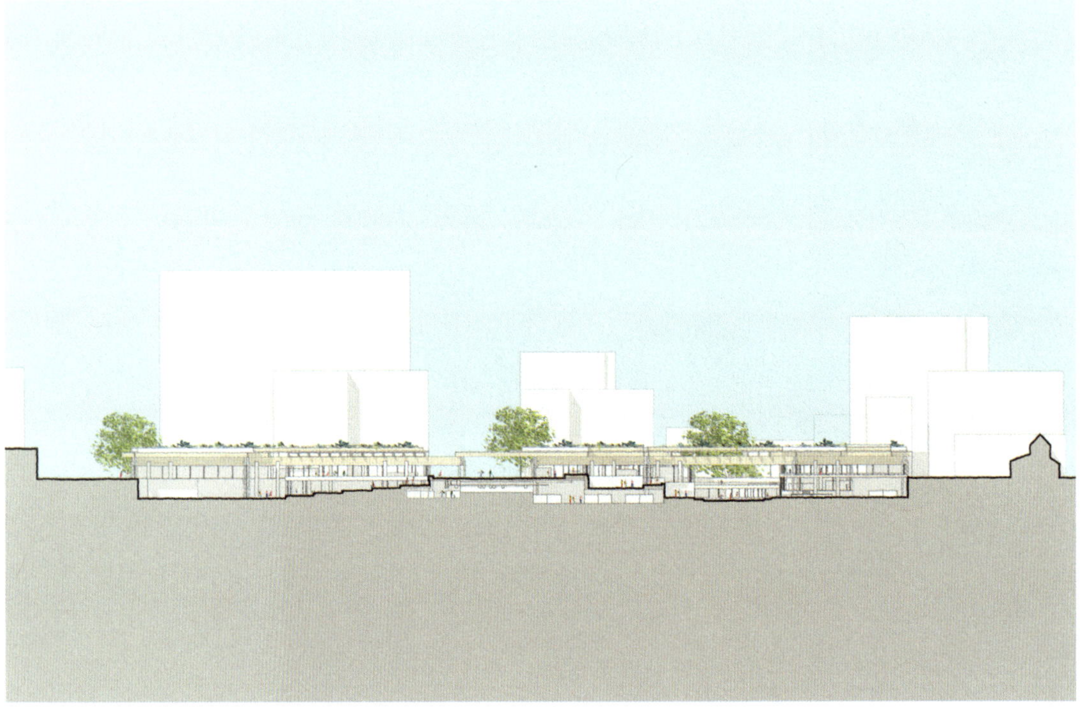

Aerial view

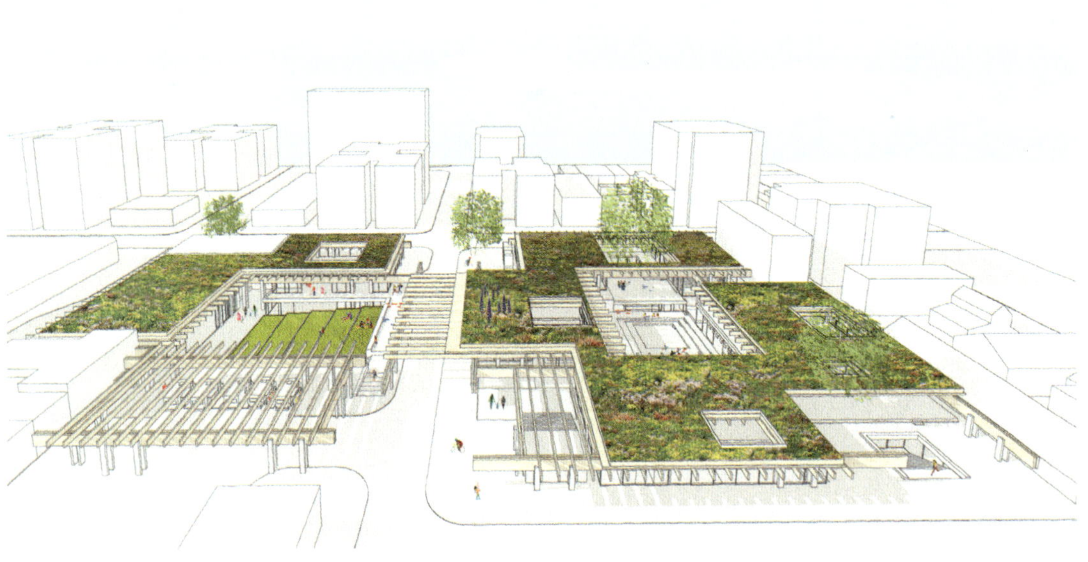

Queens Table

Courtyard vignette

Section vignette through 89th Avenue entry

Library as Site Intervention

Addressing a particular condition discovered during the site-analysis exercise, these projects challenge a singular program and organization of the library by responding directly to the site and the conditions of the immediate surroundings.

Daniella Calma: Blended

Nestled in the heart of Jamaica, the Queens Public Library (QPL) is a beacon of learning, acceptance, and culture surrounded by the haste and flux of city life. A safe space for the community and open to everybody, it is the site of numerous programs that aim to provide service and bolster collectivity between area residents. While it finds success in uniting the district, it faces the challenge of bridging the QPL with the rest of New York City.

A major hindrance for QPL is the lack of vehicular parking and access routes. There's hardly any indication of proximity to the building other than the entry point, subway routes are out of the way, and bus routes are limited. While the library has so much to offer, its visibility falls short because of poor circulation. This project aims to alleviate the transportation issue by introducing a vertical automated vehicular parking system that connects to the library. True to the numerous programs and initiatives QPL has set up for its community, this new system aims to attract a broader audience and generate more foot traffic. Inspired by the back-of-house automotive sorting system developed as part of the public library infrastructure, this new free library hybridizes vehicular circulation with human circulation, generating a cultural hub of autonomy that enhances accessibility to the city.

First-floor interior view

First-floor plan

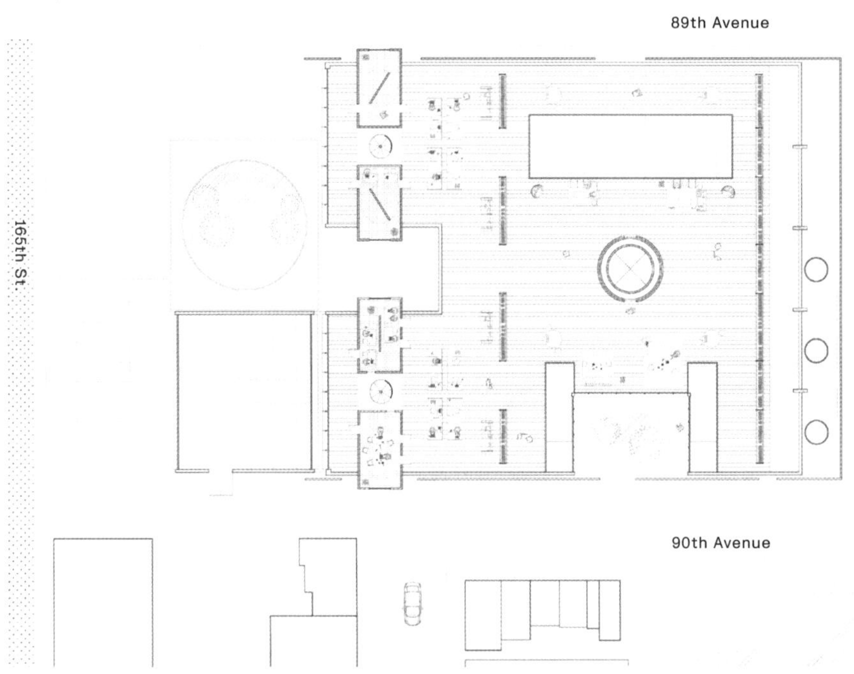

Second-floor plan

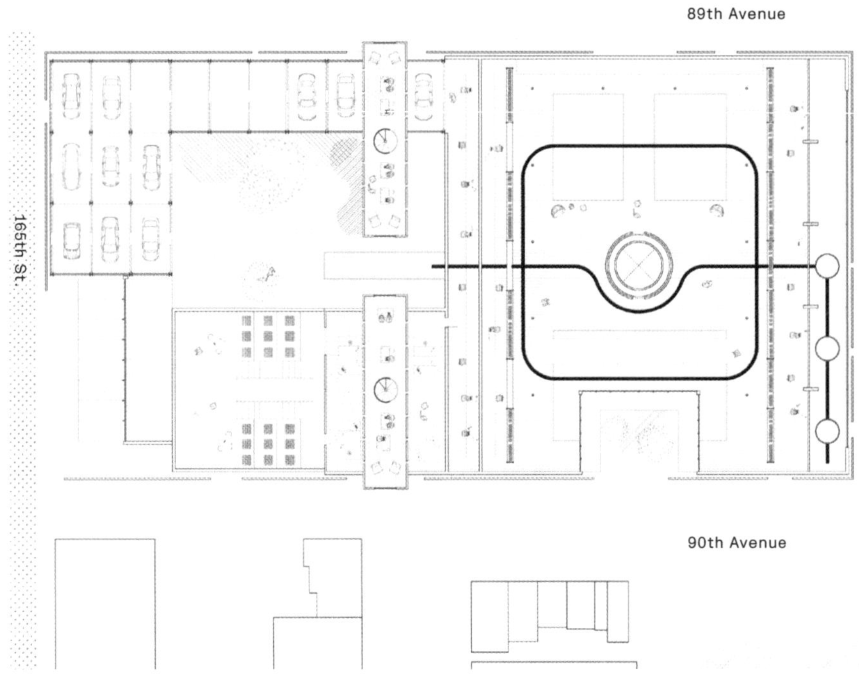

Third-floor plan

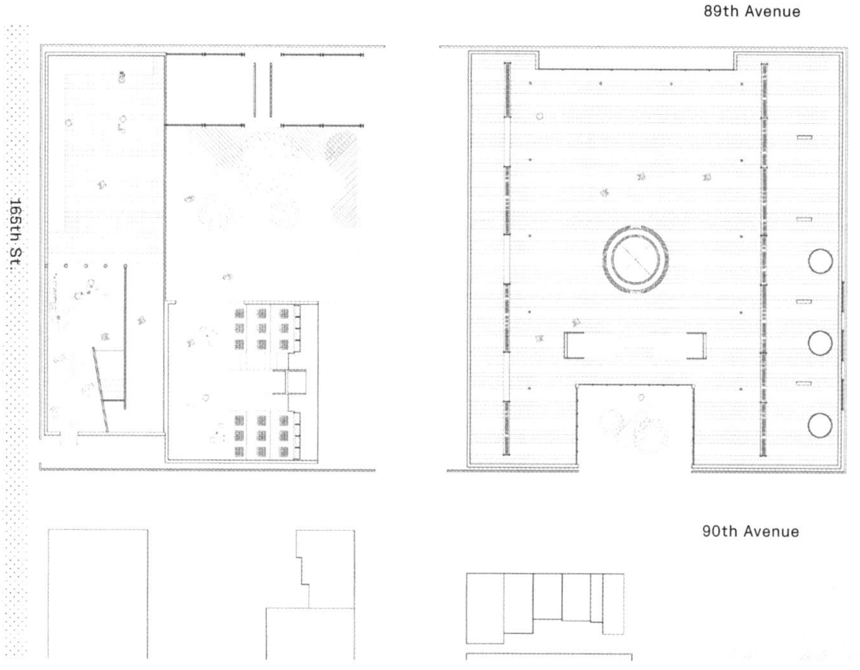

Long section

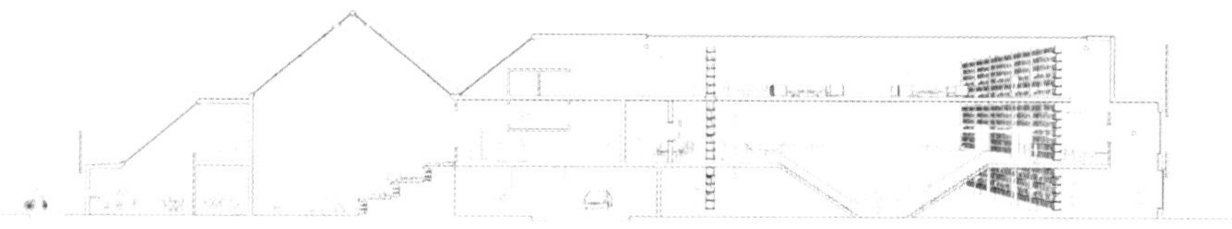

Short section

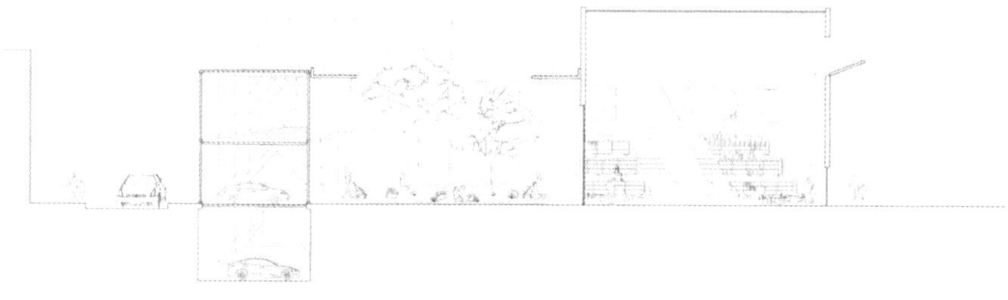

Daniella Calma

First-floor interior view

Automated parking

Blended

Interior view of book drop-off

Second-floor interior

Gordon Jiang

A free library should provide easier access for everyone. This proposal challenges the library as a single structure and instead integrates the building within the existing fabric of the city, weaving together the library, commercial, and public programs.

On the west face, the original storefronts located along 165th Street are preserved and used as secondary entrances to the library, offering direct accessibility to its program. This transforms the configurations of these shops and reorients the back-of-house, thereby creating an extended threshold condition between the street and the library. The walls of the commercial buildings are extended into the library and transformed into built-in furniture elements and a staircase to the second level. On the east side of the building facing Merrick Boulevard, the library presents a more public face. Library patrons can enter the library and walk along book walls that extend from these storefront walls.

At the second floor, the vertical relationship shifts and intertwines, creating spatial possibilities for different programs. This weaving and threading gesture of the building brings the urban context into the library and diffuses the boundary between the two the spatial realms.

Isometric aerial view

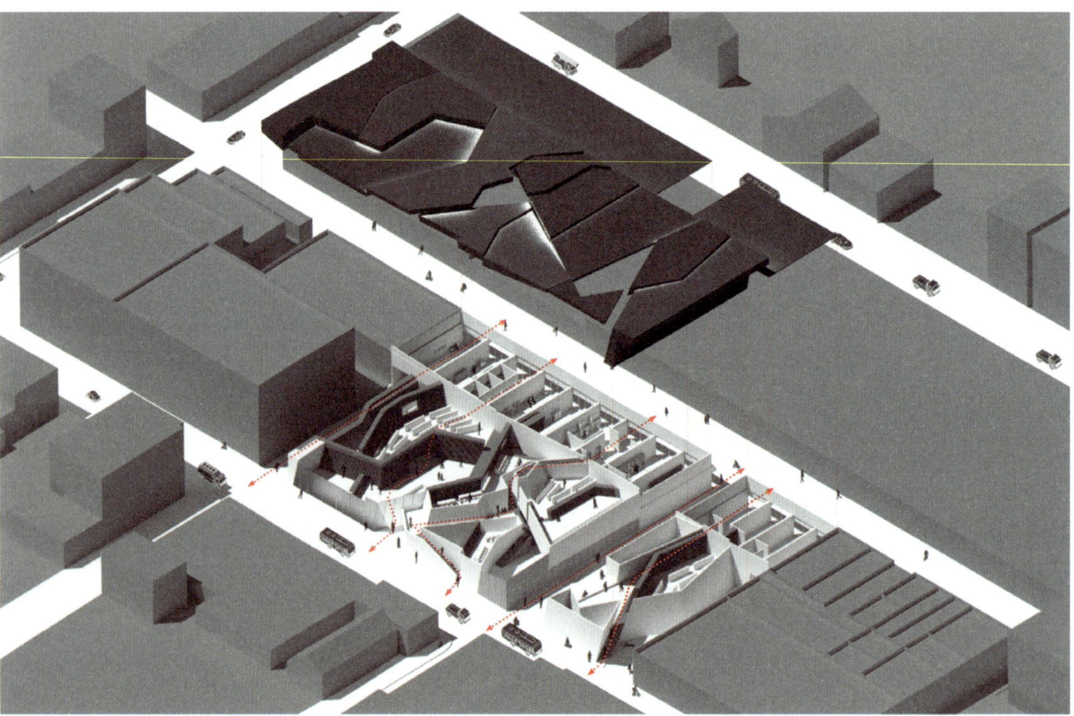

Urban Insertion in Space, Storefront to Reading Room

Plan

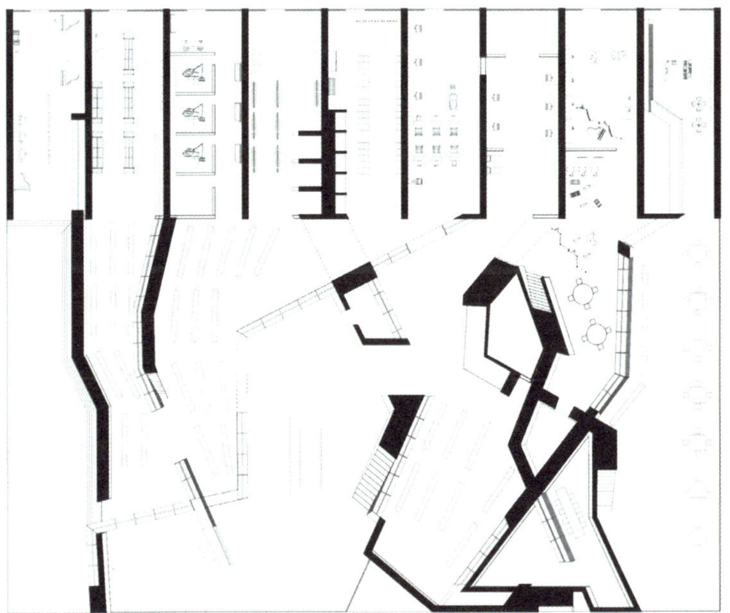

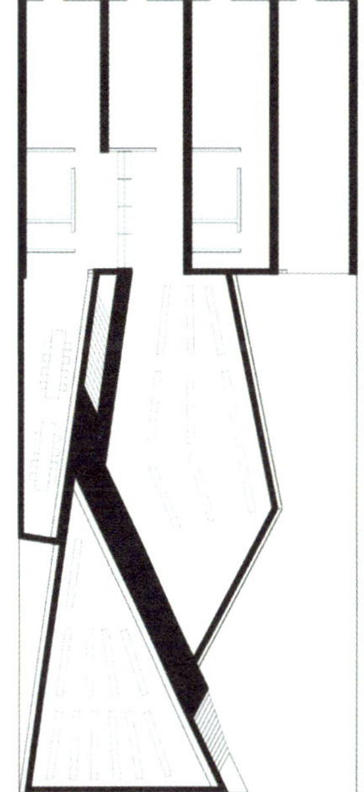

Plan sketch

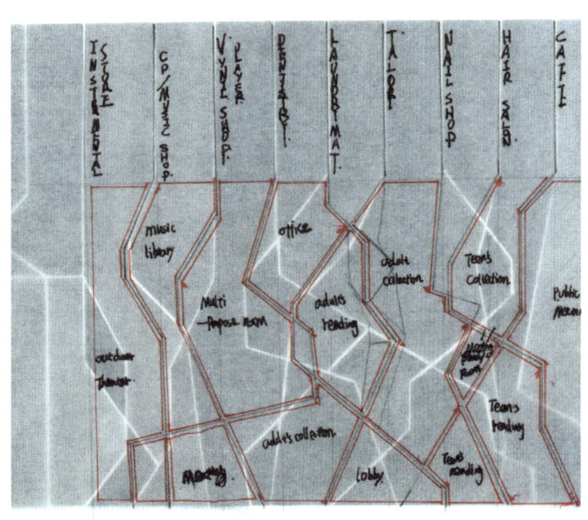

Gordon Jiang

Entry view

Interior view

Long section

Urban Insertion in Space, Storefront to Reading Room

Site model

Plan diagram

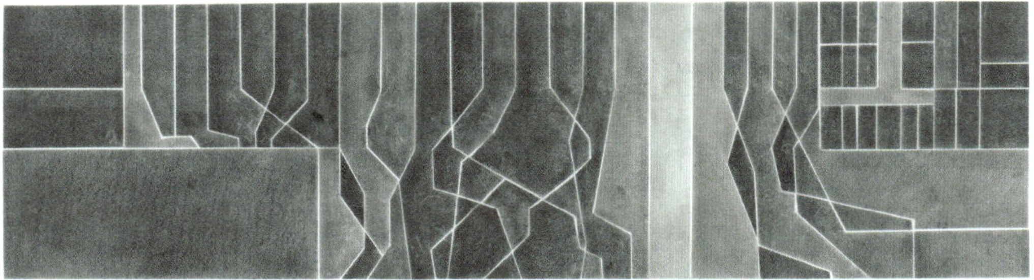

Site analysis

Jenna Ritz

The function of the public library has transcended its traditional typology—it is no longer a place only for solitary reading but for communal activities, interactive learning, and relationship building. As the programs of the library expand to address various needs of the local community, offering new activities such as maker spaces, music programs, and cafes, the acoustic landscape of the building also changes. These communal and individual activities create a diverse aural environment that needs to be accommodated to ensure comfort for users. The "Library of Soundscapes" provides a range of acoustic spaces to meet the ever-growing needs of the library program as it supports the activities of the local community.

The library focuses on improving the occupant's well-being through acoustic comfort, access to daylighting, and connection to the outdoors. Acoustic baffles are optimized for aural comfort. Areas that require the most sound mitigation are completely enveloped by the baffling system, while those intended for less quiet activities have only one wall or ceiling surface treated with the acoustic modules. The project is designed to mitigate the long-term environmental health issues of living in an urban environment. The structure's massing and interior wood baffle system, for example, are both designed to reduce the adverse effects of noise pollution.

The materials selected for the project focus on acoustical performance and embodied carbon. The wood baffle system creates a range of aural environments for the different library functions and also serves to offset the carbon footprint of the building construction. The 186,840-square-foot structural timber building is estimated to have 3,127 metric tons of embodied carbon through the overall construction. However, the sustainably harvested wood used in the acoustic baffle system sequesters 86 percent of the building's construction carbon footprint. Thus the acoustic wood baffle system is a visual manifestation of carbon emissions created from modern building construction methods.

The building massing creates an internal courtyard connected to the pedestrian street while acting as an acoustical barrier to the street. The U-shaped mass maximizes solar heat gain during the winter months, and window-shading devices provide respite from the sun during summer months. The courtyard and roof terraces provide green space in an urban environment overwhelmed by air pollution. These landscapes create a new on-site ecosystem as a counterpoint to the impervious parking lots and dense built environment nearby. The new landscape incorporates native flora and fauna to support the local bird, butterfly, and bee populations, and 32 percent of the site surface is planted with vegetation. The addition of green roofs bring total site vegetation to 68 percent.

The "Library of Soundscapes" strives to create a home for local residents that supports the needs and well-being of the community. Throughout the building a wood baffle system works to mitigate sound transmission and provide a range of aural environments to suit the diverse activities and acoustic comfort of library occupants. The organic forms of the baffle system form into walls, arches, ceilings, and furniture, playfully representing the acoustic needs of the space. This system embodies an interior environment that can provide a range of aural landscapes to accommodate all community activities and acoustic comfort for occupants.

Library of Soundscapes

Section through atrium

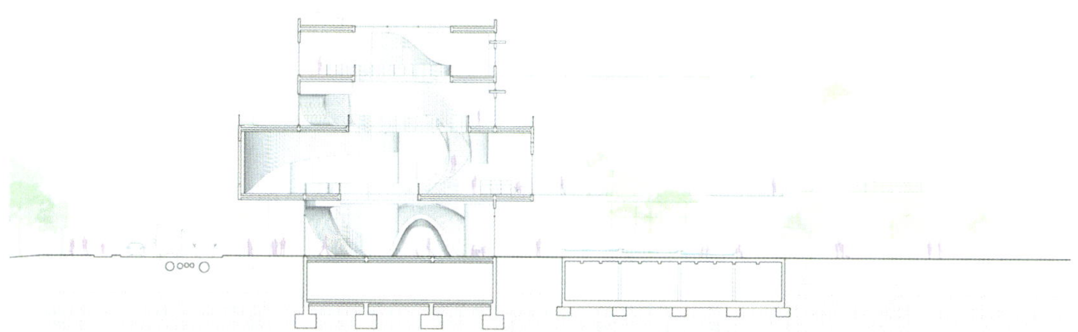

Ground-floor plan

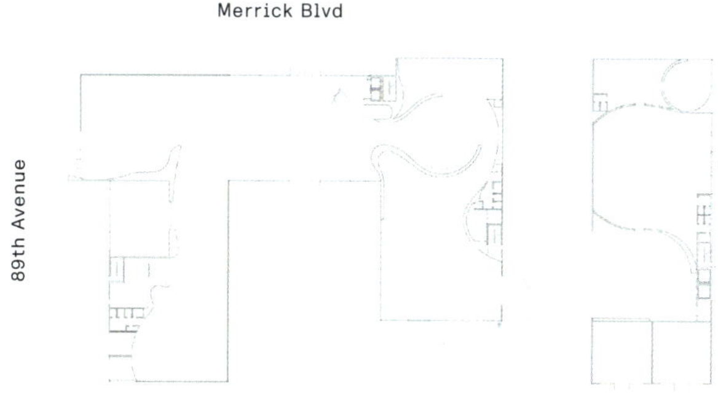

Site plan

Geothermal diagram

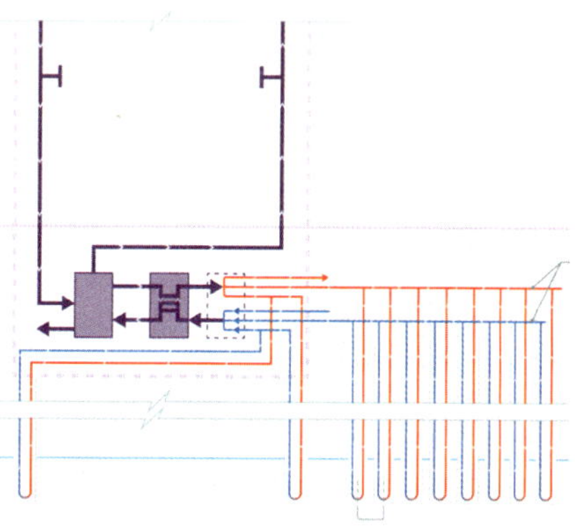

Jenna Ritz

Second-floor interior view

Aerial view

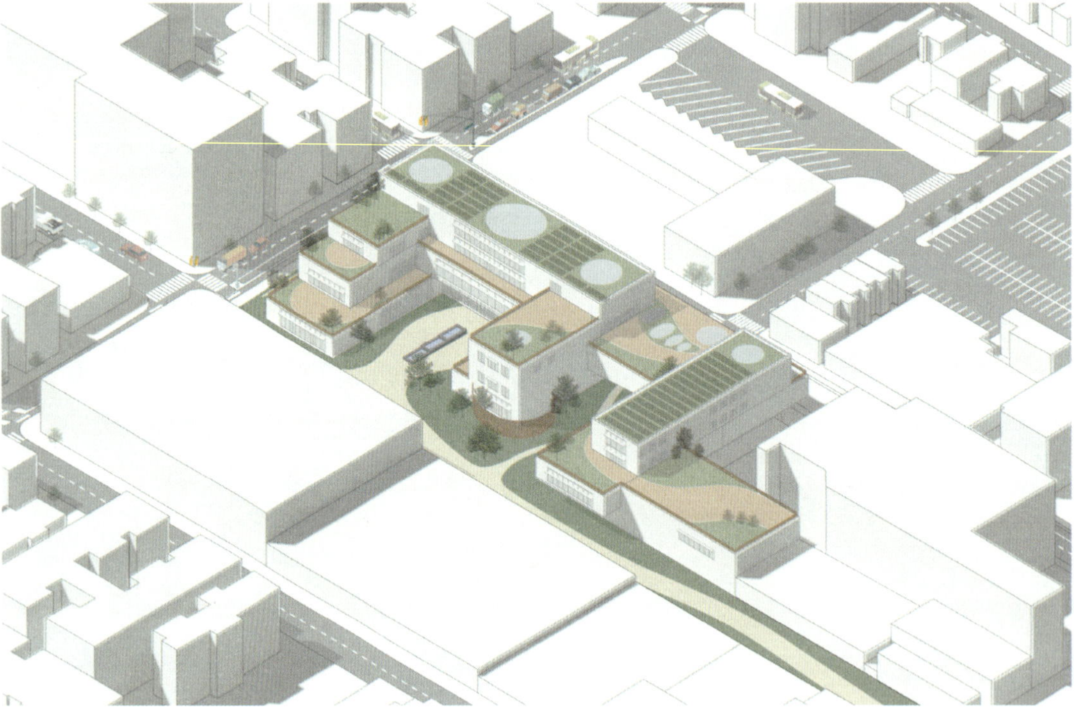

Library of Soundscapes

Exploded plans

Acoustic diagram

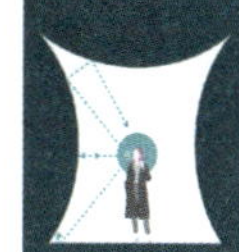

Meeting Room

Library as Third Space

Sited between public and private, fixed and flexible, static and kinetic, vernacular forms and new tectonics, these projects address the multifaceted programming and spatial conditions of the new library within not only the building but also the public civic spaces surrounding it.

James Bradley: Free Library

The "Free Library" is predicated on the principle that people have a right to free public space that offers culture, education, shelter, and myriad other amenities. As a public utility, the library is a great equalizer, and all have equal access as long as they take the opportunity.

Centered around a grand "in"-scaped plaza, the Free Library asserts itself as a keystone for every patron in the Queens Public Library network. From this grand plaza the public has access to the library, reading rooms, community theater spaces, rehearsal halls, and flexible spaces that allow for structural growth prospects well into the future.

Located on the site of an existing bus depot, the library is exceptionally open to public engagement with open-air spaces for civic programs such as farmer's markets, outdoor theater, and other community forums. The library interior harbors open stacks with reading rooms within rooms configured as elevated platforms that separate these two critical programs within a unified state.

The form of the library unfolds from a reinforced learning schema that rewards the formation of large open spaces inhabited by smaller, more complex inner chambers. The components used by the algorithm to construct this formation were derived from a singular module with geometry that could interlock and hook onto itself as a means of growth. From this growth the schema was adapted until a final form was selected as the scaffold for the library design, serving as a source of inspiration rather than end product and treating artificial intelligence as a party to design development.

East-west section

James Bradley

Library site plan

North-south section

Free Library

Plaza view

Plaza view with water

James Bradley

Aerial view

Aerial views from north, south, east, and west

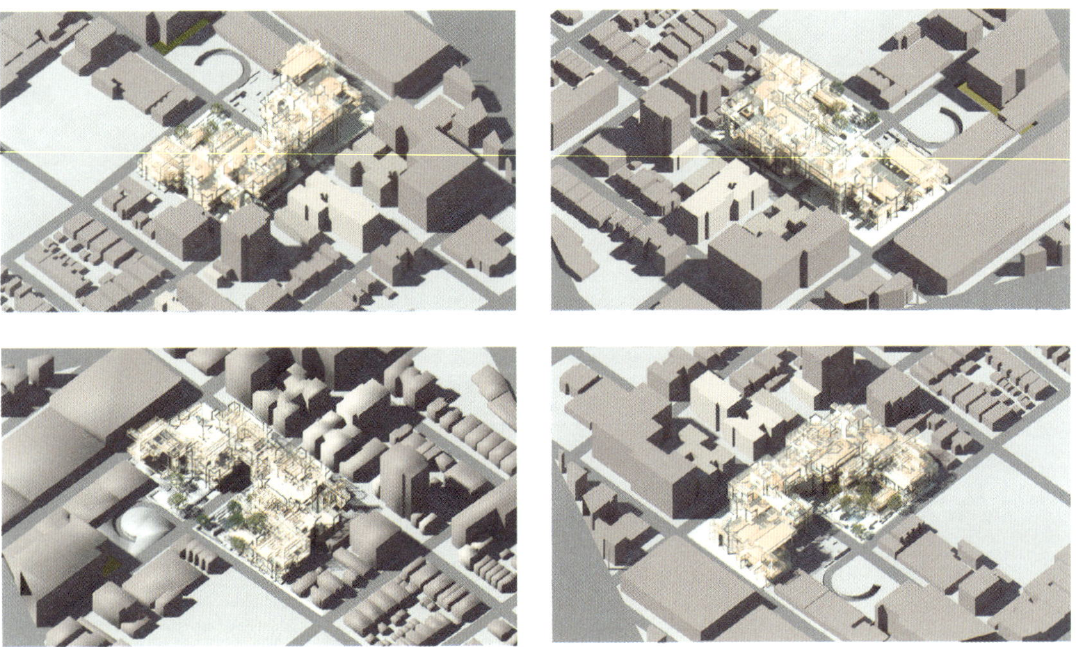

Free Library

Library interior

Library interior, lower level

Elaine Cui

The Queens Public Library's existing open-floor plan and various programs make its interior space rather disorganized. This proposal employs site binaries as space organizers. The library is divided into two zones, static and kinetic, linked by a hybridized third space serving as a buffer zone, a space of mediation, and an antidialectic approach within the system of a double helix.

This double helix creates a dynamic section through the building. Library visitors have access to multiple views of the city as they move up and through the building to the roof. The two zones of static and kinetic spaces have contrasting materials, program arrangements, and structural characteristics. The static sector is private and features traditional library programs, whereas the kinetic sector is public and hosts dynamic community programs. The double-helix structure allows the two parts to operate separately, with different opening hours. Overall the library acts like a community hub and a piece of urban furniture that can be used interchangeably by both individuals and collectives.

Urbanistically, the building addresses the many faces of the site, providing multiple entries. The mass of the building is lifted above the street level, providing an open public space amenity to the surrounding neighborhood.

Site plan

Short section

Long section

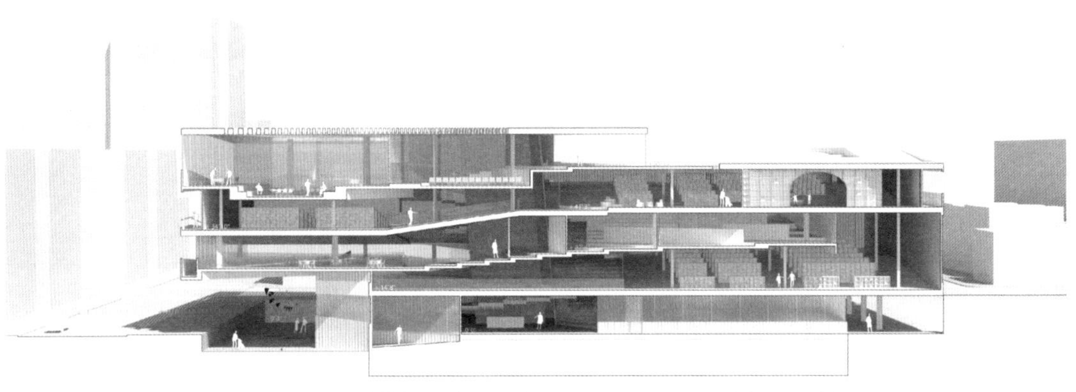

Ground-floor plan

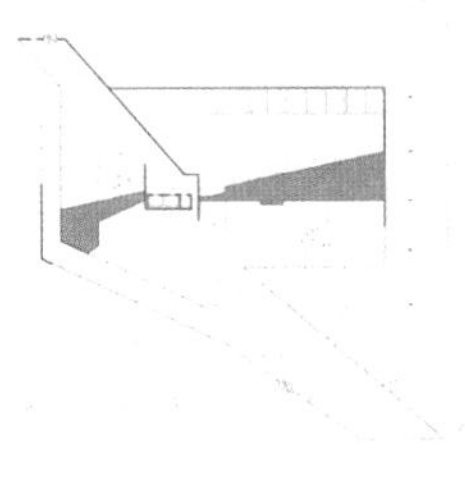

Typical floor plan

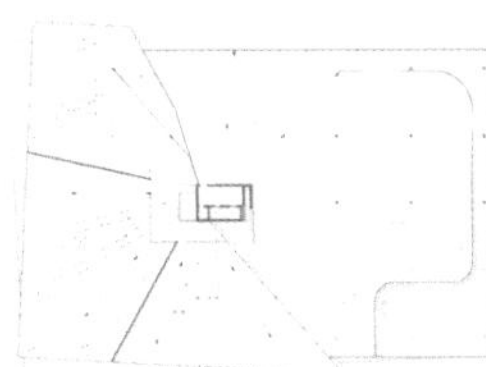

Typical floor plan

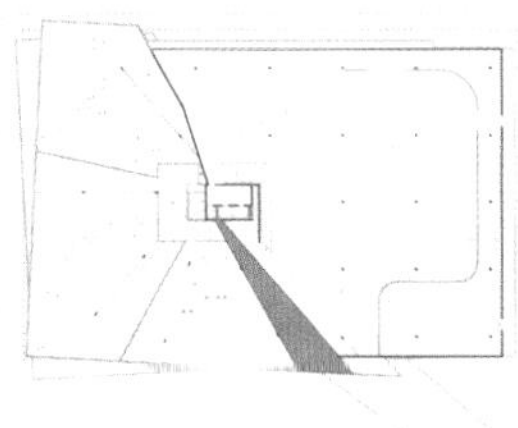

Elaine Cui

Northwest elevation

Northeast elevation

Twist

Interior view of stair

Long section

Max Ouellette-Howitz

The free public library, with functions ranging from research and community center to playground and performance space, requires both a high degree of flexibility and very specific architecture: light for reading and glare-free conditions for working on-screen, places where children can be loud and where readers find quiet, small rooms for study sessions and big areas for gathering—spaces for things we never knew the future library would need.

The library programs can be generalized as two types of space: free and figured. Free space resists walls and acts expansively; it gravitates to the outside and is inherently flexible. Figured space defines boundaries and edges; it moderates the transmission of sound and light and shapes the flow of people through the building. The Queens Central Library balances conditions of free and figured to construct a set of both universal and exceptionally specific places.

The existing library building will be partially demolished, maintaining only the belowground logistics and storage center. The above-grade portion of the building will be replaced with a public park. The green space is punctuated with a series of lightwells and courtyards inviting an exchange of ideas and allowing park visitors to peer down into the book-sorting facility that handles all 7.5 million items in the Queens collection. Across the street a set of similar figures stretch upward, becoming the legs of the new library. They circulate people up into the structure and bring light down onto the covered plaza. The new building is approachable from all sides, working as an attractor and inviting anyone hopping off a bus to step inside. It rises above its surroundings, acting as a neighborhood landmark and offering its visitors unobstructed views across low-lying Jamaica.

On each floor the vertical legs of the building land in different places and hold different functions. The fixed figures in the park and within the library sit in fields of flexible space and provide the variety of conditions a free public library requires to best serve its multiplicity of functions. As the library changes over time, floors will be rearranged and reconsidered. Furniture will come and go. Trees will bloom and die and be replanted. The figures are fixed, but the space between them is always open for invention.

Plan diagrams

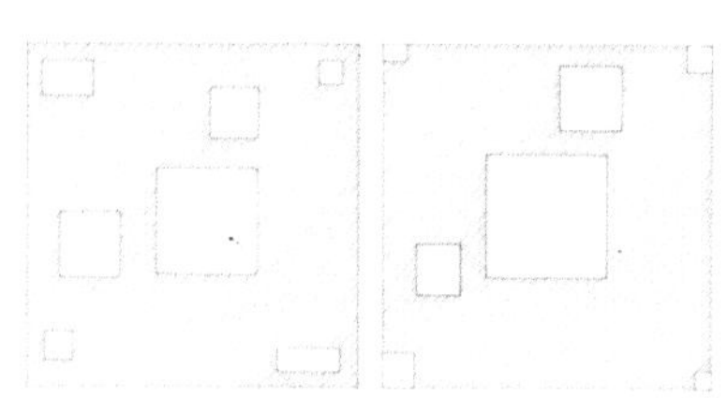

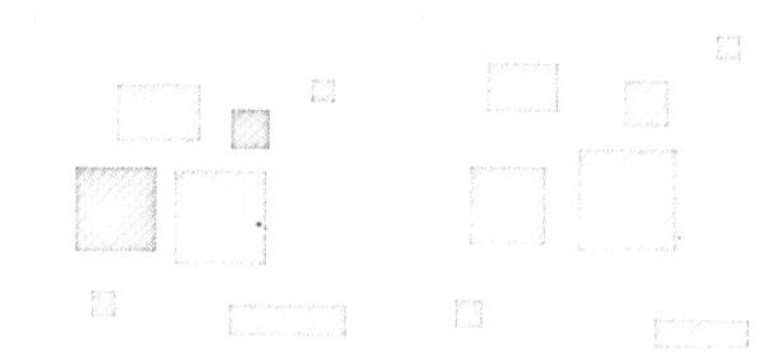

Free/Figured

Model top plan view

Model

Max Ouellette-Howitz

Section

Lower-level plan

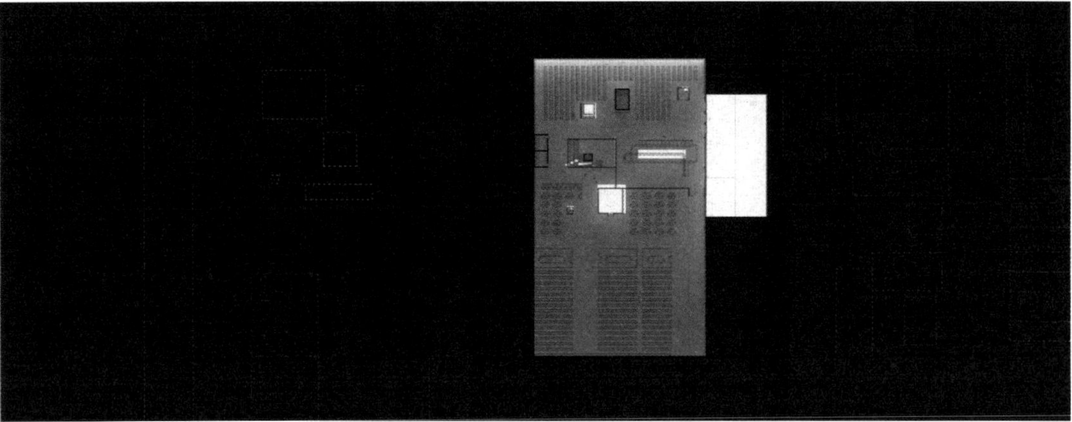

Ground-floor plan

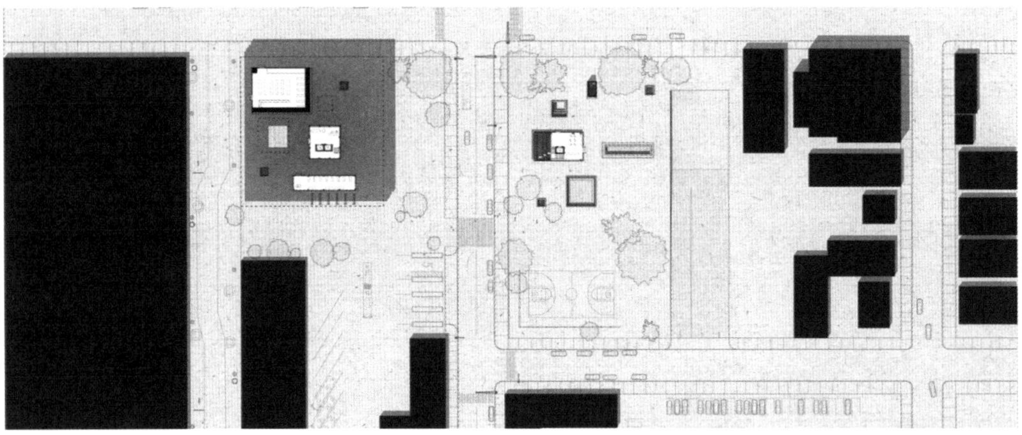

Second-floor plan

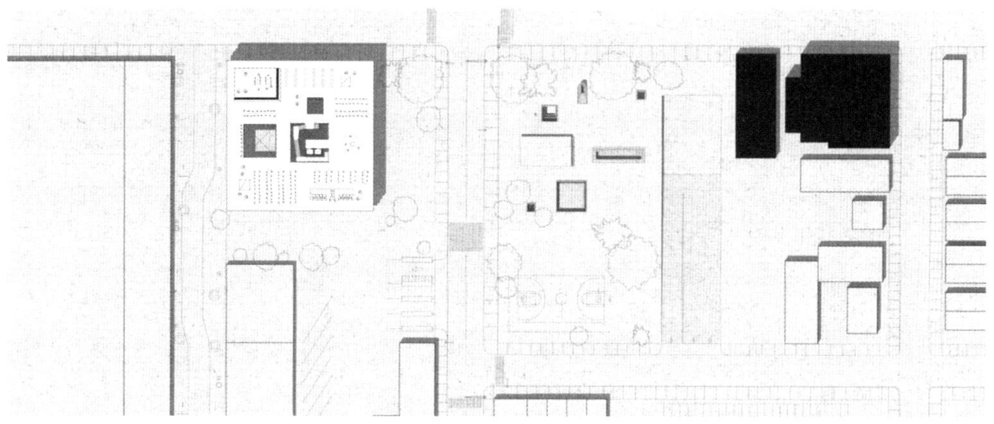

Third-floor plan

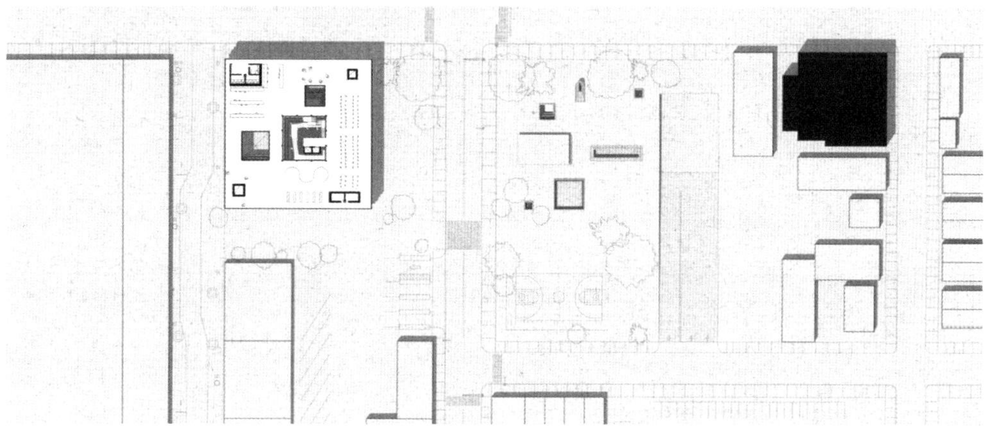

Fourth-floor plan

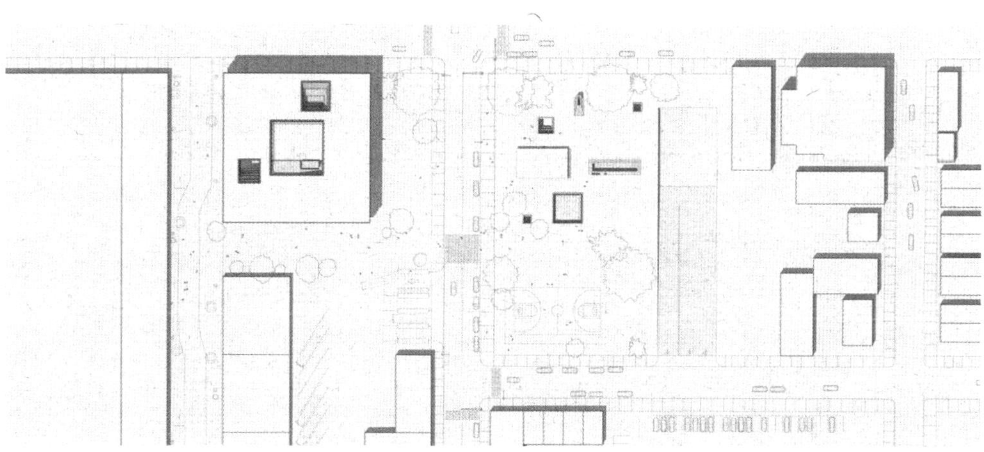

Shuang Chen

The free library is about free access, attracting people to enter after they get off the bus. Placed between the Jamaica bus terminal and the commercial street, this library is a buffer zone, a waiting room for the bus stop, and a living room for Jamaica, Queens. The waiting activities on the existing site inspired the idea of creating a library as a waiting room for the bus stop and a buffer zone between the stop and stores. The waiting function fulfills basic public needs while stimulating activities related to reading and the library.

The arched canopy derives from traditional infrastructure in New York such as the elevated subway. These arches become a splendid landscape and define the space underneath for a big market. The existing shed on the site informed the outline of the form and contributed to its role as a buffer zone. Scenarios under the shed were more vivid in front of the stores than those at the transit area against the back walls. As a giant canopy the library becomes the vivid interval.

The scheme shows a transition from light to heavy as a composite response to the relationship with the old QPL, the transition to outdoor market, and the change from waiting room to large reading areas. Multiple connections between the library, the market, the commercial street, the stores, and the bus stop have been established and integrated. In terms of materiality, the concrete shell and wooden roof manifes the contrast between heavy and light. The concrete canopy arches were designed to facilitate the sculptural sense of the whole scheme. Aloft wood floor plates and occupiable concrete surfaces provide an integrated spatial experience of the form.

Perspective section

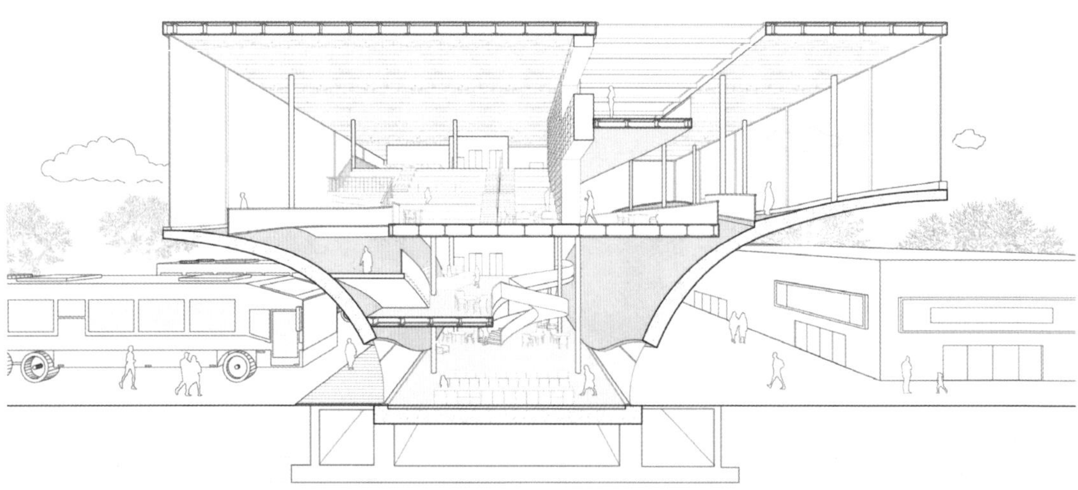

Free Library/Waiting Room

Market rendering

Elevation rendering

Site plan

Model annotation

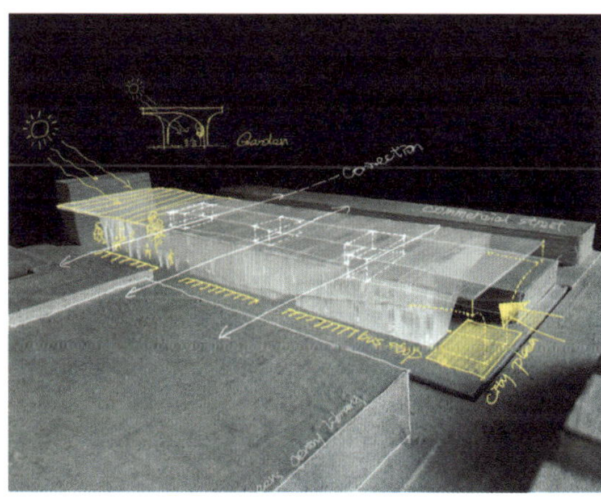

Shuang Chen

Interior rendering of reading zone

Entrance and waiting-room rendering

Free Library/Waiting Room

In-between space

Model photo

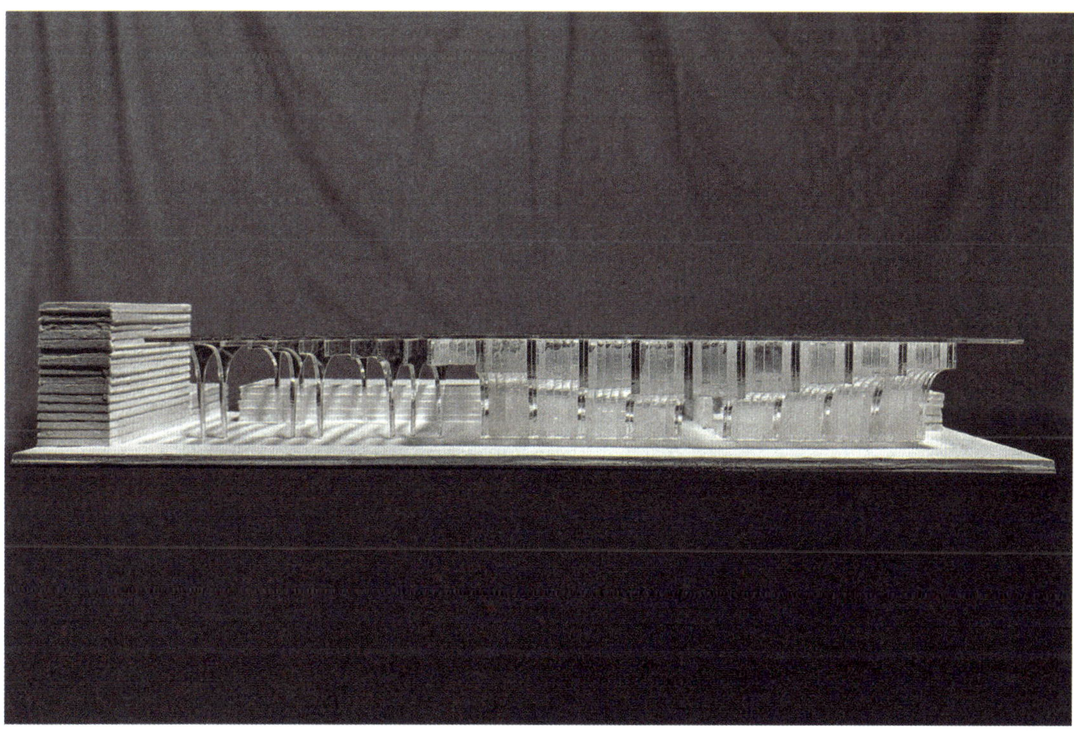

Brenna Thompson

> Third place, defined as a place between work and home that anchors community life and facilitates or fosters broader, more creative interaction.
>
> — Ray Oldenburg

A new proposal for the Queens Central Library with capacity to support the sorting and distributing operations of the network, "Nudging Vernaculars" looks to urban vernacular forms of storage and existing library branches to evoke a sense of familiarity for the neighborhood of Jamaica. The context of the site is comprised of many pieces—water towers, fire-escape stairs, brick, and signage. In view of the notion of public wayfinding, each of these elements questions how the site and program may be approached in a way that honors contextual vernaculars yet nudges them toward new potentials.

Through its many layers, the building offers an experience of discovery. On the main level, the "third place," visitors are free to use the open hall as they desire, as a space of serendipity. Workstations, cafés, reception areas, and help desks orbit the stacks while their circular silhouettes shape voids for lounging and resting. From this third place people can catch glimpses of those hunting for a book in the catwalks above or those awaiting buses in the park area below.

Acting as vertical circulation, the stacks are connected through a series of catwalks at varying levels. Deep inside the poché, shrouded by the books of the stacks, are intimate spaces of refuge, reading nooks, work and nap stations, and small-scale meeting rooms. From east to west the stacks are veiled in a metal mesh to provide sun protection for books, aided by the sawtoothed glass facade. Wrapped in several layers, the rooms within the stacks are provided with diffuse illumination from skylights.

Through its formal ties to urban vernaculars, the library expresses itself as a beacon to the public. Its many layers of materials and transparency are welcoming yet protect the neighborhood and community members. The library seeks to be a space as comfortable as home but with all the grandeur and amenities of a public space—a third place where you can relax in public, encounter familiar faces, and make new acquaintances both fictional and real.

Community garden

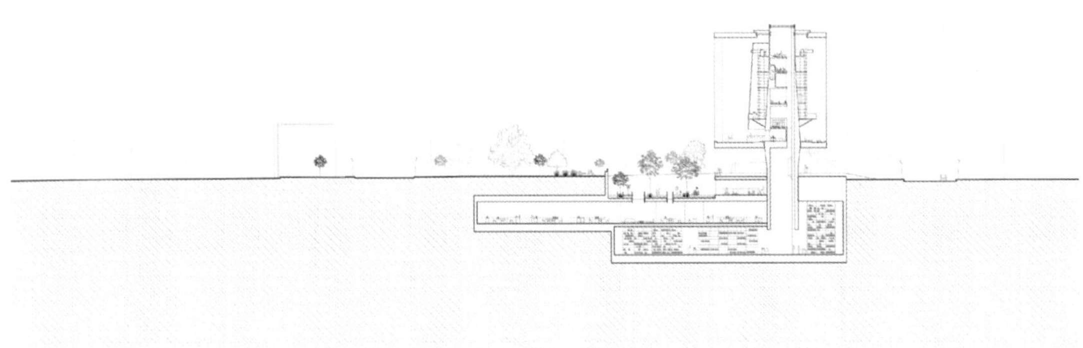

Stacks revealed

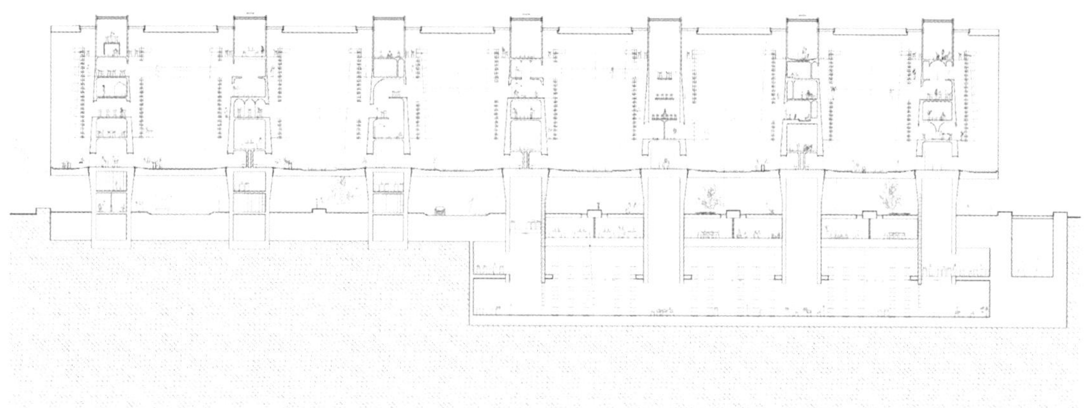

Ground-plane porosity

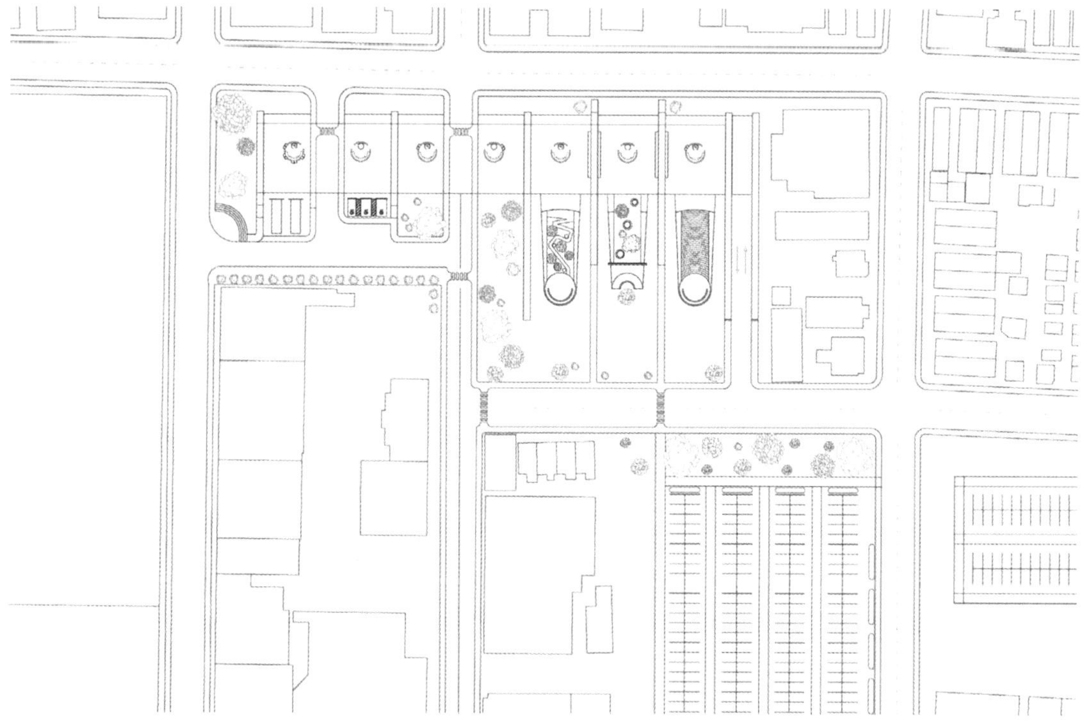

Brenna Thompson

Third Place

Approach

Bay 1: Amphitheater

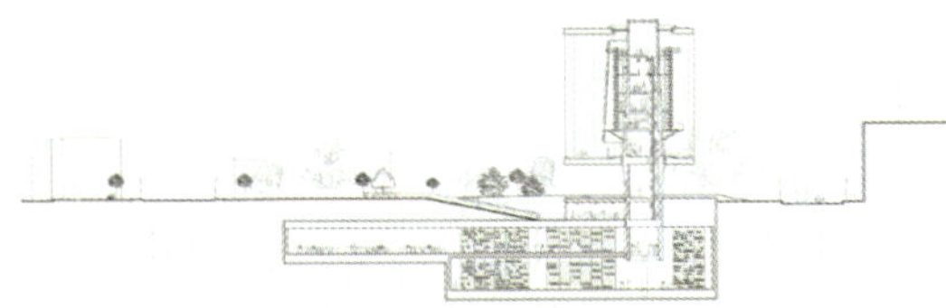

Bay 3: Playground

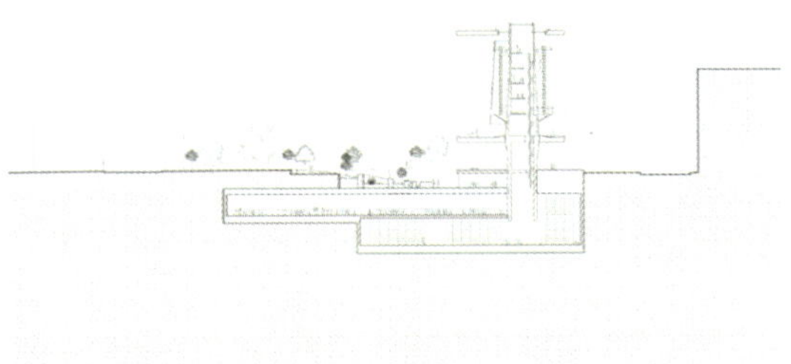

Nudging Vernaculars

Catwalk

Underbelly

Midsemester review model

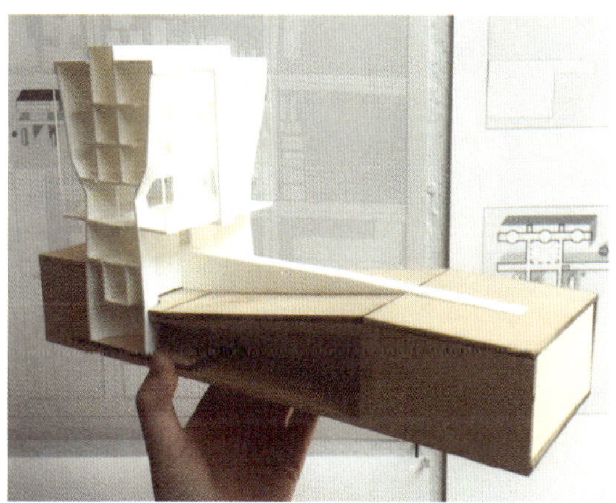

The forest clearing archetype: Three divisional model of the forest around Oslo revealing clearings with architectural significance due to their geometry and dimensions.
Credit: LCLA office with Maximilian Schob. For the exhibition *Trees as Architecture* at arc en rêve in Bordeaux. 2021.

The Forest

Luis Callejas and Charlotte Hansson

Conversation with Luis Callejas and Charlotte Hansson

Aquatic center for the 2010 South American games. Luis Callejas, Edgar Mazo and Sebastian Mejia. 2010. Photo by Luis Callejas.

NINA RAPPAPORT How did you meet and begin your practice together after having already worked independently?

LUIS CALLEJAS After meeting briefly in Oslo, we met again in Venice two years later. We decided to do one project together. When we met, Charlotte said she had a fascination for the Andes, while I had a deep fascination for the Swedish west coast and the thousands of small islands. Now that I think about it, this was very important to the decision to work together.

CHARLOTTE HANSSON Then we started working together when I moved to Boston. Our first project was an invitation to participate in an exhibition for the Neutra VDL Studio and Residence, in Los Angeles.

LC It was incredible because we didn't actually know each other for that long. While living and working in that house we got to know each other and decided to continue as an office.

CH It was a site-specific project engaging with the house in terms of experiments that Neutra did in order to bring the landscape in. Previously, the house had been undergoing a refurbishment. We discovered that the curtains were missing, so the exhibition became an opportunity to design and use the curtains as a medium to show the project in a new way.

NR Charlotte, with both an art and architecture background, how have you been merging the practices of garment construction and building, first in your own projects and then as you started to collaborate with Luis?

CH It was more important in the beginning of our collaboration that I brought different knowledge that could be used in a new way. The textile concepts we produced for the Neutra house and our installation at the first Chicago Biennale cannot be associated with fashion; it is architecture.

NR How would you define the way you work together on a project?

CH We work very much on the same things, going back and forth. It's not so divided.

NR Luis, in many of your projects with your original architecture partners, from the Heathrow Airport competition to river infrastructure projects in Medellín and Kyiv, you address the interrelationship between the built and natural environments. Would you call yourself a landscape urbanist, or do you work across disciplines between landscape, architecture, and urbanism in a way that cannot be affixed to any category?

LC I trained as an architect in Colombia, and the separation between landscape and architecture is not as important

Underside of tribunes at the aquatic center. Photo by Luis Callejas.

Guest of honor pavilion for the 2019 Frankfurt bookfair. Design: LCLAoffice + Mantheykula. Photo by Luis Callejas.

there as it is in North America, where landscape architecture is a much more autonomous discipline. Coincidentally I started to practice right when landscape urbanism started to emerge as a discourse in North America. Charles Waldheim noticed our practice after I gave a lecture at GSD in 2009, and he invited me to Harvard, where I taught for five years. This was a time when my generation was deeply interested in urbanism, and it coincided with a wave of progressive urban projects in Medellín.

In Latin America we perceived landscape urbanism with both distance and affinity, even though we didn't identify our work that way. For us, it was just a natural way to work driven more by practice than academic discourses. We were architects working with the medium of landscape, equally interested in buildings and plant life. Later our work was recognized as a Latin ripple of this North American discourse. Maybe one reason our work resonated with landscape urbanism at that time is that we were working on real urban projects, such as the Aquatic Center in Medellín, which had a clear urban impact in a tough, dense area. We were architects that used landscape media—vegetation and landforms—to deal with the problem of urban integration in a really difficult site. I have to admit that I call what we do also landscape architecture but in general our approach is project focused rather than linked to any disciplinary affiliation. We do projects and research, and the output is often recognized as landscape, and at other times what we do is clearly buildings. Interestingly the labels sometimes vary depending on the country you are working in.

NR How do Colombia's intense natural landscape and ecologies, as well as the built environment of Latin America, inspire you?

LC The cycle of life in the tropics is not really interrupted by winter: everything changes at constant speed, and architecture cannot really contain this force. It seems to me that vegetation and architecture are on more equal terms in the tropics. Most of these landscapes are not natural; they are products of urbanization or extraction as human interactions clash with the seemingly wild. Traditions are also important; architects like Luis Barragán, Lina Bo Bardi, and Rogelio Salmona were interested in landscape beyond just using it as inspiration—they knew how to tend their own gardens and had profound botanical knowledge. I have been deeply interested in modern Latin architects who had serious botanic literacy. This is also what happened with landscape architecture, which is a discipline that evolved in South America without the heavy weight of the dominant traditions (English and French), meaning that abstraction and environmentalism somehow have always coexisted. Form never became a dirty word when the ecological movements started.

NR You have designed and imagined so many projects around water, both practical and imaginary, from islands and rivers

Shower at the house in a forest clearing. By LCLA office with Clara Arango. Photo by Luis Callejas.

Terrace at the house in a forest clearing. Design Luis Callejas with Clara Arango. Photo by Luis Callejas.

to canals and pools. What draws you to water? Is it the potential for infrastructure and engineering controls, or the duality of serenity and power, even danger?

LC We do love water. Perhaps one of the reasons is that the city where I'm from is about 400 kilometers from the sea—in the middle of the Andes. It is a fascination with the ocean that we didn't have. I have discovered that water can be used to produce space as much as walls and columns. Water can be both space and material. After the Aquatic Center, we started to enter as many competitions as possible that involved water. Charlotte, on the other hand, was practically raised on a boat, in a sailing family. I suppose we are fascinated with each other's native landscapes. It was and still is very important. When we met, Charlotte was fascinated with the mountains, the Andes, another recurrent landscape in our projects, at the same time I became fascinated with Goteborg's archipelago and sailing there in the summer, a landscape that was Charlotte's playground. You ask about danger and serenity, but maybe we each are discovering new ways to engage with these landscapes, and as we don't separate life from work these fascinations end up in projects.

NR How do you engage the community when you design a public project such as the Aquatic Center, in Medellín?

LC From the beginning we proposed a horizontal landscape, because we considered the public realm more than building as an object. It was evident that the city needed not only a space for training and professional swimming competitions but also an aquatic park for the community. This was our gift to the community, and frankly it was very easy to promote. The hardest thing was to convince the mayor that he wouldn't have a freestanding iconic building. We had to convince him that a landscape could be iconic while serving more people than just professional athletes.

NR How have you been able to convince other clients to do something beyond what they imagined, such as using landscape and water for incremental public spaces in Kyiv?

LC In Kyiv we showed the client, in this case the city, that a hard-core infrastructural master plan was not actually needed. We used the project to demonstrate that the river, with 37 islands, is already a perfect structure from which to start thinking about how to link opposite sides of the Dnieper River. In smaller projects, like the houses we finished in Medellín, we convinced the client that he didn't need to live so large and that smaller fragmented pavilions would allow us to design a large landscape. It is a project that could have been one 300-square-meter house and instead became three pavilions of 70 square meters each arrayed on a beautiful slope. Obviously we liberated resources for the design of the garden by doing this.

NR How has the coronavirus impacted your practice? How have you seen life change in Norway the past few months?

The long house as a retention wall in the forest clearing. Photo by Luis Callejas.

Model of one the islands in the Dnieper river, transformed into a botanical garden linking both shores. Photo by Luis Callejas.

CH Some of our projects have been delayed, such as exhibitions and a few buildings. But since we are a small firm, work hasn't changed so much. One current project that is restarting, now finally under construction, is the design of the urban space around the former U.S. Embassy in Oslo, a triangular building designed by Eero Saarinen, which we won the competition for recently with Lund Hagem and Atelier Oslo. It was sold to a private owner a couple of years ago, after the embassy moved.

LC By now we can tell you only that the old security fence is removed and there will be public space, considering how the embassy was originally designed more like a cultural center. The building by Saarinen is a jewel, so we feel a big responsibility to build a new landscape while engaging with the restored Modernist facade.

CH Coronavirus has also affected, in an interesting way, the houses that Luis mentioned we designed in Medellín. Situated in the landscape, each of the pavilions inhabits the terrain differently. The landscape has been important as a building material, so we designed the gardens to take on a larger role than originally expected by the client.

LC There was a fortunate accident. The gardens for this project were nearly finished when suddenly the lockdown started in Colombia. This meant the gardens could not be maintained, and they went wild, so that what emerged was a strange mix of a formal manicured garden and a very wild landscape. It is what happens when you abandon a garden for a few months in the tropics—even some wild orchids appeared.

NR How did you organize the Yale studio to evolve online? Do you have methods that you think will continue to enhance teaching and inspire student investigations?

The garden and curtain at Richard Neutra's VDL house, activated as part of LCLA office site specific installation and exhibition in 2014. Photo by Luis Callejas.

LC While it is tough, the travel restrictions have allowed us to test something we might have done anyway. Studio site visits have become sources of late means of verification rather than early inspiration. At the beginning of my practice we traveled very little; in fact it all started back in 2007 with a competition for Venice, a city that I only visited later. Projects became a way to travel, and the idea of designing as a way to travel has been very important in our work. We introduced students to advanced modeling techniques, from remote sensing to more traditional physical models, but also to narrative and literature as a way to create mental models of sites that have potential to be more powerful than the real one. There is a kind of taboo, especially in landscape, about designing a site without visiting it. We believe that when you trust a model you can be inspired by that abstraction. We wanted to teach students how to read a site you cannot visit and to construct creative mental and physical models when it is not possible to travel.

The archetypal clearing, or the form of an idea.

One of the most fascinating and recurrent spatial metaphors employed by philosophers, both Eastern and Western, is the forest clearing. As much as this image can be precise and sophisticated, such as Martin Heidegger's *Litchung*, it is a visual metaphor that takes shape within the mind of whomever is imagining it. Although Heidegger employs the German word as both verb and noun, the clearing has no form or dimensions in his writing.

A precise description of the clearing is absent in most literal constructions of this spatial archetype. Is it that the form of the clearing as an archetype doesn't really matter when discussing it with words? Or is it that the attempt to crystallize a precise perimeter or shape runs the risk of killing its beauty as a pure idea, that of the open space in a field of trees. A powerful image without a form, a space guided by an idea, takes shape in the individual memory of whoever is engaging with the literary description. Furthermore, as there is often no scale in memory, we can assume that the dimension of the clearing also doesn't really matter for philosophers.

Houses in a forest clearing. LCLA office and Clara Arango. Photo by Luis Callejas.

From Heidegger's depiction of the clearing as a metaphor

of the mind to Taoist principles framing the cosmological qualities of emptiness, the clearing is loosely described as a space of enlightenment with undefined edges. The forest clearing has been a persistent abstraction that seems to work across cultures and time, implying that the endurance of the metaphor may depend on evading questions of geometry and dimension. Its descriptions thrive on the elusiveness of a jagged perimeter that we know is there; we have seen it, yet it resists rigorous geometric study.

For architects and landscape designers, the forest clearing has been framed as a preeminent archetype giving origin to the most basic spatial formulations in landscape architecture. The clearing and the walled garden are often presented as preeminent archetypes for the Western landscape. In descriptions by authoritative design scholars the clearing is often drawn as a simple circle with blurry edges. A powerful image, the circle is also a visual placeholder for the myriad shapes that might be of interest to a designer. In contrast, the walled garden is linked to the sophisticated Persian archetype that inspired the contained paradises of the West, for which extensive and precise geometric studies exist.

Curated clearings and irregular plots around Oslo in the urban forest. Photo by Luis Callejas.

The primitive reasons why forest clearings are created are perhaps not worth aesthetic inquiry; forestry's often brutal extractive practice clearly conflicts with the poetic ideal of being in a clearing, an

Curated clearings and irregular plots around Oslo located in the urban forest. Luis Callejas and Dale Wiebe

experience that needs a renewed evaluation in terms of form. For designers to discuss this archetype as a kind of proto-architecture, a set of formal principles are required to evaluate spatial qualities and define geometry beyond the purposes of pragmatic forestry.

For architects, the shape of the clearing embodies the poetic qualities of the metaphor, therefore form and dimensions cannot be elicited from its conception as an archetype. From all the examples of real clearings that can be studied formally, it is in Norway, close to Oslo, where the sophisticated rules for forestry make it possible to sharpen the understanding of it as a valuable spatial archetype for designers.

The Norwegian Clearing

The forest around Oslo is a carefully managed plantation of trees that many locals still describe as wild nature. Centuries of development between the forest and the sea have produced a unique European capital with a sophisticated relationship to its natural surroundings. Many residents of Oslo acknowledge the forest as a civic space; a weekend in the forest is a unique urban experience, and not just because of its natural beauty, ease of accessibility, or sophisticated networks of facilities and amenities. The sophisticated urban forest is an urban space that outcompetes the plazas and boulevards of the city because its role as a civic space is more specific as well as unique to Oslo. It is also a space with particular importance for the construction of the Norwegian national identity, for instance, the myth of the urban forest as a free zone, “a space where one could escape the city, escape modernity, and escape the Nazis.” From wartime refuge to meeting place for romantic trysts, the forest has a rich history as an arena for civic life.

Selected clearing chosen for spatial qualities, later edited to act as civic spaces for Oslo. Luis Callejas and Maximilian Schob

It is essential to clarify that the forest around Oslo is not all public; there are significant areas that are private property. However, decades of discussion and active public participation, along with environmental movements and vocal activism from hiking and skiing associations, have presented a continuous resistance to actions that would impede free access to the forest for everyone. This strong civic sentiment has been influential in perpetuating an image of the forest based on national romantic ideals. In other words, public participation has worked in synchrony with sophisticated regulations to perpetuate the particular look and feel of the forest and afford free open access to all, even in areas used primarily for wood harvesting.

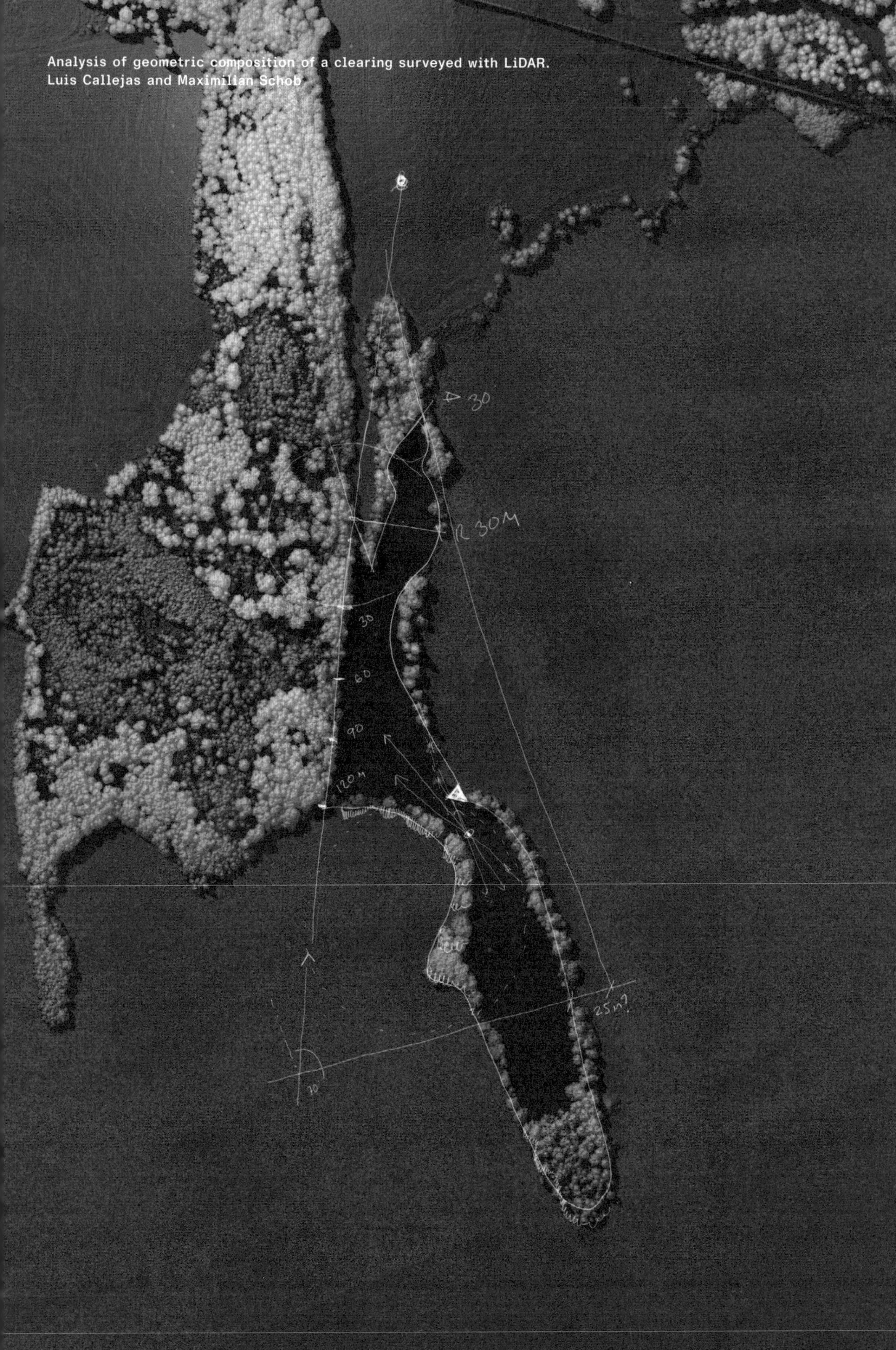

Analysis of geometric composition of a clearing surveyed with LiDAR.
Luis Callejas and Maximilian Schob

Around Oslo the particular shapes of clearings are guided by decades of discussion, reconciling public use with forestry. As a consequence these spaces present myriad sophisticated, quirky forms that contrast the brutal clearings for forestry in other parts of the world. The figures are a result of the early environmental principles that informed Norwegian forestry practice, such as the understanding that biodiversity can be strengthened by allowing natural succession. The clearings in Oslo present us with a set of circumstances that enable designers to work effectively within the constraints of sophisticated shapes. Practitioners must obey the rules passed in 1993, which focus mainly on maintaining the recreational and aesthetic values of the forest. The rules: Limit the size of clearings; allow and encourage natural succession where possible; avoid planting trees in new rows, especially close to lakes or paths; follow natural topography for felling sites; avoid straight, square-shaped clearings; and let trees mature spontaneously along lakes and rivers.

Finally, understanding the quirky shapes of the Oslo clearings is possible only because of the aerial LiDAR surveys that are publicly available from the municipality. With a minimum resolution of eight points per square meter, the laser survey gives an accurate three-dimensional perspective that architects can start to instrumentalize in order to evaluate this vast, difficult-to-survey space. The archetype crystallizes not in direct experience on the ground or in the sophisticated spatial metaphors employed by philosophers, but within the space of the drawing as a formal reality. The act of giving form to the archetype and manifesting ideas as primitive and universal as the forest clearing start by creatively editing the forest survey.

Studio Brief

Fall 2020, with Marta Caldeira

Introduction

For the past five years our practice, LCLA, and teaching studios have challenged prevailing ideas about site-specificity by considering drawings and models as the sites. We focus on five canonical landscape types: mountain, desert, island, forest, and ocean—always attempting to reach the point where certain landscape conditions can be generalized to design for site-specific situations.

The Forest

The studio developed projects in forest clearings in Norway, while focusing on the clearing as an archetype present in different forms of cultural expression such as literature, art, architecture, and landscape.

As illustrated in Franz Heske's writings of the 1930s, practices as mundane as forest management can reflect, if not embody, prevailing religious beliefs and practices. Myths and traditions that emerge by looking at forests endure as influences for architecture in many design cultures.

The studio explored how architects could take inspiration from this landscape type. The idea was to challenge phenomenological approaches prevalent in Nordic design cultures and engage renewed questions about the representation, modeling, and surveys of forests, particularly how surveying technologies such as LiDAR imaging shape how the forest is managed and envisioned as a designed space. We engaged with the design problem of freestanding architecture in a forest clearing, in the framework of Heidegger's proposition that all architecture somehow starts this way. The poetic force of this image is persistent across cultures. For Heidegger the clearing is closely connected to the term's original meaning in German—lighting, or letting the light in. The manipulation of light in the design of the forest is not entirely alien to forest managers and landscape architects; however, architects rarely engage in manipulation of a site's landscape and generally focus on adapting to found conditions.

In Norway the boreal forest is a cultural landscape that has long influenced designers. Yet designers often ignore the fact that most forests are managed spaces or objects of design. Ultimately the studio engaged the forest as a cultural landscape and spatial metaphor informing architecture. Students investigated the need for an updated set of forest representations around Oslo. From forest management to myths and spatial metaphors, the studio investigated the persistent yet evolving love affair with the forest in Scandinavia.

The History of "Thing"

From the Iron Age through the Viking and Middle Ages communities in Scandinavia were organized around a governing assembly called "thing" (*ting* or *folkmoot*) that served as both parliament and court. It was the forum for conflict resolution, tax collection, marriage alliances, and legislation and a place where all free women and men could speak their minds. Events would happen regularly and could last from one to three weeks, so it also served as a seasonal marketplace.

The meeting place, called thingstead, was often in fields or clearings close to land or water routes. These sites would often have a man-made mound marked

Reconstruction of the Oslo forest based on LiDAR data. Exposing the clearings with architectural interest. LCLA office and Maximiliam Schob. For an exhibition at arc en rêve, Bordeaux. *Trees as Architecture.*

with large stones, from where the law speaker would preside.

The thing was the precursor of the modern parliament, and the name still refers to the governing structures of Scandinavia: Althinget (parliament of Iceland), Stortinget (parliament of Norway), Folketinget (parliament of Denmark), Landsting (regional governing structures of Sweden).

Studio Methodology

COVID-19 travel restrictions presented an extreme condition to test the limits of a methodology often used in our practice: modeling the site as an operation of higher importance than direct experience. The reality of the site was the constructed model.

As part of the studio's remote methodology, Nordic architects and landscape architects were invited to share their work with our students at Yale, while a group of researchers and students from the Oslo School of Architecture worked on-site and shared remote-sensing surveys of the forests.

Phase 1: Research The research stage focused on two seemingly polarized scales: persistent spatial metaphors originating in studies of forests across different design cultures and their links to architecture, and projects of territorial afforestation with clear nation-building agendas. Embracing this dichotomy, students explored the spatial consequences of themes ranging from the forest in literature to the forest as a complex ecosystem.

The projects were located in the privately owned forests of Normarka, surrounding Oslo. Students had to first edit the forest to produce space before attempting any architectural proposition. As the studio assignment makes no distinction between the design of interior and exterior, all projects started with producing a partially open-air parliament. They dealt with an architecture of subtraction and addition and developed structures as

Geometric principles in a clearing in Oslo, LCLA office and Maximiliam Schob.
For an exhibition at Arc en Rêve, Bordeaux. *Trees as Architecture.*

freestanding objects whose logic is related to how the forest is edited.

Phase 2: Translation of Research Themes to Space The students reflected their research in an atlas of forest imaginaries and a single shaded plan drawing conveying space and form through rendered shadows and planimetric projection.

Suggested Techniques

Based on aerial photos, the students invented topographies that estimate the forest's tree height, planting distance, dominant species, density, and other parameters determining spatial conditions. These were not meant to represent reality but rather to construct a model as a prototypical landscape to be rendered in plan. The model was a base for spatial experiments and a careful modeling of the trees covering 70 percent of the invented site. For the remaining 30 percent, the students developed subtractive techniques and applied them to the design of a forest clearing to form an initial idea about architectural space.

Manipulation of Trees

In considering how to model trees carefully, the following principles were offered.

1 Designing trees This far-fetched assertion has, in fact, an important precedent in many gardening traditions. The students analyzed how trees are bent while they grow to produce beams for ships and how they are ornamentally trimmed by nurseries to understand techniques from ancient shaping to genetic manipulation.

2 Color Students could suggest interventions affecting the color of bark and leaves. Trees are often painted for different purposes, from repealing pests to marking trails.

3 Cutting height It is common practice to cut trees high above standard stump height to promote biodiversity.

4 Trimming of the canopies

5 Balance between deciduous trees and evergreens

The project's last phase was to design by editing what was produced in Phase 2. Students proposed what a contemporary version of the open-air parliament should be, along with the structures that would host or support such activities. They edited the clearings and designed buildings tailored to individual agendas. Architectural interventions were to be located at the edge of a clearing, with building and planting of equal hierarchical status.

The trees were to be considered members of the parliament, not just a backdrop for human assembly. This open provocation required an architectural interpretation. The design of a landscape, the planning of a structure, and the formulation of an architectural program were all tied to how the clearing was edited and shaped. Geometries generated during Phase 1 were to have traces in the architectural elements of the buildings, ranging from the large-scale plan to the proposal of at least one special detail. Finally, some projects associated the idea of the parliament incorporated contemporary programs such as a school. For most students the concept of the parliament was enough to formulate a proposal for a new definition of a cultural landscape.

Student Projects

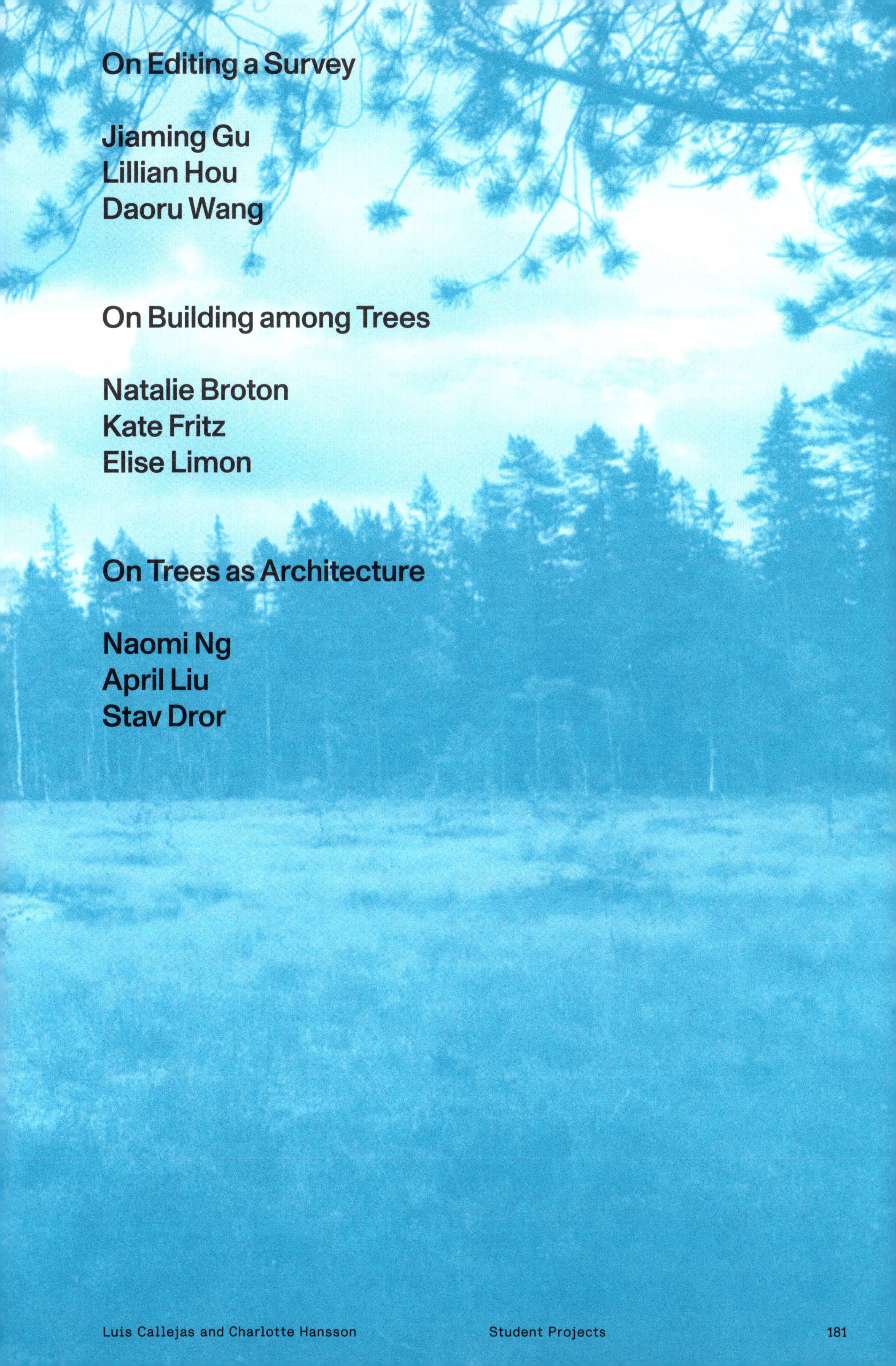

On Editing a Survey

Jiaming Gu
Lillian Hou
Daoru Wang

On Building among Trees

Natalie Broton
Kate Fritz
Elise Limon

On Trees as Architecture

Naomi Ng
April Liu
Stav Dror

On Editing a Survey

Projects for which the edition of a preexisting topographical survey privileges trees and clearings over the addition of inert architectural form.

Jiaming Gu: Anchor in Nature

Preliminary analysis examined the typological and morphological qualities of the forest. The outline of the forest landscape was traced and the volume of trees and plants was read as an extrusion of different heights and depths. The volume of the vegetation was transformed into a 3-D model, and the trees were planted in lines to test and represent a similar spatial quality to the extruded 3-D model. The second step was to analyze various field conditions formed by different densities, sizes, and formations of trees.

The site slopes down from south to north and is covered mainly with spruce trees. The dimension of the site is 500 by 700 meters, with one main road to the north and two main clearings next to each other.

Images from previous extrusion studies were applied to the site as height filters. One test among these was chosen as the base for the final project, as it creates gradient boundary conditions in between clearings and different textures on the ground. The final plan started with modifying the height of trees and boundaries of clearings based on the test from AerioLOD software.

People could wander around the forested area and experience different perspectives while encountering small-scale structures anchored in the clearings with meeting spaces organized around them. The parliament is not intended as a forum for one person to speak while others listen, but as an unstable environment that stimulates as much discussion as possible.

The rules for the plan were as follows:

1 The trees were edited so that the original site condition is in the upper part of the image. Trees of various sizes were planted at the same time and grew into random conditions. Some trees around two clearings were replaced with smaller trees that gradually transform into bigger ones to create gradient conditions at the clearings' edges.

2 Anchored structures were inserted around two clearings as gathering spaces, both covered and not covered, to stimulate the exchange of political ideas and discussion.

3 A focus on circulation was created in an entrance from the main road on the upper-left side of the site and a pathway surrounded by trees that arrives at the first clearing, called "gathering in between trees," and an observation tower. A less dense tree-covered area leads to the second clearing, with a "seat for interchange," the platform for people to sit and talk.

Perspectives

Surrounded by lines of trees on two sides, you enter the first space and see a wooden house in front of you, in which seats are placed between treelike columns. This creates a covered space for people to put their bags and sit down to talk or rest.

The observation tower has a restroom and outdoor seating on the first floor. The benches reflect the simplicity of the patterns on the ground, following the change of contour lines to be in harmonious relationship with the surrounding landscape.

At the top of the observation tower you see the change from birch and English oak trees to a big group of spruce trees that gradually rise in height. After walking across the tree-covered area you arrive at the second clearing, where the seating for interchange and activities is marked by trees on four sides.

Jiaming Gu

Editing the forest

The walkway

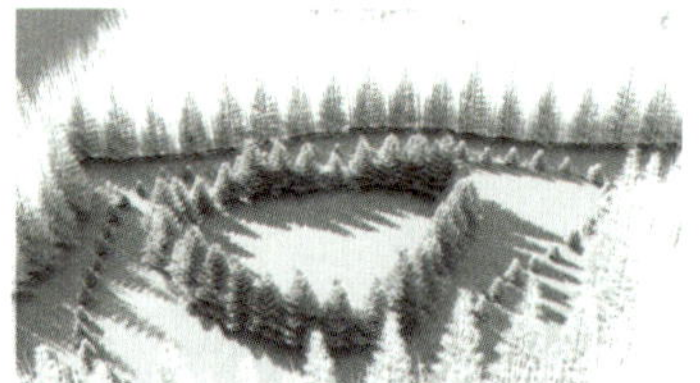

The “maze” gathering space

The field

Editing the clearing

Editing trees

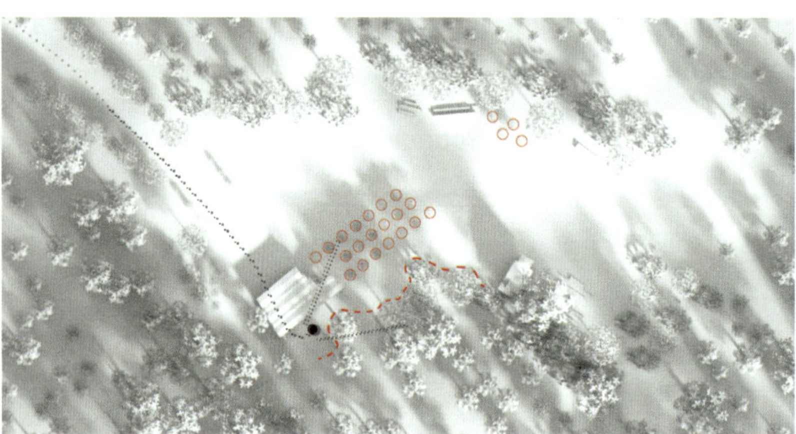

Anchor in Nature

Treelike structure

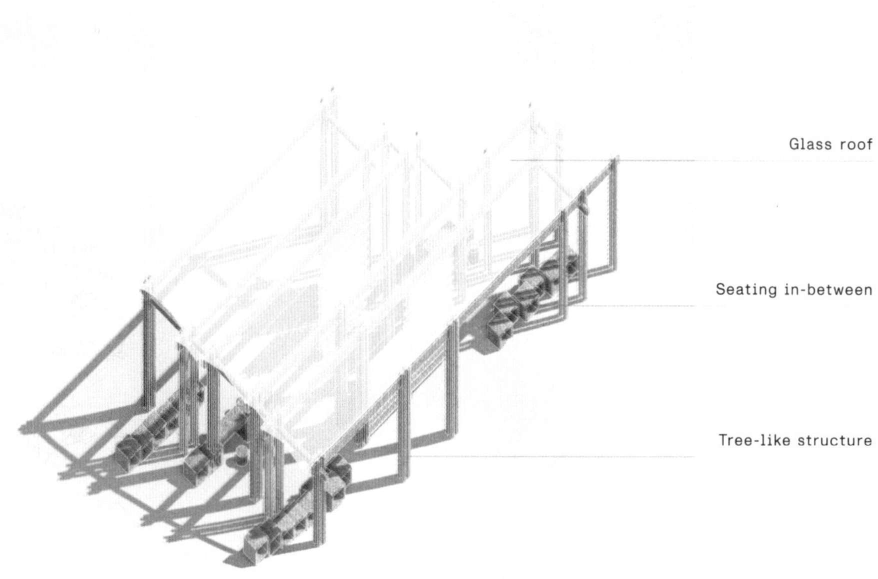

Observation tower

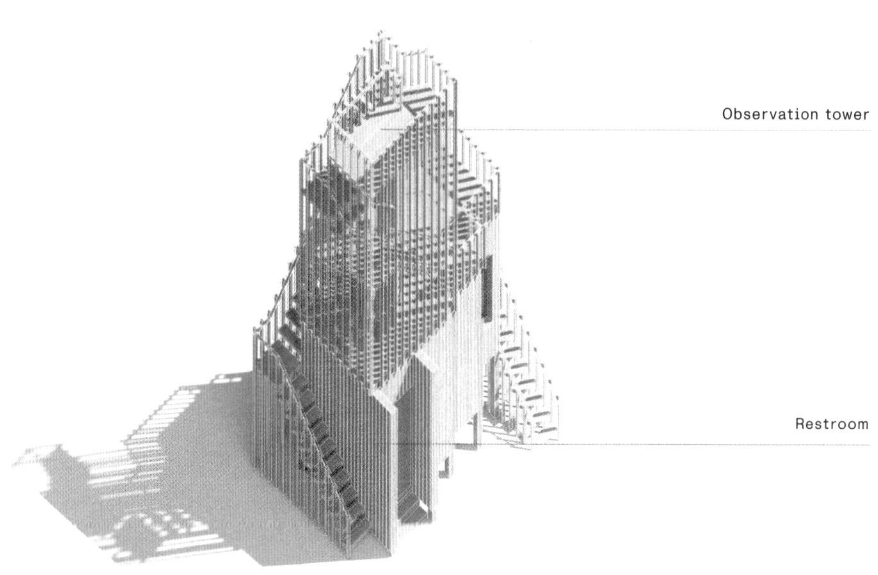

Jiaming Gu

Plan

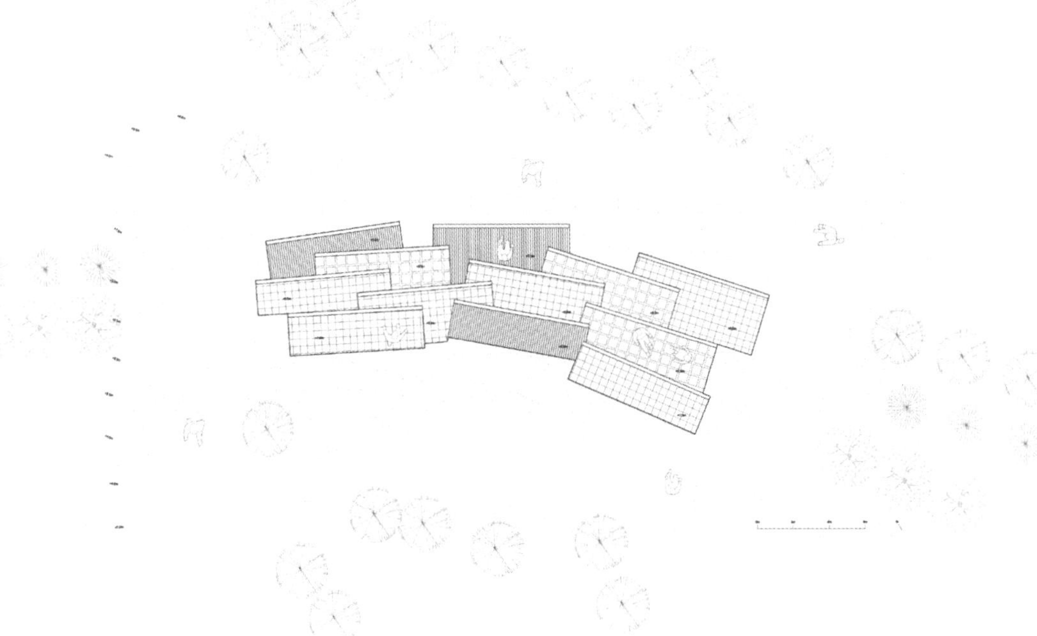

Plan

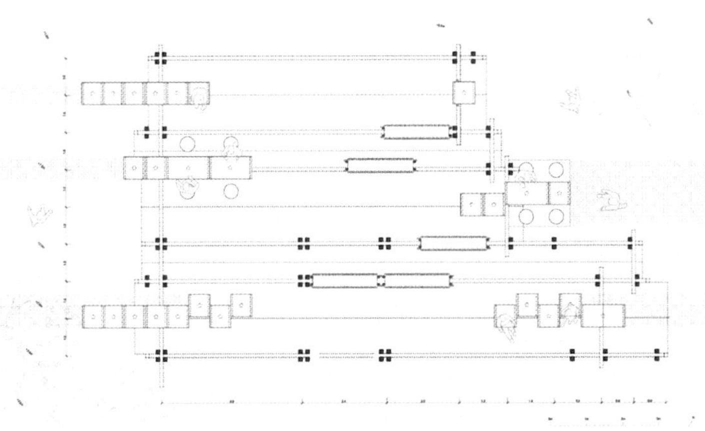

Anchor in Nature

Plan

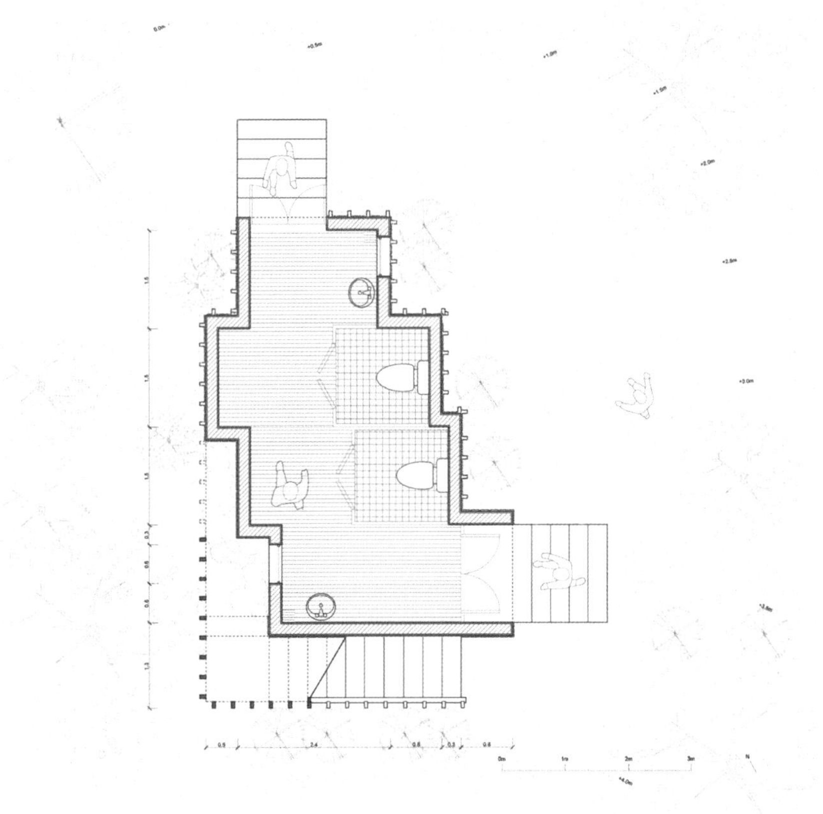

Structure in clearing

Lillian Hou

In phase one of this project, trees were treated both as individual qualities and as topography in a hypothetical forest plan. A technique of "overlapping" was introduced in the process of "trees making space." Three layers overlap each other in trees of different qualities—ages, species, colors, ways of planting—and types of clearing blur or define edges. In this way spaces are created to reflect the dynamics and changes in tree quality and topography.

Public bathrooms and benches are proposed in a contemporary interpretation of the "parliament" in the forest of Oslo, Norway. The site, with a lake and an intersection of two driveways, intrinsically encompasses the contradictory forces of nature and civic life. While implementing the techniques of planting, subtracting, and trimming in phase one, the plans of the trees were reedited by proximity to the lake or the road. The designs of the toilet structures were categorized into three types to respond to each tree plantation. Unlike the ancient parliament, the thing, which functioned as a meeting place in fields and clearings, here the interplay of toilets and benches, as well as trees, redefines the space for gathering while challenging the boundary of private versus public and individual versus democratic.

Overall site plan

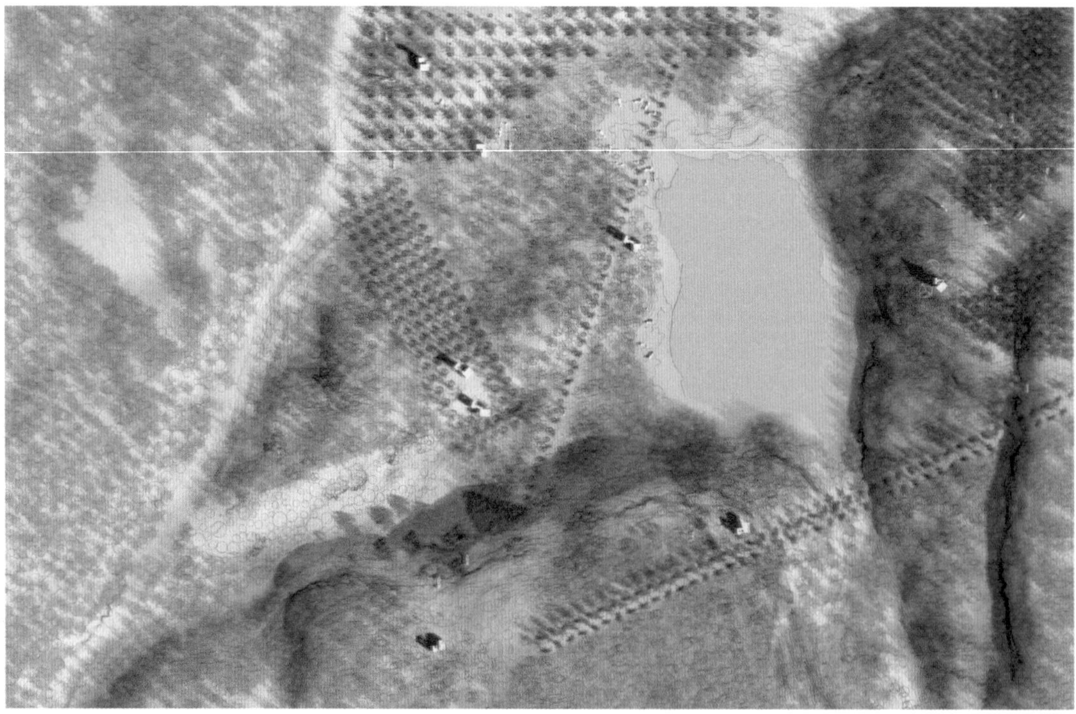

Trees Making Space

Plan: type A bathroom and benches in orderly planted trees

Plan: bathroom at the edge of a clearing

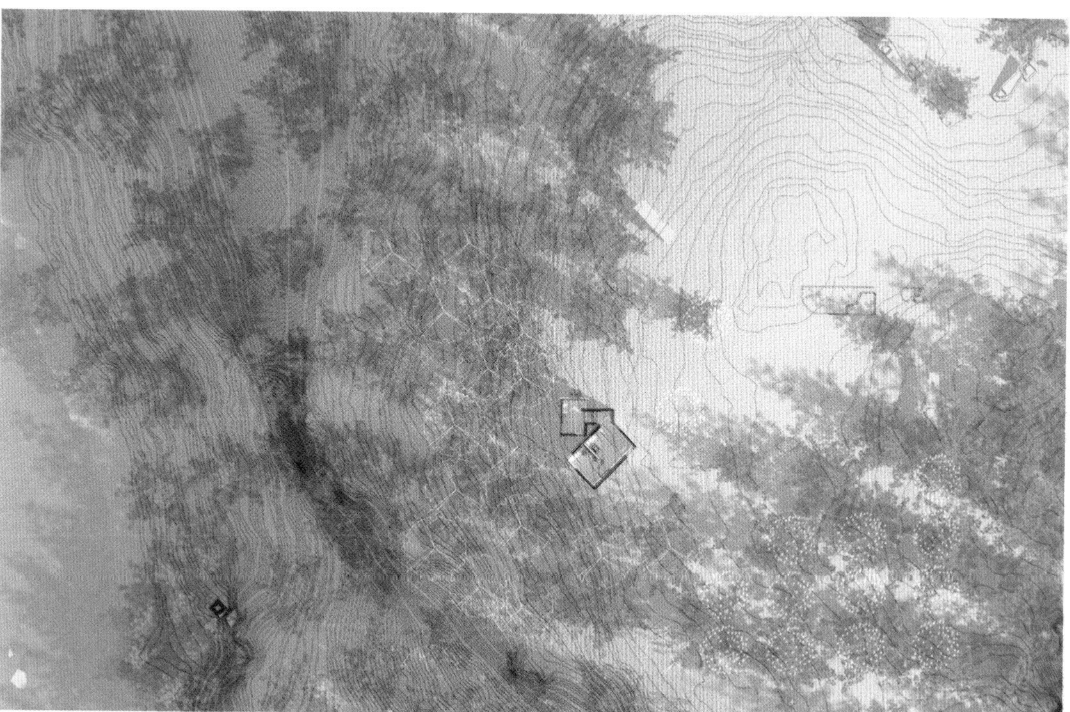

Lillian Hou

Typical floor plan of type A bathroom

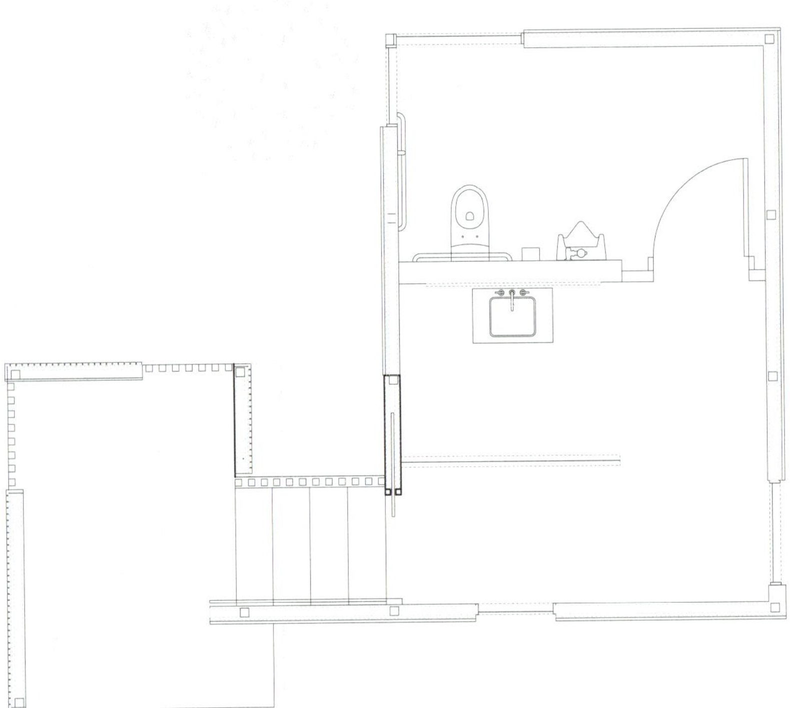

Section: type B bathroom and tree editing

Trees Making Space

Site plan: tree planting in landscape

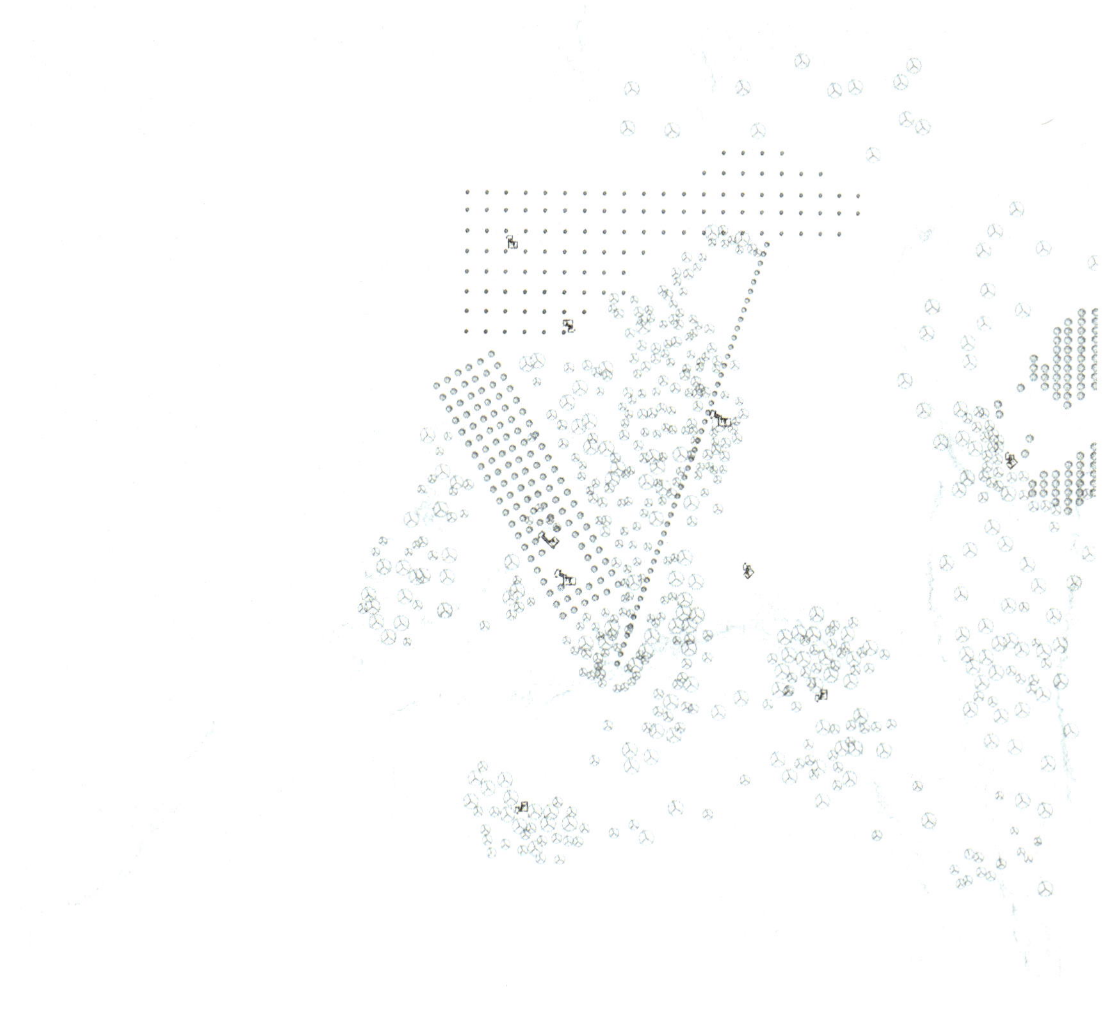

Daoru Wang

The forest is one of the most invaluable national resources in Norway, covering nearly 40 percent of the territory. While providing natural and economic resources to the populations of Nordic countries, it also provides design inspiration and insight into the regional identity and culture. That inspiration informed the landscape design strategies for the project. Throughout the design process the work of Norwegian artist August Cappelen was used as the main reference. As the paradigm of Norwegian national Romanticism, his work depicts the beauty of the Norwegian forests and natural environment. There were three phases to the project: first, identifying the distribution pattern and growing logic of the forest in Norway, in which numerous statistical tools were used; second, developing the clearing method within the forest and applying the techniques to the site for landscape interventions; third, developing those interventions based on the study that was done before completing the project.

Editing the forest clearing

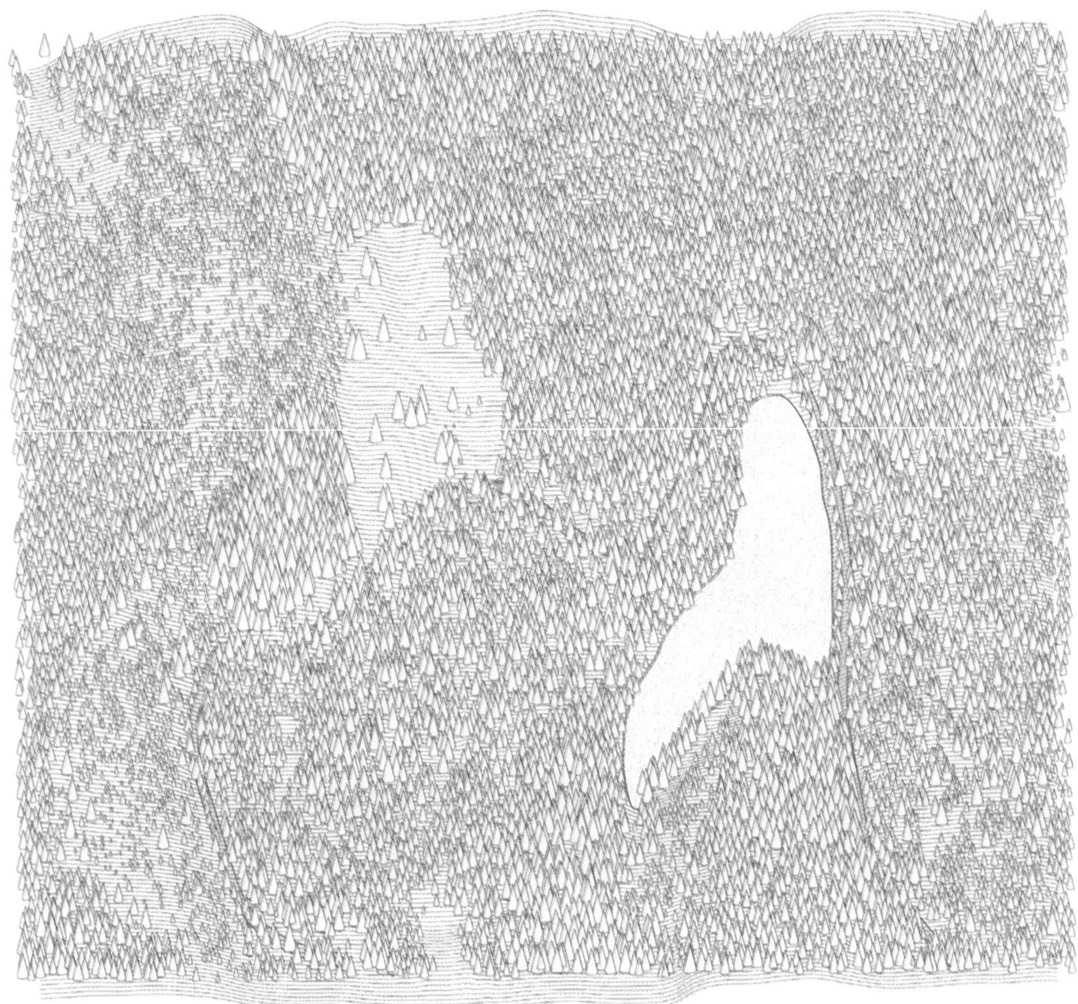

The Real and the Ideal

Editing the forest clearing

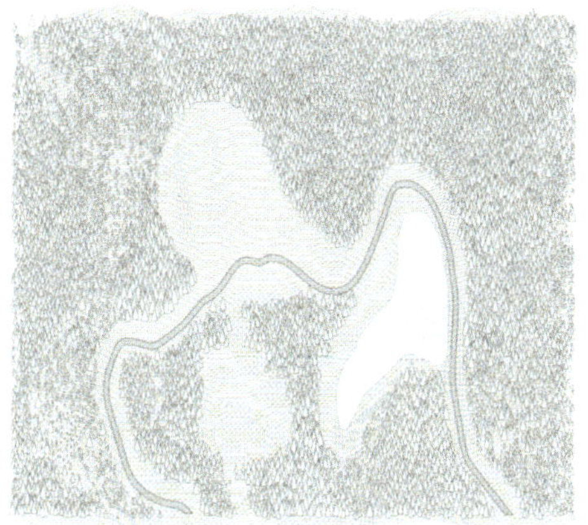

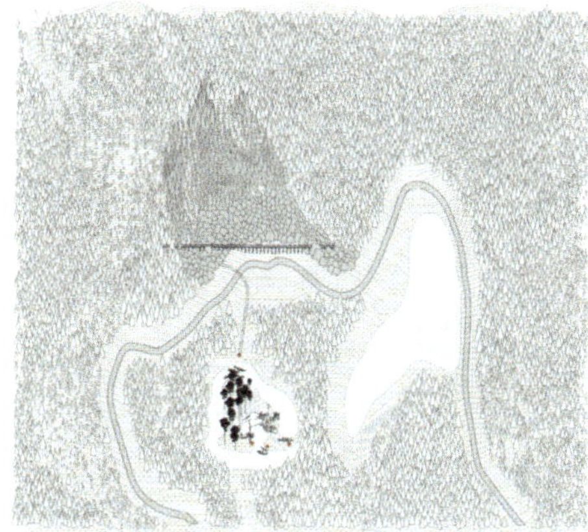

Constructing the image of the forest within its own clearing

Daoru Wang

Rendering a model of a painting

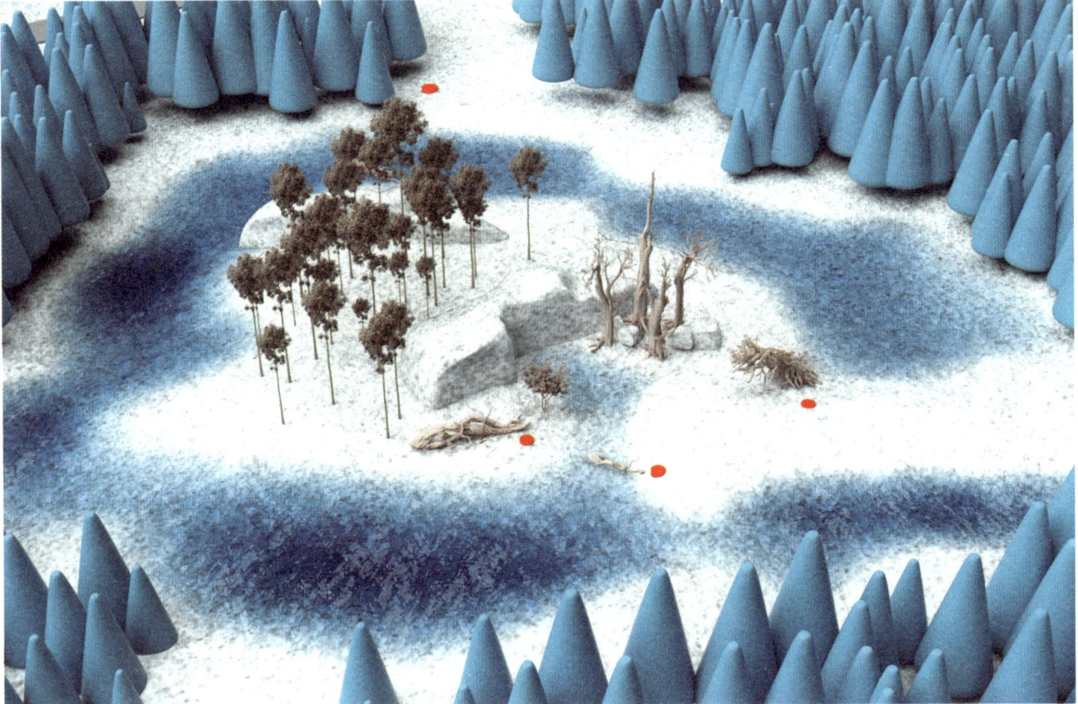

Site model

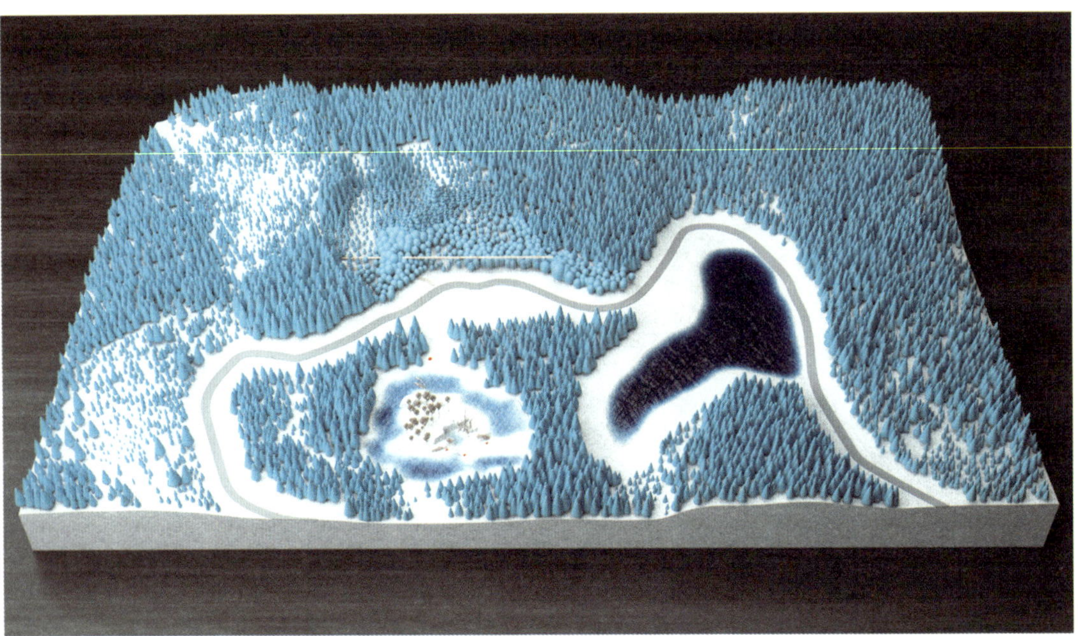

The Real and the Ideal

Modeling of the Norwegian forests based on paintings by August Cappelen

Daoru Wang

Modeling the paradigm of Norwegian national Romanticism

Buildings at the Edge of Clearings

These projects creatively position buildings at the edge of edited clearings, generating an architectural language that acts in coordination with the new visuals opened by the edited trees.

Natalie Broton: Forest of Fire

Vitruvius asserted that the first form of architecture was not the construction of walls and roofs but the act of gathering around a fire. This project centers on fire and its different uses for the development of structures focused on warmth, cooking, and gathering. Our most primitive necessities inform a permanent and public infrastructure within the forest. Three structures are dispersed around the clearing and fall into localized sites of small, medium, and large scales.

The small site is focused on warmth and isolation with primitive infrastructure promoting intimate moments for guests seeking comfort. The trees are planted densely and grown tall to amplify intimacy within nature and among people. The medium site is focused on fire for cooking and has the infrastructure needed to make meals. It incorporates informal trees that are comfortable but not intimidating for a range of guests. The large site is equipped with infrastructure for large formal gatherings such as an interior fireplace and formal trees lining the exterior.

Forest patterns

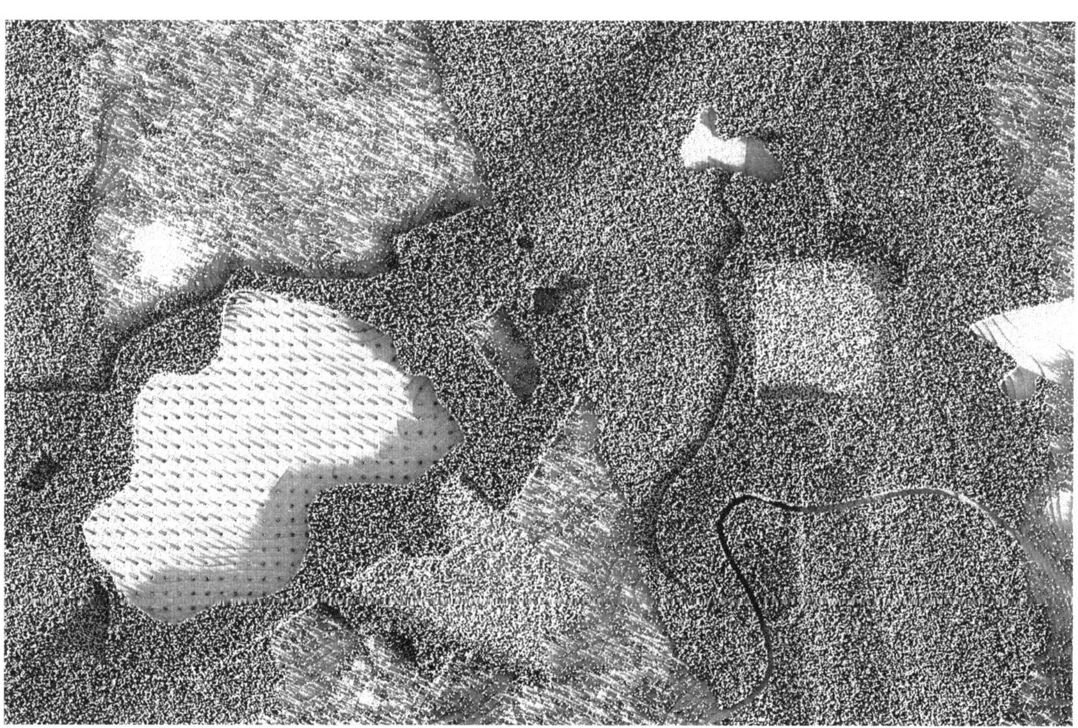

Natalie Broton

Site plan

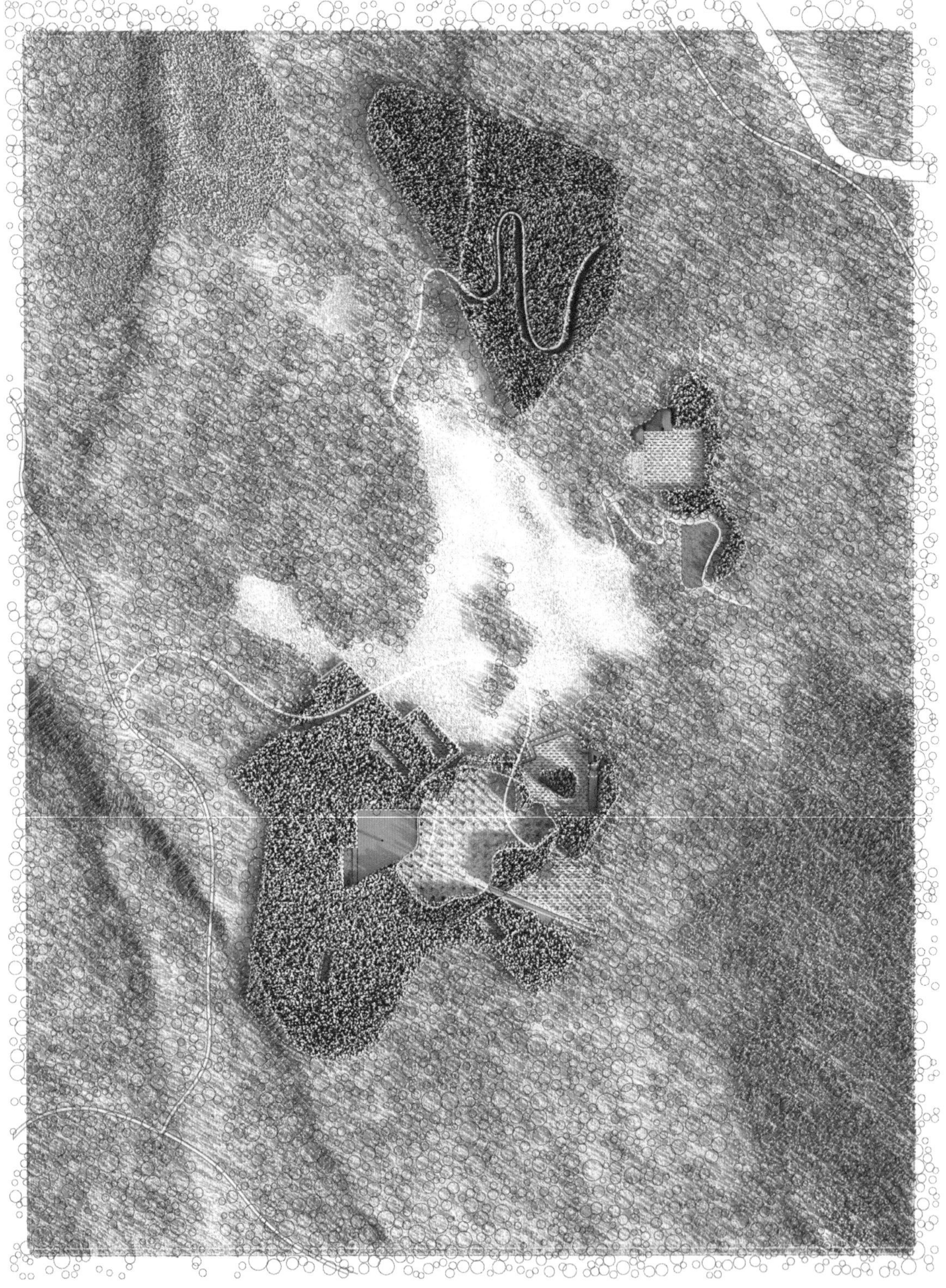

Forest of Fire

Catalog of sites

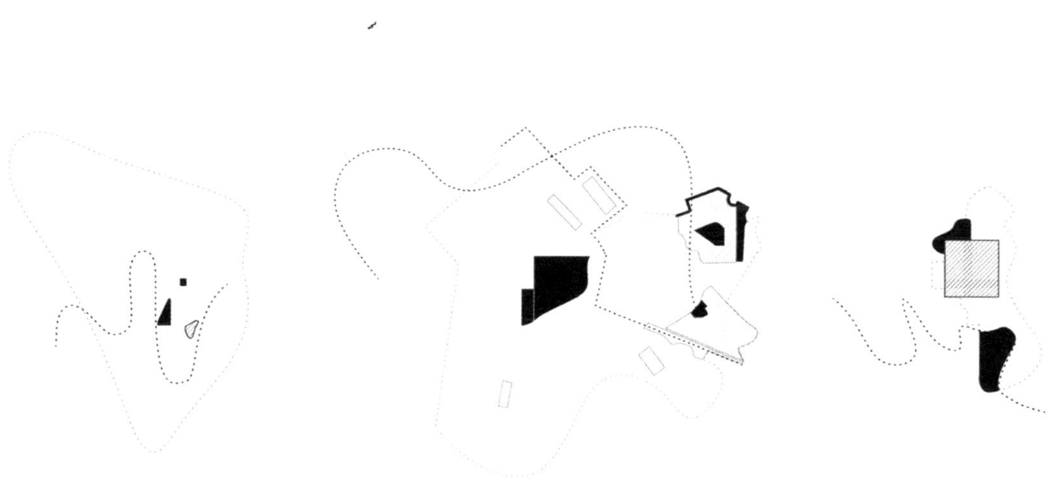

Structures for fire

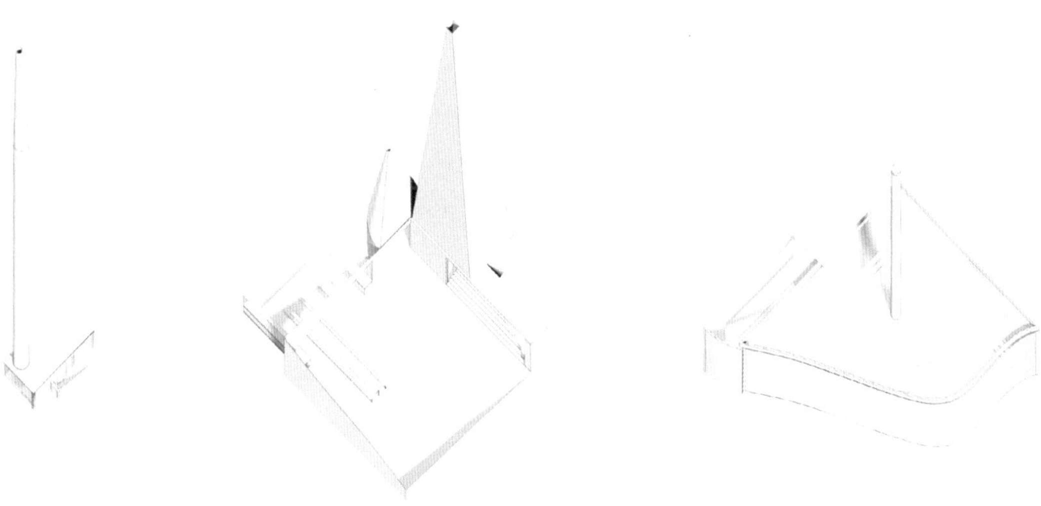

Natalie Broton

Small site plan

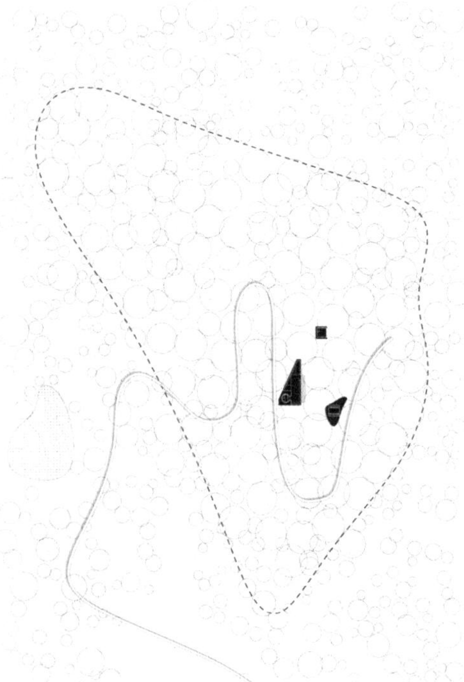

Medium site plan

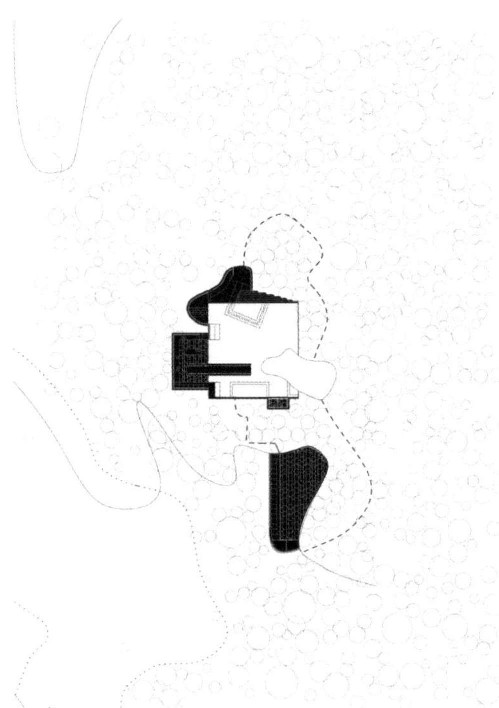

Large site plan

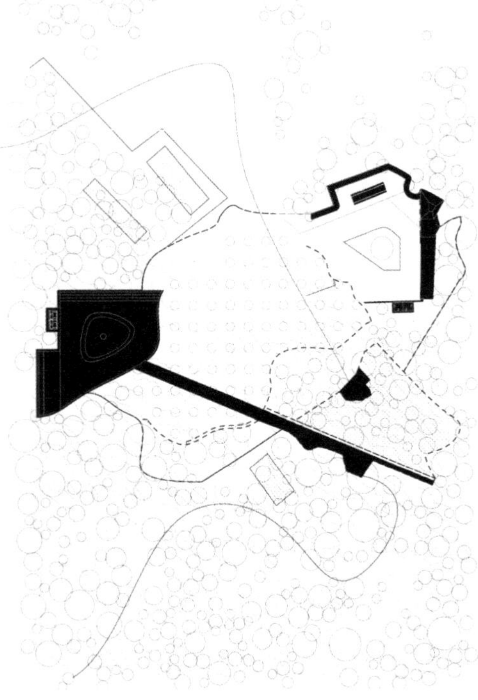

Forest of Fire

Small site section: structure for warmth

Medium site section: structure for cooking

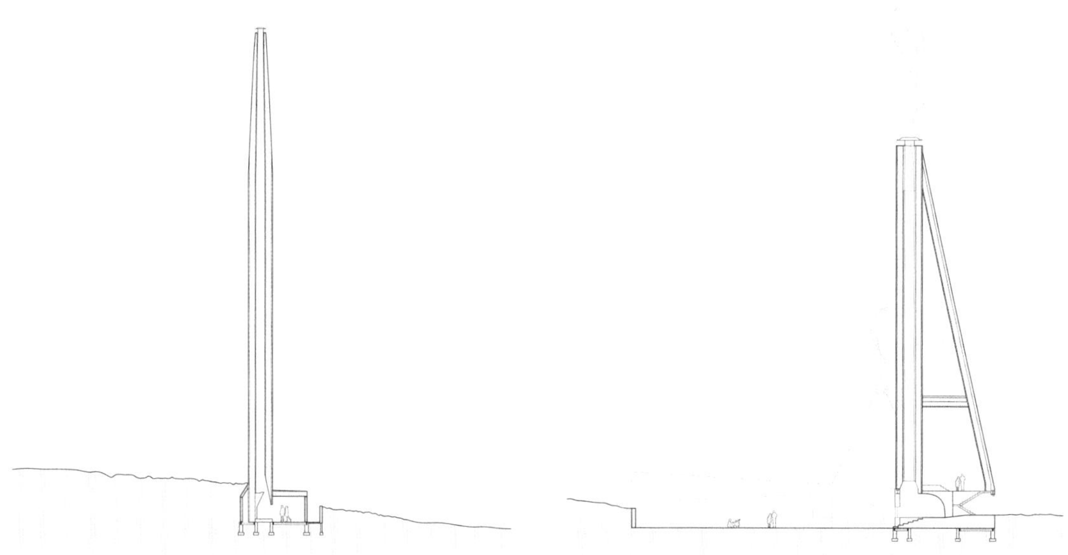

Large site section: structure for gathering

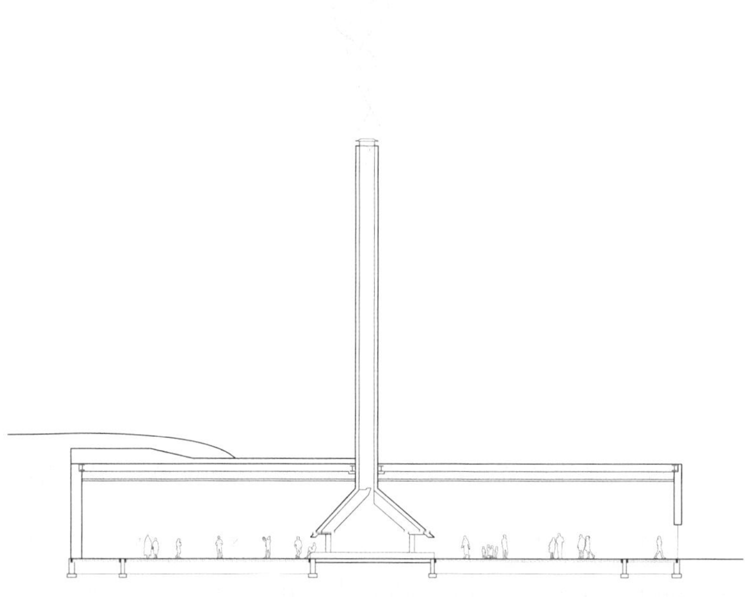

Kate Fritz

Initial research for this project was focused on silvicultural practices within the forest, analyzing the different techniques and resulting spatial effects that these practices have on the resulting clearings. A catalog of triptychs served as formal exploration and informed design decisions for the project. These studies produced an understanding of how to create the desired bosquets through the execution of silvicultural subtractive practices.

Three traces introduced cycles in the forest, which are understood through the scales of time and permanence: the bracket (felling), the clearing (succession), and the garden (parliament).

The bracket directly references the cycle of time of the Norway spruce harvest. Following tree felling a trace is embedded in the landscape through techniques of soil resurfacing, resulting in the form of mounds that accumulate over the years. The bracket cycle is understood to be generational. A boy comes to plant a tree and then visits it each summer, walking along the path. As his cycle advances so do those of the trees, and at age 40 the tree is harvested. The boy, now a man, returns with his son and together they replace the earth where the tree was felled, and another sapling is planted. The man's son is now the keeper of the tree. The bracket is the first trace a traveler experiences upon visiting. There is a prescribed path and directionality that indicates a place within the otherwise vast forest landscape. From here the traveler moves onto the clearing.

The clearing exists and is bordered by both infrastructural and geological traces on the earth. The clearing is a trace of silvicultural practice left behind; it was last felled between the years 2001 and 2011. It will continue to regrow without interruption through natural succession that will occur around year 150. Within this time almost four generations of trees will have been felled along the bracket.

The garden is the final trace left at the site. A space for gathering and a parliament, it exists at the northernmost edge. The introduced cycle is episodic; the parliament commences on the first weekday of October and every four years for elections and the end of the parliamentary term. Mounds are displaced to recall earlier felling of the bracket; however, there is no cycled silvicultural practice on the site. Norway spruces are planted along the mounds, and concrete retaining walls are introduced as both structural and programmatic elements. Concrete walls support a wooden structure that recalls early Norwegian vernacular design and longhouses. The wood subtracted from the site is recycled into its construction. Within the wooden structure the traveler is lifted and walks among the trees.

Bracket

Overall site plan. Three components of the design intervention (bottom left to top right): the bracket, the clearing, and the garden

Plans of the garden. A series of site walls derived from initial studies of silvicultural practices and the French bosquets serve three primary purposes. At ground level these walls frame the gardens and serve as retaining walls for the surrounding earth while providing structural support for the bar of the "Parliament of the Forest."

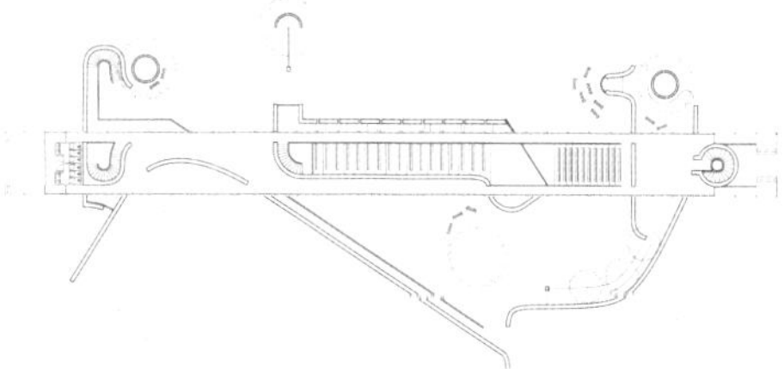

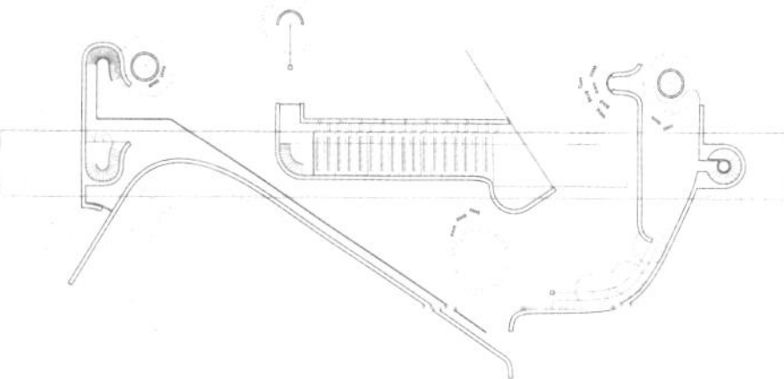

Kate Fritz

Model of primary entry sequence along the site wall edge

Model of facade. Trees subtracted from the surrounding gardens are used and repurposed in the construction of the long parliament structure.

Bracket

Model of facade and site wall relationship. The undulating depth of the facade correlates with the span of distance and depth of beam used to support the longer spans between site walls.

Model of parliament building structural elements and their relationship with the site walls. Site walls penetrate and inform further internal organization of the building above.

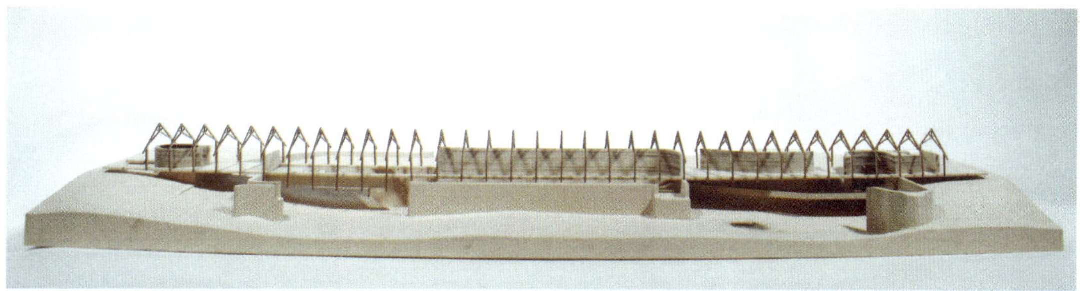

Model of an entry into the parliament building. Stairwells recall elements of the existing parliamentary building and wrap along the supporting site walls.

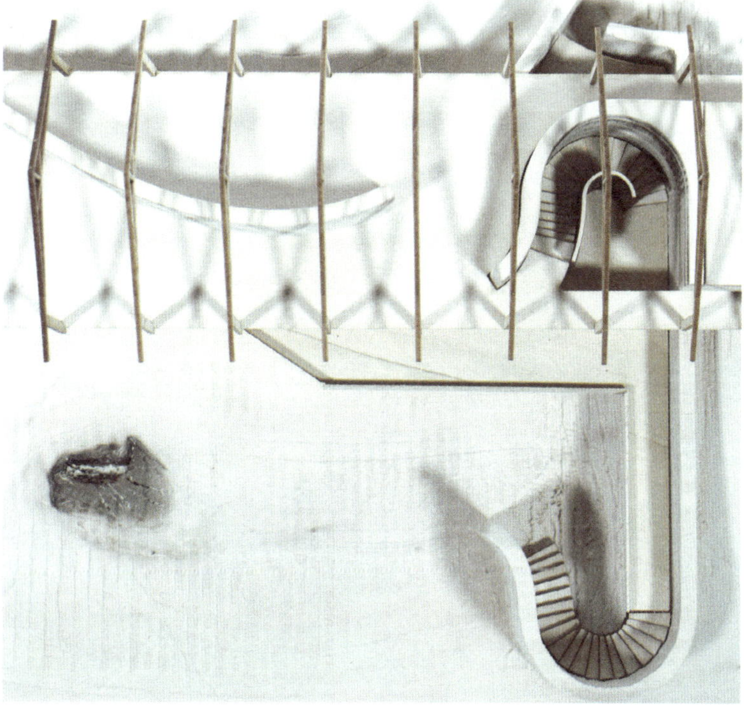

Kate Fritz

A series of triptychs created to study the relationship between case studies of silvicultural practices (left) and paintings of French bosquets (right). A series of renderings (center) tested the formal relationship between the two.

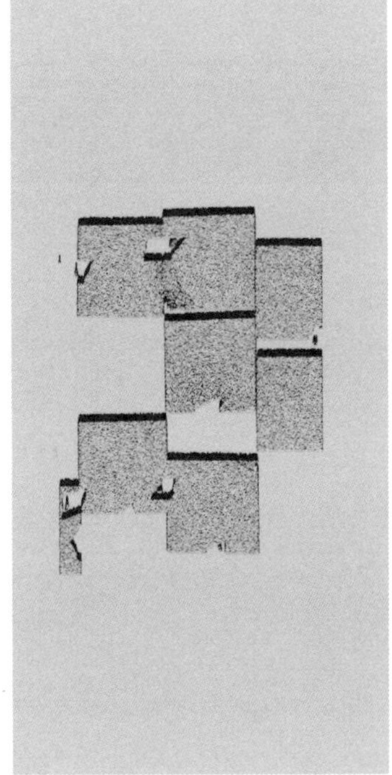

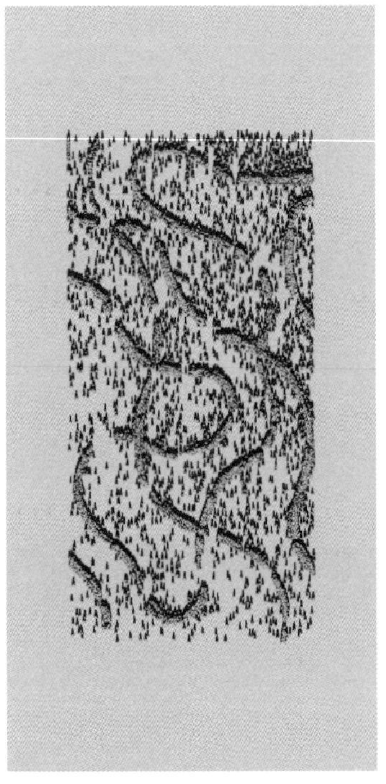

Study model and rendered representation of the forest in continued exploration of the French bosquets and resulting spatial qualities of silvicultural practices

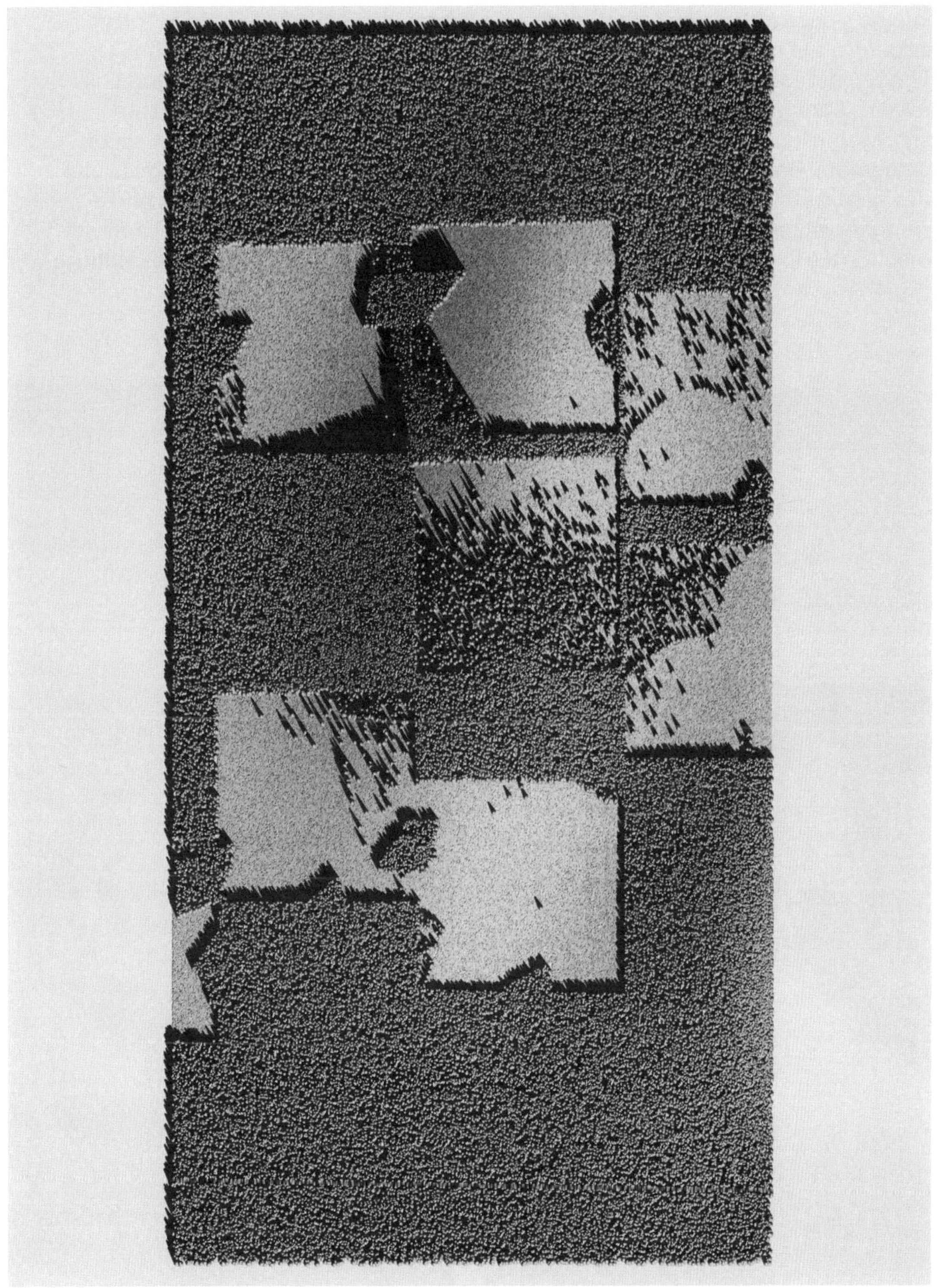

Elise Limon

"An Unfamiliar Forest" explores what a new language for intervening in the forest surrounding Oslo might look like beginning with the rules, acts, and regulations—such as the Markalov—that structure and manage the forest space. The project asks how an unfamiliar forest clearing might come to be. The site, Maridalen, is an old agricultural settlement. One of the characteristics designating this part of the forest as a conservation area are cultural monuments in the form of "farm environments, homesteads, stone fences, clearing piles." Building and construction are prohibited in Marka. On a patch of plantation forestry among agricultural fields, the project plays with a loophole in Norwegian forest law that permits construction for agricultural measures. The project speculates on a new set of unfamiliar objects—buildings taking after agricultural structures and a *skigard* (a round pole fence) that welcomes plants other than trees to thrive.

The size of clear felling in Nordmarka is limited, meaning patches of cleared forest appear brushing up against one another.

Trees close to roads and rivers are not to be felled in Nordmarka. This preserves the aesthetic experience of an untouched forest.

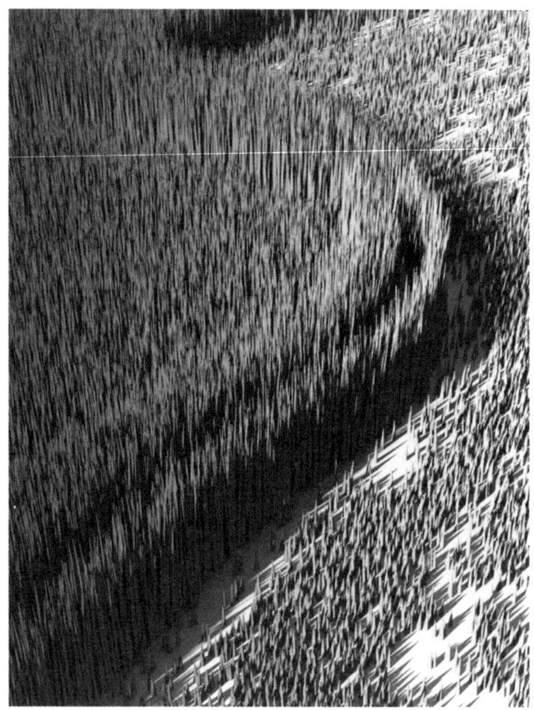

An Unfamiliar Forest

A set of “familiar” clearings make legible the rules and regulations governing space making in Nordmarka.

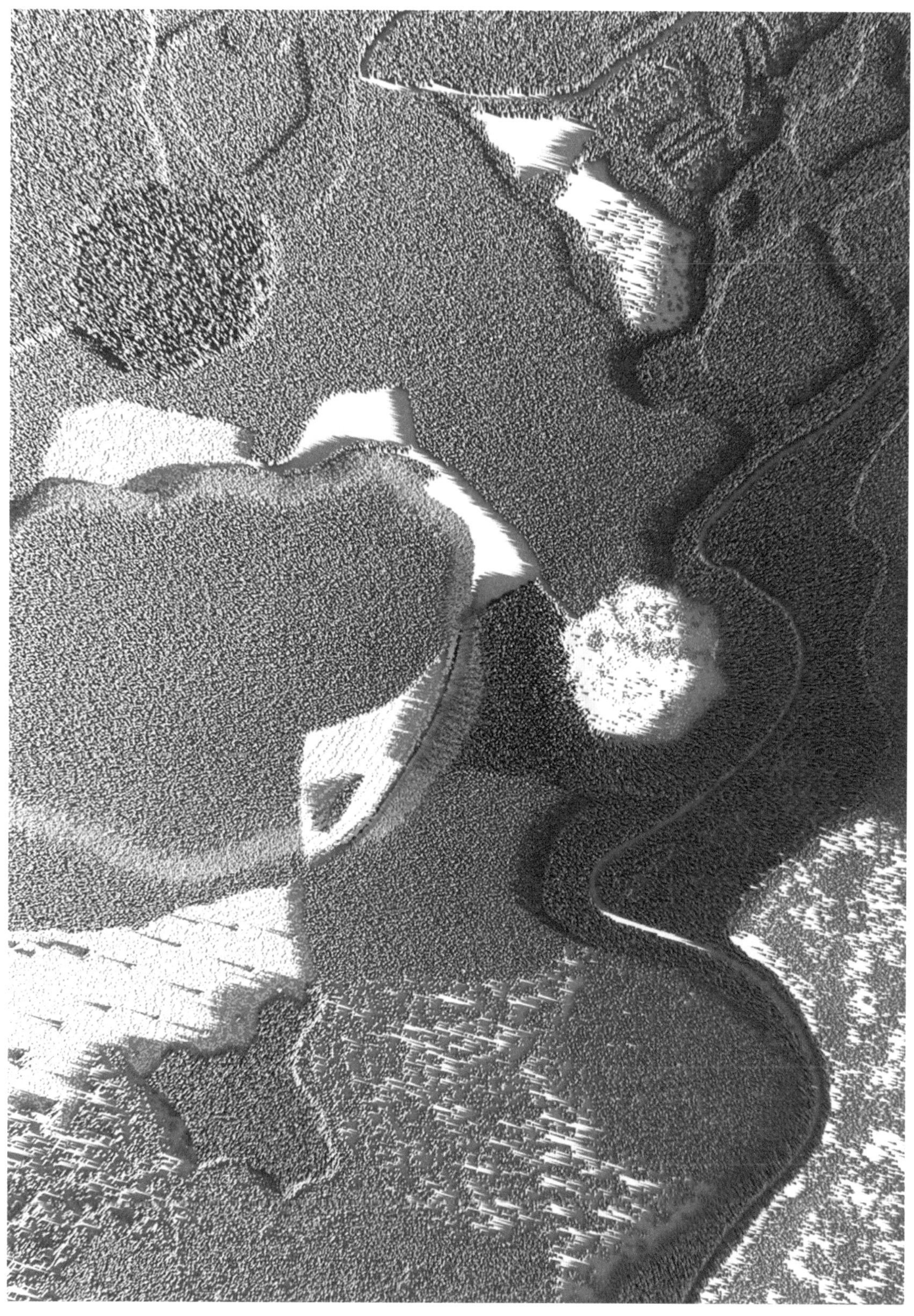

Elise Limon

Editing the forest after Hilma of Klint

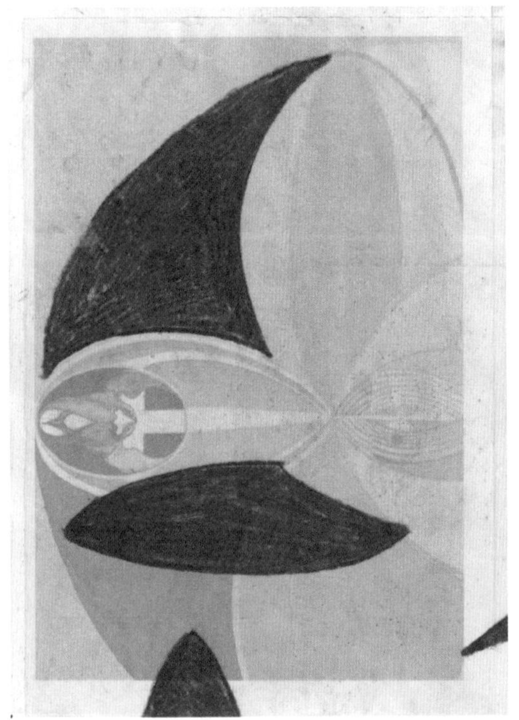

An Unfamiliar Forest

Editing the forest after Hilma of Klint

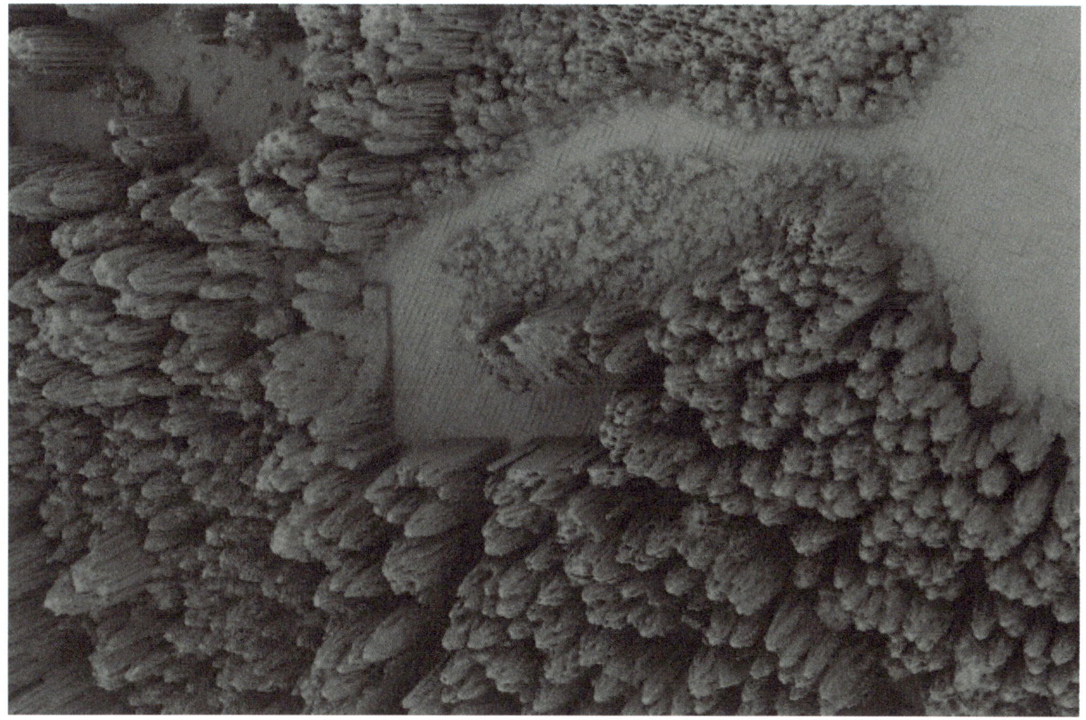

The silo: A group of buildings for gathering take on the agricultural character of the surrounding farms.

Elise Limon

The storage: Each building makes use of the natural topography of the site.

The feeder: A long building serves as the main gathering space.

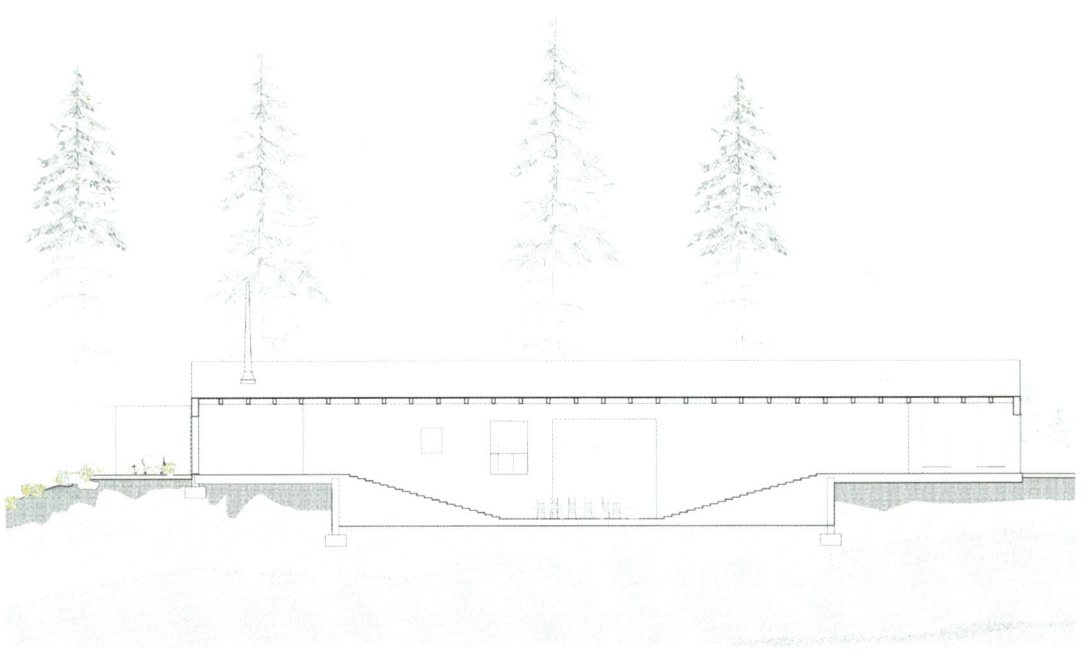

The barn

The shed: Edited trees are incorporated into each structure.

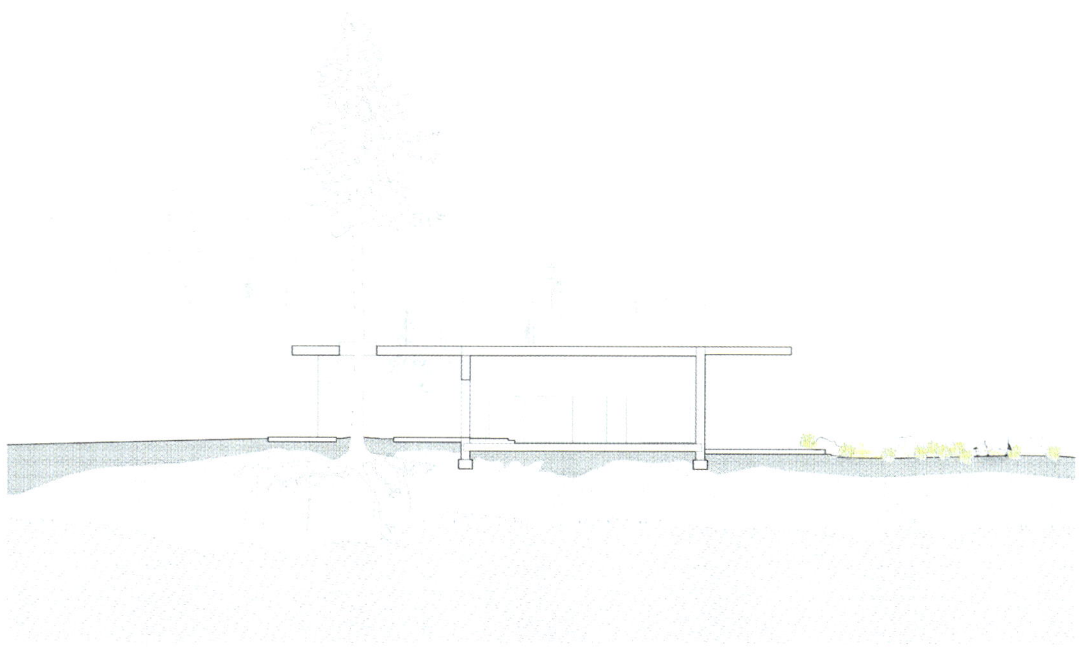

On Trees as Architecture

These are projects that see the forest clearing as architecture, where program and roofed structures are secondary to the primitive civic spaces defined by the trees.

Naomi Ng: Nine Gates

The Scandinavian parliament archetype has not changed in centuries, with hearings often taking place above a flat ground within the enclosed walls of an unforgiving monument. Architecturally this project questions what it may be like to bring the familiar archetypal forms of the parliament back to the forest, and in doing so confront the open landscape. Socially this project questions how changing the spatial arrangement of the parliament may change how decisions are made. Inspired by the nine gates lining the facade of the Norwegian parliament (the sorting building) and adapted from the fragmented Icelandic thing, this parliament primarily includes nine fragmented pieces scattered across the site. The forms derive from a mixture of geometries interpreted from the parliament in conjunction with the ruthless geometries of forest-management practices. Ultimately this project goes forward and backward simultaneously—forward in breaking the ancient parliament archetype and backward in terms of bringing the assembly back into an open landscape like the Icelandic thing.

Catalog of five silvicultural systems

Strip cutting

38.4191082,
-120.3778067

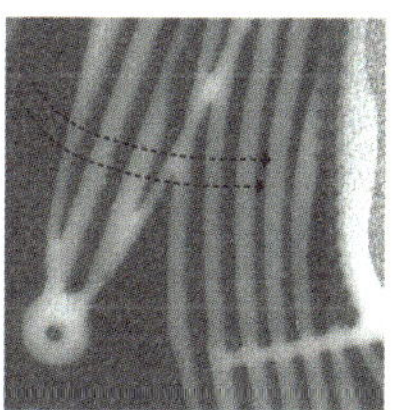

Clear cutting
(North & South america,
International

66.5779691,
25.9664833

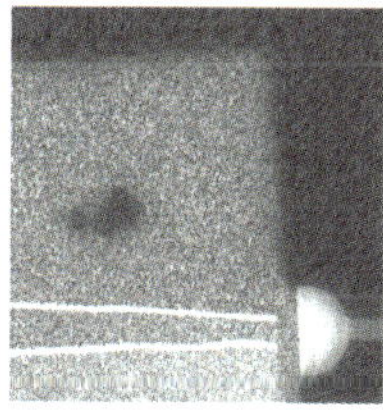

Shelterwood/
Femelschlag (german)

56.8787669,
14.5923393

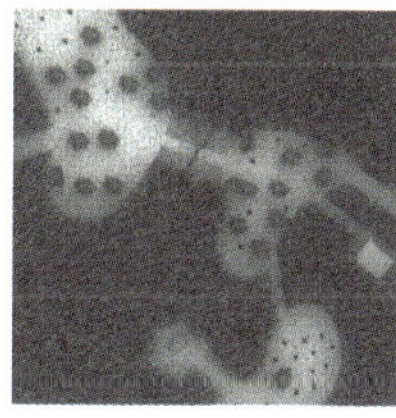

Slash & burn
Svedjebruk
(Sweden/Norway)

60.8146489,
4241116

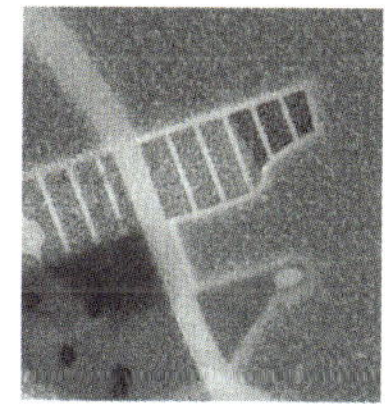

Cultural burning
(Australia)
fire stick burning
(North America)

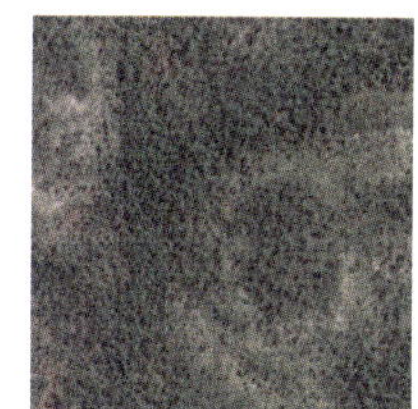

-11.4066333,
132.2769984

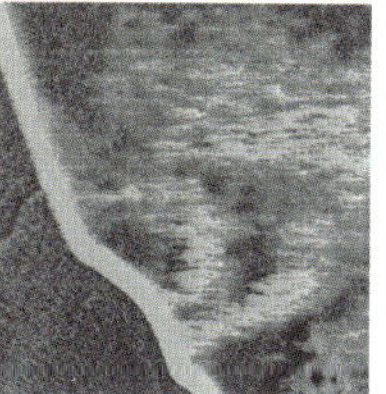

Naomi Ng

1:750 Site plan

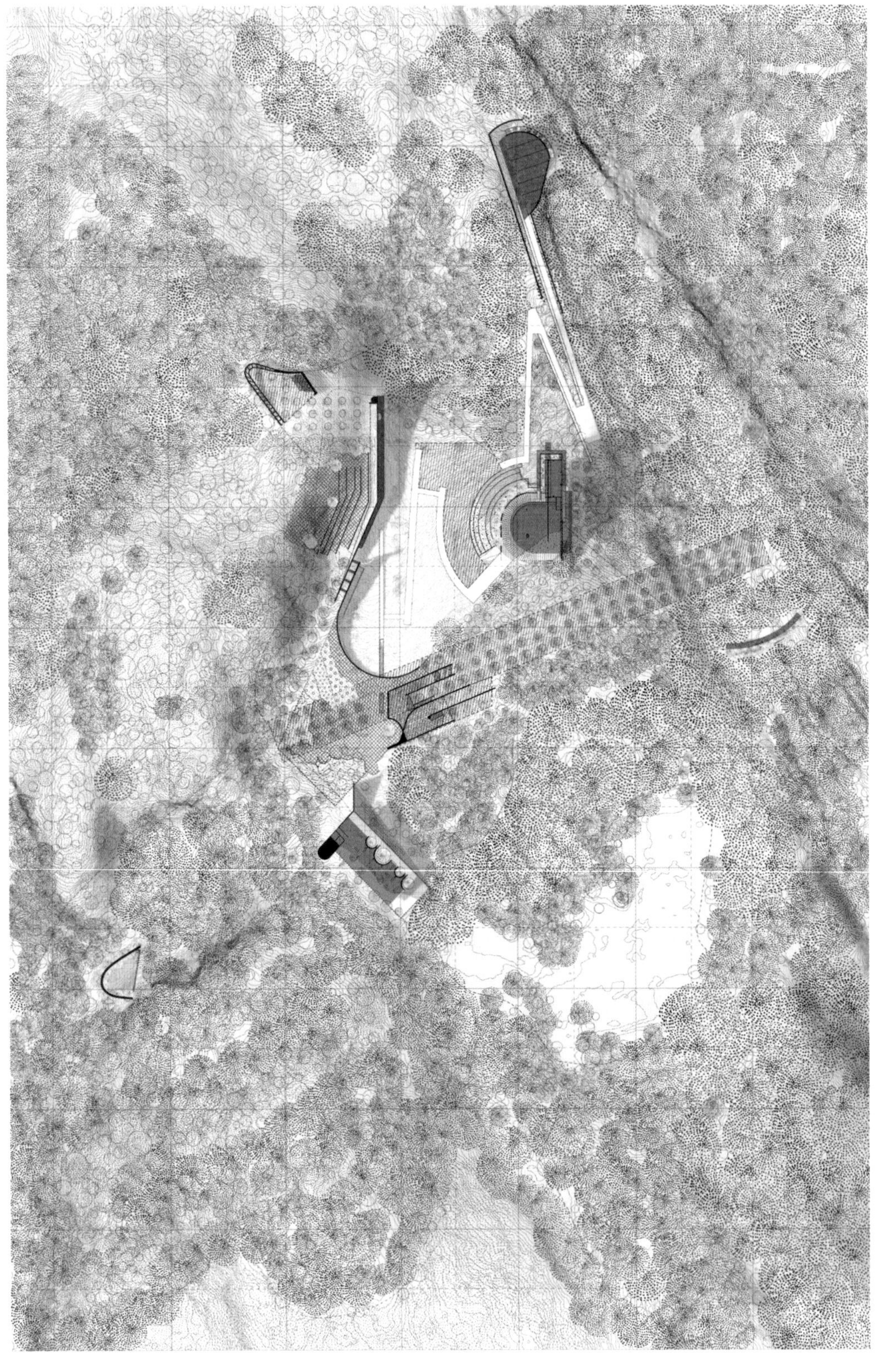

Nine Gates

Forest clearing based on silvicultural systems

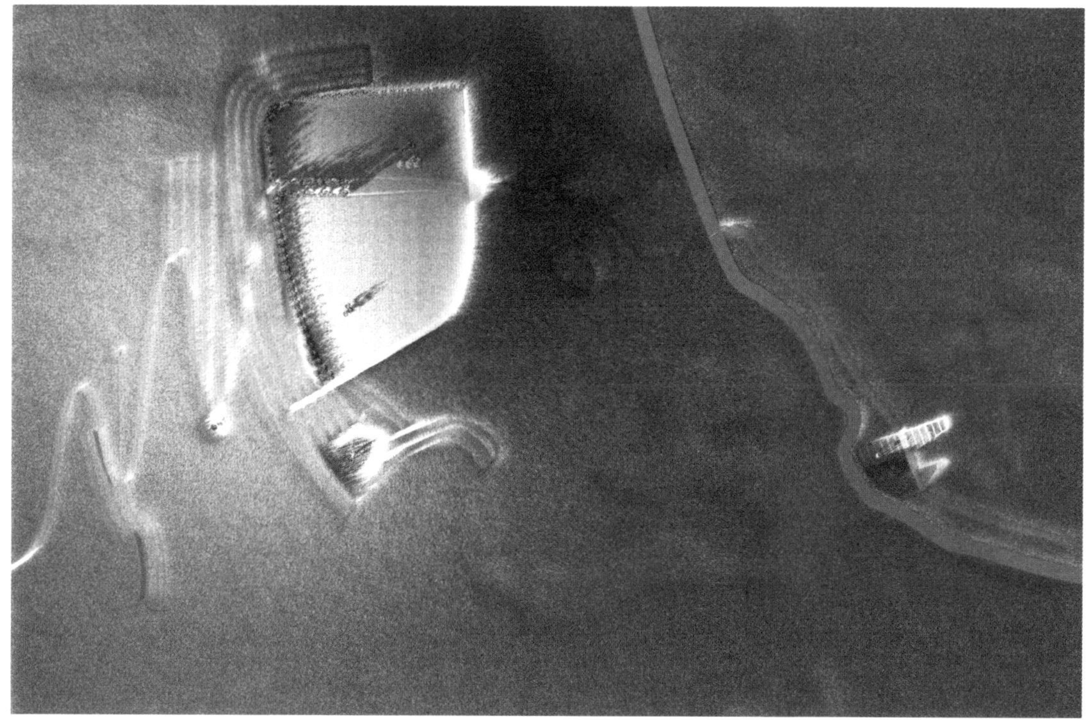

Overall rendering

Naomi Ng

Entrance of gate one: parliament

Nine gates: sections and plans

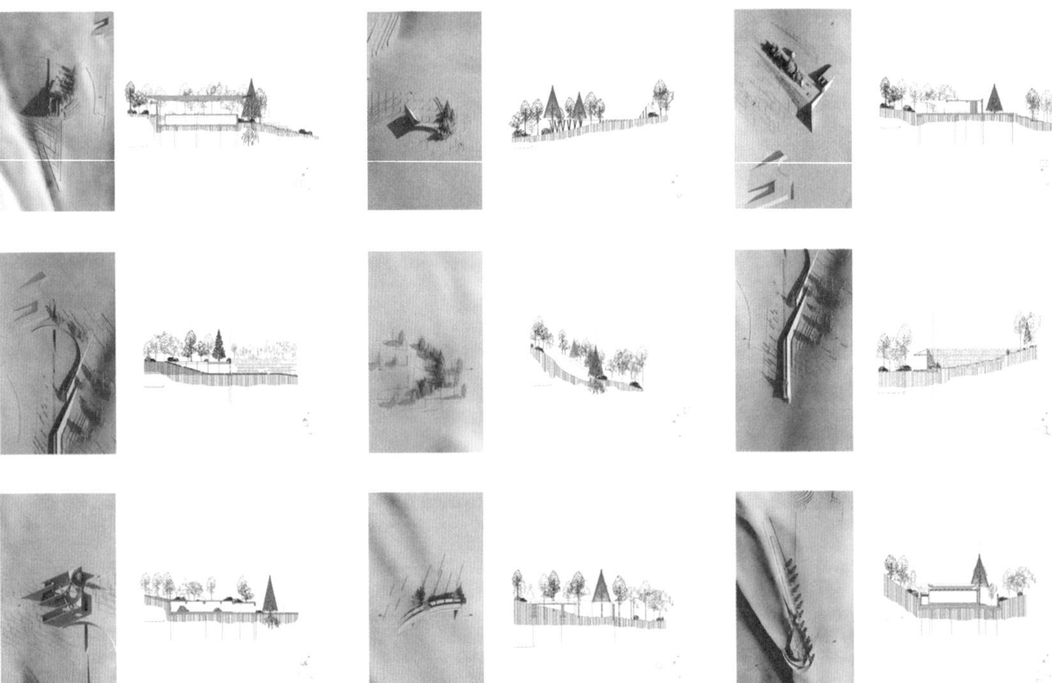

Nine Gates

View from gate two: public assembly

View from gate three: Log storage/plantation

April Liu

The goal of this project is to test the collision of distinct cultures by investigating the sophistication of Chinese gardens and employing their spatial principles on a site in Oslo, Norway. The idea of a parliament is redefined to accommodate the contemporary programmatic need in the forest aligned with the functions of traditional Chinese garden architectural elements. The five essential elements of a Chinese garden are distilled and applied on site 23 through the manipulation of local vegetation with spatial principles in mind.

Contrary to the vast pleasure gardens built by Chinese emperors, the Suzhou gardens are intimate spaces created for reflection and escape from the outside world by scholars, poets, former government officials, soldiers, and merchants. They are idealized miniature landscapes meant to express the harmony that should exist between man and nature. By moving through the site visitors view a series of carefully composed scenes unrolling like the scroll of a landscape painting.

This type of sequential experience is created through various spatial strategies that entail the manipulation of indoor and outdoor elements such as water, rocks, vegetation, paving, screens, doors, and walls. The organizational principles include contract and expand, borrowed landscape, hidden and visible, dense and sparse, and penetration of indoor and outdoor. In addition, the five essential architectural elements in the Suzhou garden are distilled as the concept of evolving tree branches transforms a traditional pavilion into a growing system of infrastructure that continues to adapt to the site, providing an increased amount of focal points, spatial experiences, and indoor-outdoor exchange.

The nine structures were inspired by the five essential architectural elements in Suzhou gardens: Ting, Lang, Xie, Qiao, and LouGe. Based on relative location, size, and form, each structure's activity defines its unique function. Together with the man-made landscape inside the clearing and the unedited forest outside, they form a contemporary open-air parliament that strives to serve different user groups and adapt to evolving needs.

Buildings will be constructed with timber from the edited clearing. Each has three branches varying in width from 4 to 12 meters. The branches are constructed based on a 1.2-by-1-meter grid and connected through a triangular support system, with the structural load transferred to the central column. Any branch larger than 8 meters long delineates its envelope to create an open-air corridor as a second spatial layer.

Editing the forest

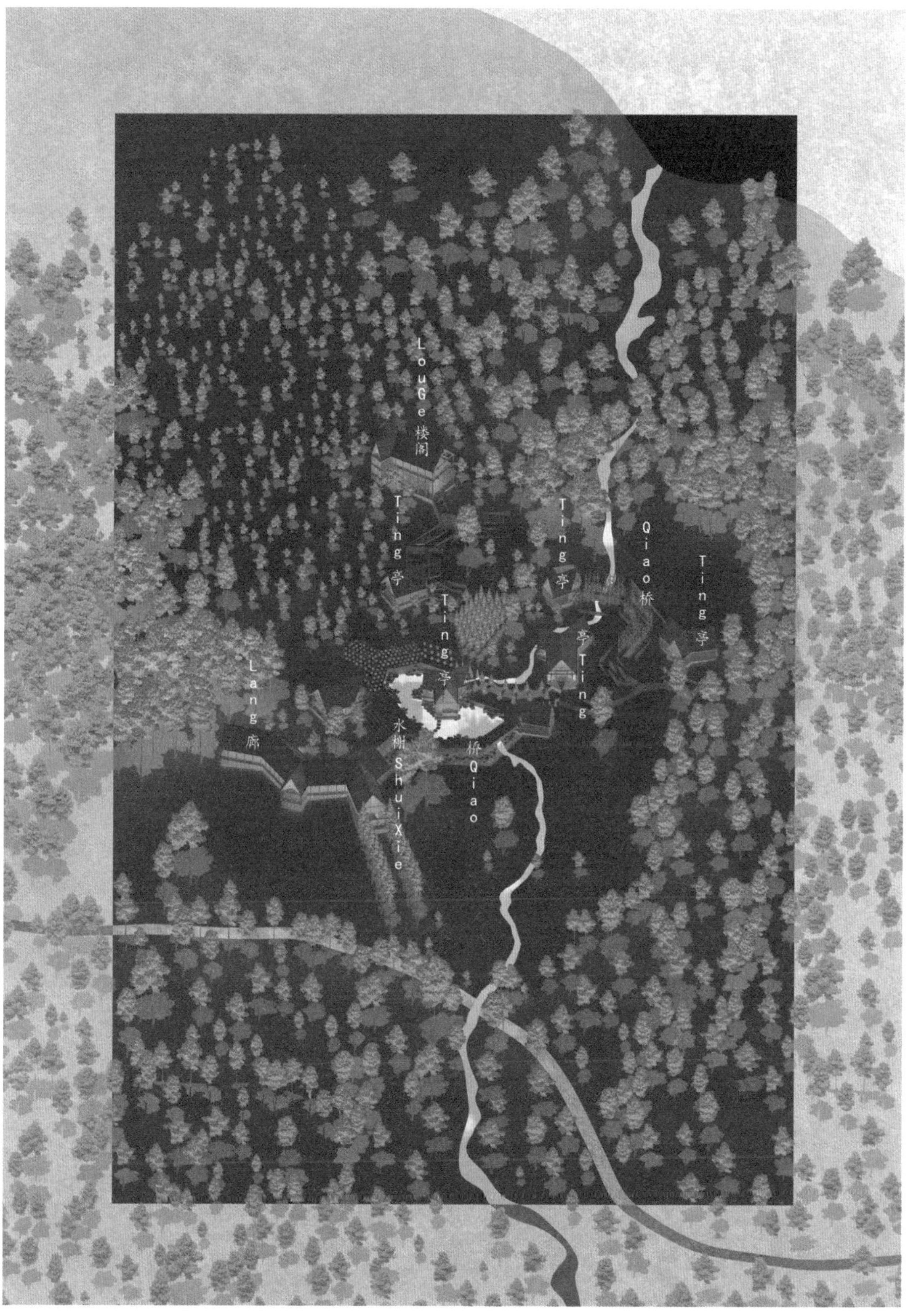

April Liu

Spatial contrast: facing inward and outward

Borrowed landscape/framed landscape

Contract and expand

Borrowed Landscape

Site plan

Programmatic plans

Trade/Gather/View/Circulate

Educate/Gather

Exhibit/Rest

Rest/Sleep/Circulate

View/Social/Play

Store/Read/Play

Discuss/Meet

Tea/View/Social/Circulate

Rest/Sleep/Circulate

April Liu

Structure and detail

Borrowed Landscape

Structure and detail

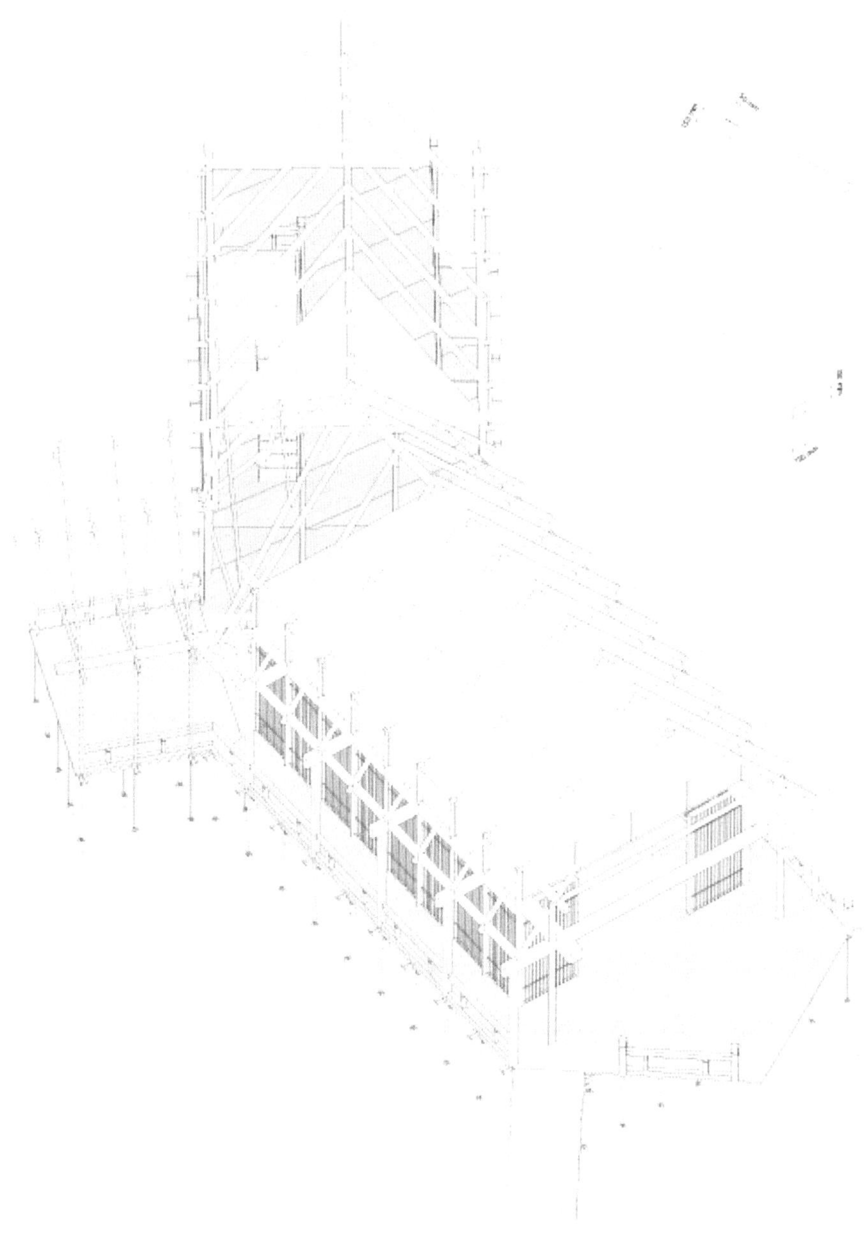

Stav Dror

The Norwegian forest is a site of fantasy and home of monsters. It is defined by an imaginary dimension and plasticity of scale ranging from true to untrue. A clearing within the Oslo woods, the project site, is an ex-territory whose existence between narratives constructs a neutral space out of context—a clear ground.

The program of the clearing is conflict. It is rooted in the ancient definition of thing as a parliament—a conflict conducted in the landscape. The proposed schedule of the clearing as a site of conflict takes place in three phases: arrival, filling space through negotiation, and emptying.

Only a single edit was made to the site—one straight tree line cutting alongside the clearing edge, measuring a landscape that resists being measured. Surround the clearing are 2,177 trees, 9 of which participate in the formation of a parliament space; 180 trees provide raw material for the fabrication of chairs, the basic movable programmatic unit that allows returning the clearing to its essential neutrality.

The clearing and its inherent quality of emptiness are the spatial and programmatic starting points of the linear parliament structure. Its purpose is to uphold the clearing's edge while supporting the program of conflict. The tectonic logic in the structure is reversed: there are no rooms enclosed by walls opened by windows and doors; rather the exterior is never fully enclosed and remains in an almost interior state.

The parliament structure houses some of the forest's monsters. The tiger, the horse, and the lion are essential parts of the Norwegian narrative and array of urban symbols. I stole the animals—I did not borrow them. They are reclaimed from urban space to be used as constructive and programmatic building parts—the tiger as a constructive element, lions as fireplaces, and the horse as a bench reintegrate the city's representation of landscape into real landscape.

Like urban space, the chair in Norwegian culture commonly includes depictions of landscape, animals, and narratives as it has its roots in literalism. It performs as symbol, object, and space simultaneously. Instead of merely a sitting body, the chair in the project is based on the sum of all parliament members' actions: sitting, sleeping, and fighting. It is the accumulation of all body positions translated into the choreography of the parliament as a superposition of the chair's physical and symbolic dimensions. You sit, you fall asleep, you lean; there's a shape, there's a bar connected to the legs. They hold up the surface that supports you, sitting asleep.

Conflict in Clearing

Parliament room, almost-interior

Service platforms

Stav Dror

Parliament, chair workshop

Model: tectonic fragment

Conflict in Clearing

Chair sketches: sit, sleep, fight

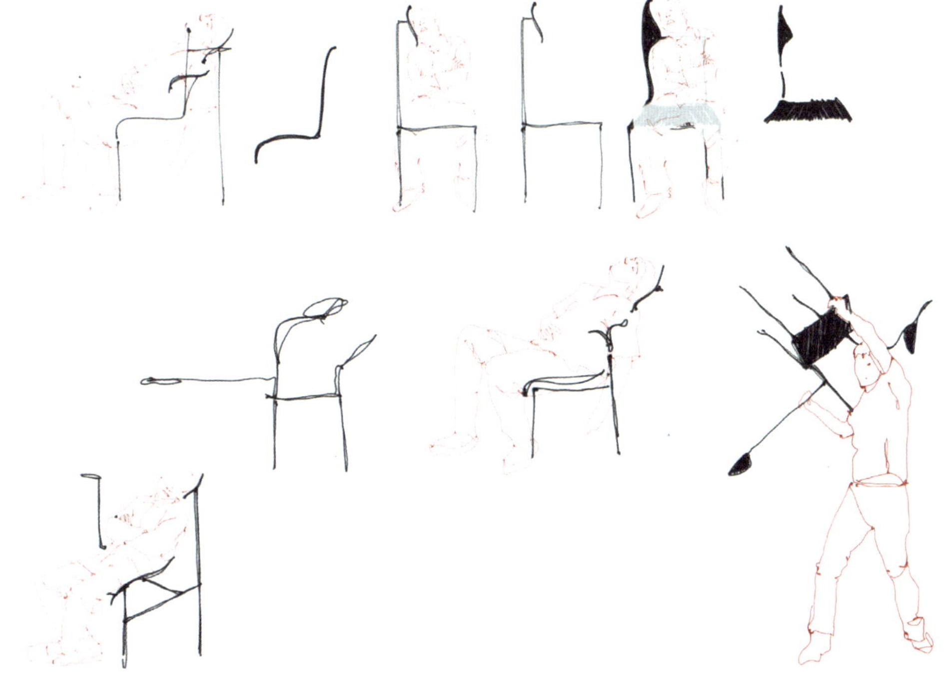

Mock-up: chair body parts

Stav Dror

Sections: bench and parliament

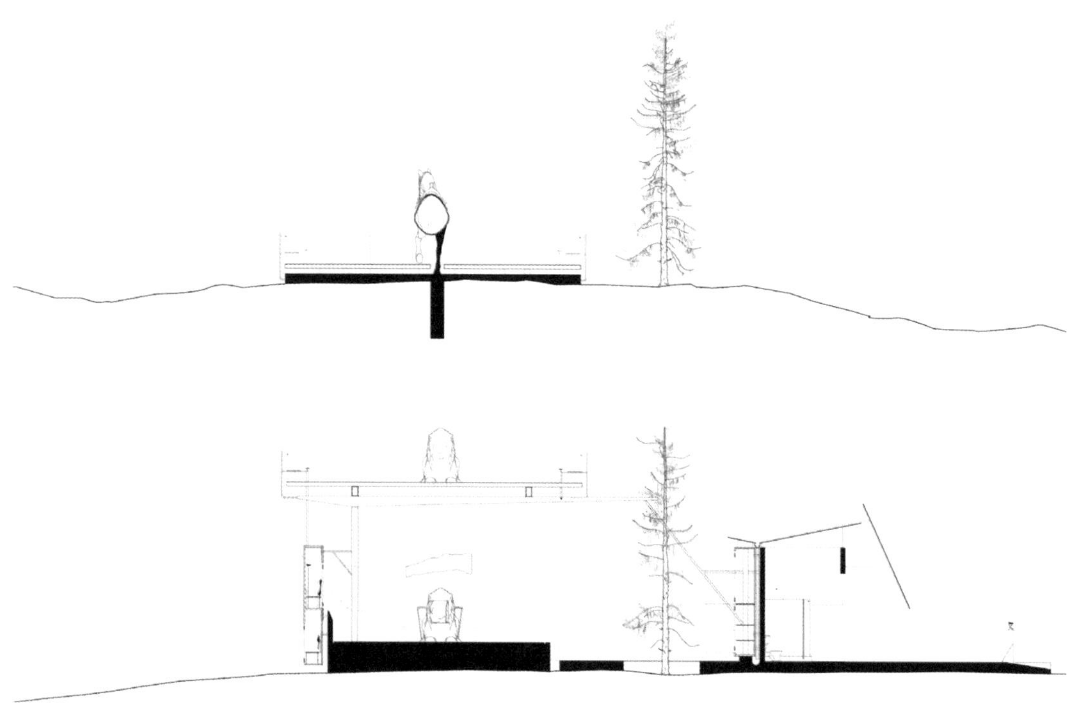

Plan edge structure: bench (horse), parliament (lion), workshop (tiger)

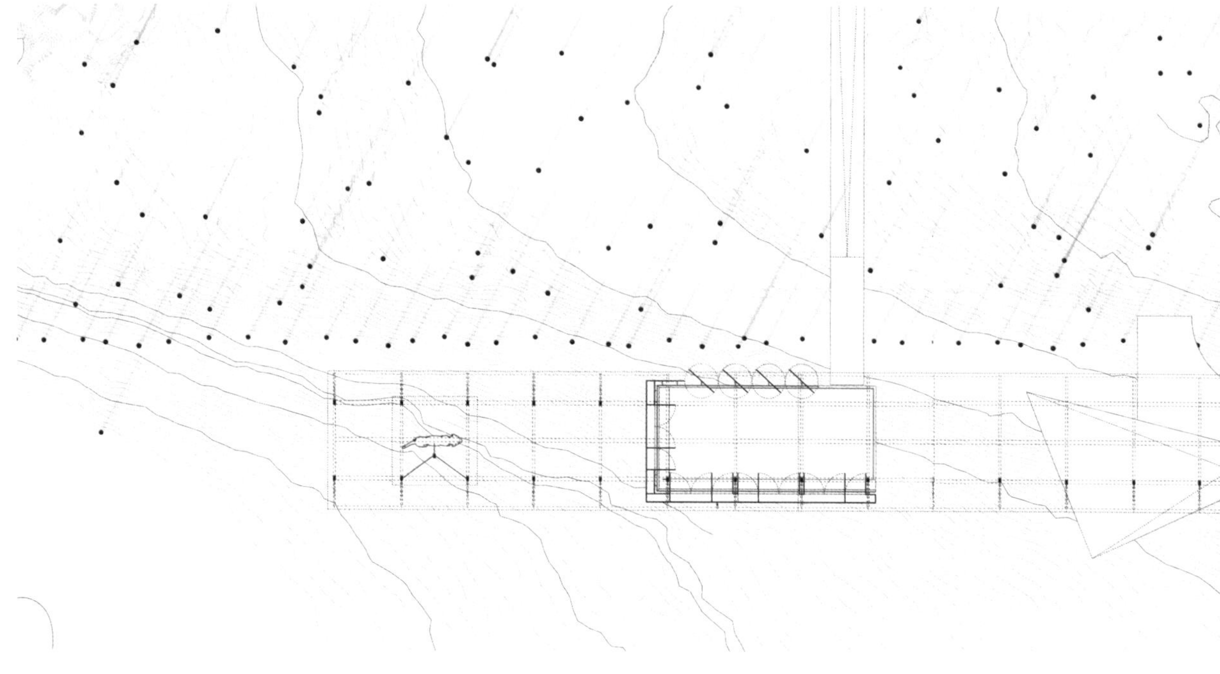

Conflict in Clearing

Plan: stolen city animals

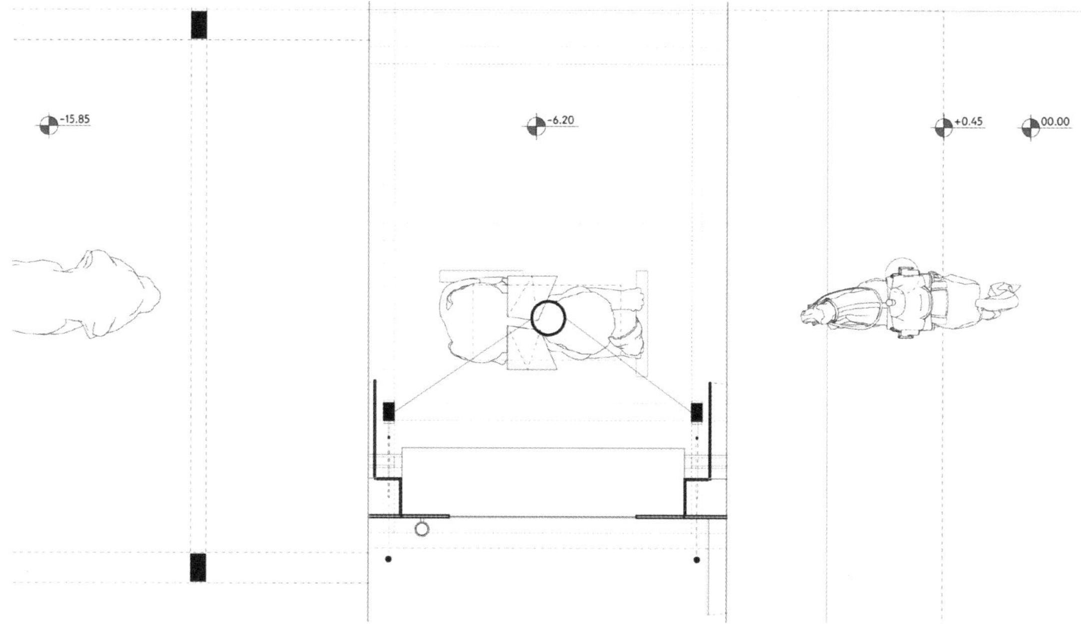

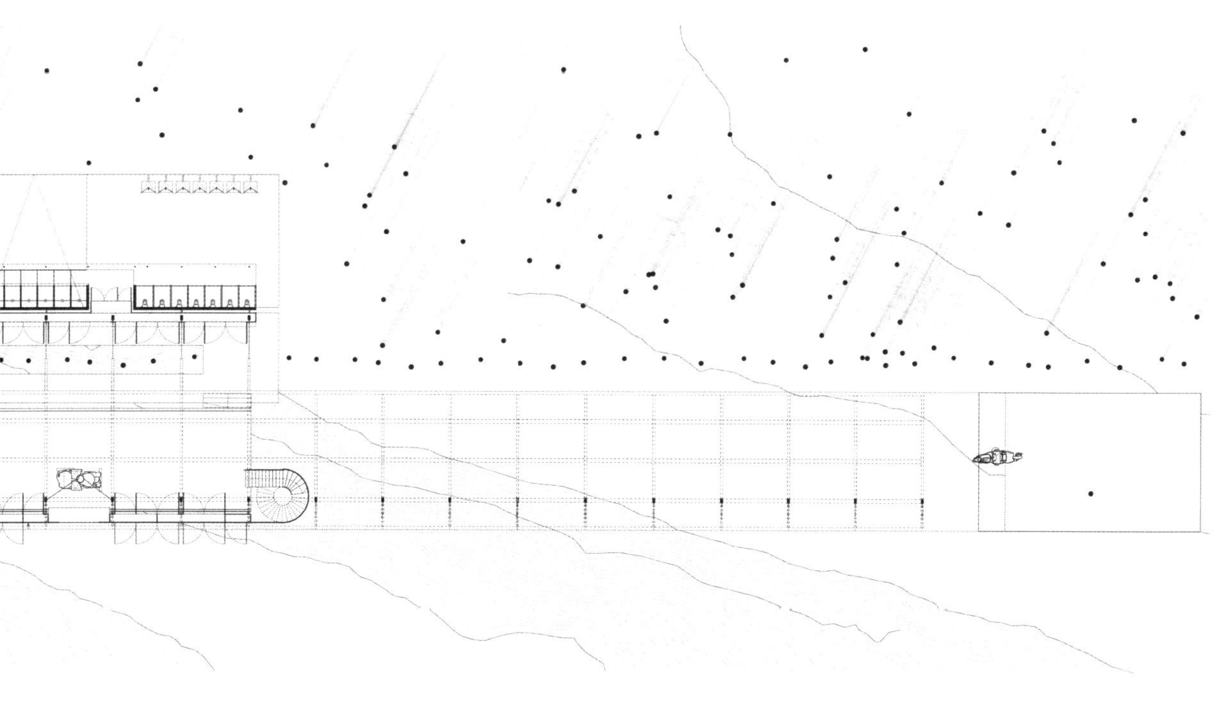

Image Credits

Google maps
20, 24 top, 30 top

David Turturo
21, 25

Fernanda Canales
14–15, 22 top and bottom, 23 top, 24 bottom, 26, 30 bottom, 31, 32, 33, 34, 36

Archive Francisco Serrano
35 top

Jorge Taboada
23 bottom, 29, 35 bottom

Maison Lucien Gau
96–97, 103

United States Library of Congress
102, 116–117

New York Public Library
104

Wikimedia Commons
105

Ramon Prat
106 top

Helena Ariza
106–107 bottom

Tomio Ohashi
107 top

LCLA office with Maximilian Schob
164–165

Luis Callejas
166–171

Luis Callejas and Dale Wiebe
182–183